sic

A

series

edited

by

Slavoj

Žižek

SIC stands for psychoana-
lytic interpretation at its
most elementary: no dis-
covery of deep, hidden
meaning, just the act of
drawing attention to the
litterality [sic!] of what precedes it. A "sic" reminds
us that what was said, in-
clusive of its blunders, was
effectively said and cannot
be undone. The series SIC
thus explores different
connections to the Freud-
ian field: each volume provides a bundle of Lacanian
interventions into a specific domain of ongoing
theoretical, cultural, and
ideologico-political battles.
It is neither "pluralist"
nor "socially sensitive":
Unabashedly avowing its
exclusive Lacanian orientation, it disregards any form
of correctness but the
inherent correctness of
theory itself.

Perversion

and

the

Social Relation

Molly Anne Rothenberg,
Dennis Foster, and
Slavoj Žižek,
editors

sic **4**

DUKE UNIVERSITY PRESS   Durham and London 2003

© 2003 Duke University Press
All rights reserved
Printed in the United States of America on acid-free paper ∞
Typeset in Sabon by Tseng Information Systems, Inc.
Library of Congress Cataloging-in-Publication Data appear
on the last printed page of this book.

Contents

Acknowledgments

We owe a debt of gratitude to Bruce Fink
for his generosity in allowing us to re-present
his work on perversion, which forms such
an important theoretical foundation for our
work. The editorial staff at Duke University
Press, especially Reynolds Smith, Sharon
Parks Torian, Leigh Anne Couch, and
Christine Sweeney, has offered professional
and timely assistance. Many thanks to
Louise James, Department of English,
Tulane University, for her help in preparing
the manuscript.

Perversion

and

the

Social Relation

Molly Anne Rothenberg
and Dennis Foster

Introduction.

Beneath the Skin:

Perversion and

Social Analysis

We conceived of this volume as a way of asking some fundamental questions from a psychoanalytic perspective about how the social relation functions, how it is that we can live together. Admittedly, we don't always live together well. In fact, considering the many ways we humans have found to despise each other and to act on that feeling, it is surprising that we find any pleasure or comfort at all in the company of others, particularly of strangers. It seems likely that if Freud were writing his analyses of group psychology today, he would find more reason than ever to imagine we had grown out of a primal horde, seeing how ready we are to return to some similar social organization, closed within an ethnic identity, ruled by tyrants. His story of a primal father whose terrible governance was replaced by a gentler, if more pervasive, law has functioned with great persistence to explain our ability to repress our more destructive impulses and to sublimate them into socially productive activities. However, such a model is inadequate to describe varieties of social relations in post-Freudian communities, perhaps as neurosis has ceased to explain the ills or health of our contemporaries. That is, the Oedipal subordination of instinct to law may not be the only way of managing instinctual impulses in socially productive ways, and the resistance to law might not be the only way of going wrong.

In 1980, Hans Loewald wrote a striking essay entitled "The Waning of the Oedipus Complex" in which he attempted to preserve traditional Freudian interpretations even as he lamented their failures to address the passions of his era. Discussing what he seemed to imagine were simpler times, he argued that the Oedipus complex was resolved when one came to terms with patricide, the killing of the father in order to take up one's own desires in the world. But the evident tone of nostalgia in the essay reveals less that each of us must get over the guilt we experience for betraying the father than that there is no father left worth killing. The Oedipus complex wanes because it no longer functions when the law has faded. In this essay's echo of *The Waning of the Middle Ages*, we hear Johan Huizinga's longing for a time he imagines before the Enlightenment, before the Renaissance, just before, when feelings were more immediate and people, ruled by men of violence, lived with a passionate intensity. In both writers, the wish for a father's law reveals its absence as well as the emergence of an analysis based on something before the law. Many have called such a wish the perverse.

The emergence of perversion as a description of behaviors and desires, as discursive constructs, as fundamental psychic structures, and as political positions has been accompanied by an increasing valorization of the perverse for its analytic possibilities as well as for its revolutionary potential. For most earlier writers, there was little question but that the perverse belonged to a class of ills to be avoided or cured. The Kantian pervert acts, to the detriment of all, on inclination and pleasure rather than the stricter dictates of duty, soul's reason. The Freudian pervert fails to leave behind the polymorphous pleasures of infancy for the narrower utility of reproductive genital sexuality. While the normal neurotic wrestles with the inability to find true satisfactions within the boundaries of lawful encounters, the pervert remains in a world left frighteningly open by the father's failure either to close the door on early pleasures or to promise a future to compensate for the awful discoveries of childhood—of mutilation, loss, and death. And yet the resistance (or perhaps even subversion) that perversion offers to the father, to the law, seems for others to promise freedom. This ambivalence surrounding the category of the perverse suggests both the richness and dangers of using the term.

The Perverse Foundation

The story that psychoanalytic theories tell of psychic development indicates that certain capacities for social life derive ultimately from the necessary passage through a perverse stage, which installs structures and tendencies that persist in the mature psyche. From within a Freudian frame, the polymorphous character of infantile perversion suggests the openness of the child to multiple avenues of cathexis. That is, the category of the polymorphously perverse suggests that we are highly motivated to have varying forms of satisfaction and attachment to objects, including both human and nonhuman object relations. The stage during which the child has to find a way to separate himself as an independent entity from the engulfing, if secure and pleasurable, universe of the dyad sets up the basic forms of the adult's social ties, the satisfactions he will seek, the sufferings he will undergo and in turn inflict. Whether the absolute bonding between the child and mother actually occurs, or whether it is a retroactive construction by the child, or, again, whether it is fantasized by mother and child, and therefore lived as real, at the heart of perversion is the disavowal of the knowledge that separation is permanent, that mother lacks, and has always lacked, the power to make the world whole—again. Disavowing, as the pervert does, the knowledge of limitation, of castration, makes it possible to act on and enjoy the candidness of a polymorphously perverse body and mind. Normal neurotic pleasure is attenuated for good reasons, and if you can live within these limits, you are lucky. But that doesn't mean perverse pleasures are necessarily unavailable to the normal adult: as a stage of development, the pleasures of the polymorphously perverse remain embedded in the transformations we undergo to get civilized. The delight many of us feel (and the disgust and disapproval some others feel) in bodily movement, in song and rhythm, in the patterning of words, in looking, in eating, and in other activities learned prior to the Oedipal period and outside of social meaning suggests how the perverse persists in normative behavior. We might even ask if the meaningful activities of social life would be possible without their perverse foundations.

For the ordinary neurotic, *jouissance* must remain unconscious lest the experience recall too disruptively the lawlessness of polymorphous perversity with its suspicion that in fact there is no law. We encounter, however, a negative reflection of that jouissance in the contempt we so often hear in complaints about the disgusting pleasures of others: their horrible, smelly food; their loud and disorderly music; their irresponsible sexual extravagance; their profligate rates of reproduction. Perversity seems to saturate the social relations of others. Michel Foucault and

Jonathan Dollimore argue that perversity is actually a discursive construct generated to define normative life. But the purpose of this construct may be less to implant an arbitrarily generated perversity than to provide cover for the specific pleasures that sustain and threaten the law. That is, I can continue to believe that my world is orderly and enjoy the covert pleasures of that world so long as I denounce the perversity that so obviously dominates the lives of others. At the level of skin, I can allow myself pleasure within the intimate society of a shared fantasy; that same skin, however, marks the limits of the social relations and, as it functions in politics, becomes the ground for racism, homophobia, and other expressions of disgust at others' enjoyment. Our observations here suggest that the perverse is implicit in at least some aspects of normal neurotic social life and that there is some advantage in accounting for its presence in attempting to understand social relations. But for those individuals or communities more fully structured by the perverse, the negative implications are more serious. In effect, perversion allows one to continue to live in a world suffused with enjoyment after the point when the Oedipal law of restraint should have taken effect.

The Perverse Predicament and the Imaginary Law

By addressing perversion as a psychic structure—a specific relation to the paternal function—rather than as a description of behaviors, we avoid the traditional stigmatizing of perversion, which has served to obscure its significance for all "normal" psychic development. In order to assess the way in which the perverse functions within most of us as part of the motivation for and dynamics of the social tie, we need to understand the pervert's predicament, the enjoyments and the sufferings of the perverse position. As Bruce Fink argues in his chapter on perversion that we reprint here, those who do not undergo the Oedipal compromise remain bound to the horror, as well as the pleasure, of living within the mother's domain of jouissance, never free to enter the ordinary world of more temperate, symbolic desires and disappointments.

   The precise problem of the mOther's jouissance is that it threatens to pull the subject back, not into wholeness and unproblematic enjoyment, but to the presymbolic world in which the self is engulfed by the mOther's demands, where jouissance circulates at the expense of subjectivity, where encounters with the real are traumatic. What we call the perverse structure marks the developmental moment when some notion of a law beyond the idiosyncratic, unsymbolized world of the mOther is glimpsed: there is a place for the law in perversion, unlike in psychosis. But the Law of the Father has not been articulated, and therefore it cannot articulate the subject with other subjects: it can furnish neither the space within which subjectivity can come to be as separation nor the channeling of enjoyment that moves the subject to seek objects for its own pleasure without negating them in the process. Absent the intervention of the paternal function qua function, the only law that the pervert can bring into being is a set of rules and fantasy scenarios about limiting jouissance. The law as imagined in the realm of the perverse is thus imaginary.

We can think of the difference between the perverse law and the Law of the Father as follows. The law imagined by the pervert, the law he thinks he can bring into being through his probing transgressions, is fantasized as being completely regulative, covering the entire field of relations and parceling out "goods." Like Blake's Urizen, it divides the world up into positive categories, possessions, and entitlements. Regimes of such laws can indeed be challenged through transgression, but when I violate the law through some illicit act of violence or pleasure, the punishment I endure reveals, unnervingly, the fictitiousness and impotence of the law. In its limitation, it cannot liberate me from the demand to enjoy. By contrast, the law as Name of the Father exists as a mere function—a crucial function, to be sure—that does nothing more than open, by means of negation—the father's "No!"—a crack in the smothering universe of the mOther's demand. To the child, the addition of this negation means that some other space exists, some other order or law (potentially) governs the mOther as well as the child. A child may get trapped at this stage if the Law of the Father is not articulated. Desperate to find limits to the mOther's jouissance, perverts try to bring this Law of the Father into being through "transgressive acts" and disavowal. They simply do not realize that the *Non/Nom du Père* they seek cannot be brought into being in this way.

From this vantage, the pervert's disavowal should be conceived not simply as a defense against castration, against the realization that the mother has no penis, but also as the means by which the pervert attempts to open a hole in the world of the mOther. That world is "full" in the sense that there is no perceptible lack in it and, therefore, no space for the child as separate from the mOther, nothing missing that can mobilize desire. As Fink puts it, "One never sees or perceives the lack of anything: one sees what is there to be seen, not what is absent . . . there is no lack at the perceptual level—there the world is full."[1] So the fetish does not just fill in for the missing penis in the same way as a plug fills a hole. On the contrary, the fetish is the pervert's way of *making* a hole, of making visible the fact of a lack (the lack that the Oedipalized adult has had to accept). Although the fetish cannot actually add anything to the Real, since it already exists *as itself* (a shoe, a pair of panties, a piece of fur), at the same time, it does supplement the Real: in its role as stand-in for the missing penis, it negates the fullness of the world of mere phenomena.[2] That is, we could say that it adds the concept of lack, that its negation functions in a positive way. When the pervert says, "I know well that my mother has no penis" but persists with his fetish, he is making it possible to see that his mother has no penis, that his mother lacks, rather than simply seeing what mother does have, in positive terms. In this way, the pervert tries to use disavowal as a substitute for the father's "No!" to open a space, one that will function to set limits to jouissance and allow him to emerge as a subject among subjects.

This tactic lashes the individual more tightly to the circuit of jouissance; it cannot provide the limits to the mOther's jouissance. Still, it testifies to the orientation of the pervert *toward* some law. This is why it is possible to say that, even if the pervert never moves beyond this stage of the Imaginary law, nonetheless he is constantly gesturing beyond it, seeking to bring the Law of the Father into being. This glimpse of the necessity of the paternal function is the pervert's link to the social, while the lack of its articulation is what keeps the pervert enmeshed in the jouissance of the mOther. But we are not trying to suggest that the social relation involves the elision of jouissance. On the contrary, without jouissance the subject has neither the motive for connection nor the means for disconnection. For this reason, we consider it worthwhile to keep our eye on the pervert, at this moment of nascent sociality, to see what energies, what barriers, and what enjoyments accompany the propulsion toward the social relation.

The Potential of Perversion

Given the violence that is so often a part of societies structured by the Oedipal dynamics of repression and the ethics of a band of brothers, many writers have promoted some non-Oedipal, perhaps pre-Oedipal, or perverse structure as an alternative basis for social arrangements. The forces that might enable such a society could include, for example, the intimacy established through the semiotic chora Julia Kristeva theorizes—a bodily sense of connections instilled in the rhythms of the voices we share. Or we might think of the polymorphous perverse as a rich source of interconnection opening a sexualized body to a larger community than that which follows the genital reduction of the Oedipalized body. We might imagine here that in some ideal world, the law would lay a light hand on us while we lived within a harmony of like voices and bodies. The dream of a perfect community, maybe in Utah, as the Coen brothers suggest in *Raising Arizona,* seems to be founded on an idea of sameness, of a shared spirit, history, aspirations, and values—an archaic, unified community. But not even in some golden past did such communities exist, and the totalitarian implications of such imaginings should make everyone leery of seeking them. What, then, are the pre-Oedipal, or perverse implications for social relations?

It is not always easy, after all, to tell on which side of an argument the perverse lies. The beauty of Kant's formulations concerning virtue and duty is that one can find the good without reference to one's pleasure. The more romantic injunction to "follow your heart," or any other leading body part, betrays "reason, God's viceroy in us," and hence is by its very inclination perverse. The categorical imperative derived from Kant's commitment to reason and duty provides the basis for all social relations, uniting all under a golden rule where all would choose the same action: act as you would have all others act in the same situation. The clarity is stunning, its utility less so. Lacan has pointed clearly to the secret enjoyment hidden in the Kantian formula.[3] Even so non-psychoanalytically inclined a critic as Richard Rorty sees "sadomasochism" in those who are committed to a Kantian need for absolutes.[4] It is impossible to dismiss enjoyment or to contain it in the duties we owe to society and reproduction. In denying those pleasures, we risk becoming the sort of monsters who are convinced that the thrill that runs through them as they enforce their discipline upon others is the suffering of righteousness, approved by the father. And yet we would not want to discount the possible virtues of a community structured by perversion.

Here we want to distinguish between two realms of interaction, the *social* and the *political*. The crucial distinction between these two realms concerns the function of fantasy. What we call political interaction is prompted and shaped by a fantasy of wholeness, omnipotence, linear causality, and/or the recovery of lost essence. Each individual participates in this fantasy in his own way, to the extent that he is involved in the political action. Each "hooks" into the fantasy using his or her own personal psychodynamics, which means, in effect, that the political fantasy looks quite different from the vantage of any given individual: I may join an anti-war march because I imagine myself as being part of a powerful movement that will change the world, or I may participate because I enjoy confrontation. In political action, the symbolic space becomes a field in which, under an Imaginary vision, the defenses and jouissance of individual psyches can be activated. In other words, each individual will stage his or her enjoyment differently by means of the political fantasy. The successful political action is what enables the participants to believe that they share the *same* fantasy, that is, have the same interests, agree on the same reasons for joining, and seek the same means and ends *when they don't,* when their access to jouissance derives from strikingly different sources. In this way, the political fantasy allows individuals to experience themselves as maximally particularized and narcissistically omnipotent ("*This* is *my* destiny, *my* power, *my* vision of the world") under the sign of commonality. Of course, the core political fantasy may represent some other group as abject or abhorrent, but this representation serves, as we well know, to reinforce the identificatory processes within the political group and, more importantly, to mobilize what Žižek calls "obscene enjoyment." At bottom, however, the political fantasy orchestrates narcissism by way of a structure wherein the individual imagines that his compatriots are like himself, enjoying in the same way.

The social realm does not function by way of this fantasy. Individuals do not have to be lured into believing they share the same fantasy, the same enjoyment, in order for the social relation to obtain. The social relation transpires in a symbolic space, but no overarching fantasy of group identifications and exclusions is in play. Fantasies abound; in fact, they are necessary to provide the motivation for innumerable transient and variable points of contact as well as to mobilize the equally important forces that delink individuals, that keep individuals sufficiently separate to function as subjects. So, the individual enters the social realm when he finds that a space exists for him in linkage with others. But this space emerges only when the Law of the Father enables a psychic separation from the mOther, with whom the subject has been locked in an interplay of jouissance.

From this perspective, the fantasy of wholeness/sameness implicit in all political, as opposed to social, dreams emerges as a regressive fantasy, one that promises a return to the mOther and enjoyment without the loss of separateness, autonomy, and self that actually subsists in the presymbolic realm. The fantasy behind all calls to political action promises maximum jouissance to each individual and at the same time denies that the jouissance of others is a problem for the subject. In other words, the political fantasy, by disavowing what we know very well in our daily social lives, falsifies the experience—both the dangers and the rewards—of the developmental stage we know as the perverse. This fantasy claims that in politics, the Law of the Father is suspended in the name of a unifying cause.[5] It is for this reason that this volume explores the contributions of perversion to the social relation prior to assaying claims for its political valence.

The Perverse At Work

As we have said, when the Law of the Father is articulated, it articulates the subject, providing the means for both connection and disconnection. The motive for these manifold linkings and delinkings is supplied by jouissance, but such jouissance must be channeled by social forces. Unchanneled jouissance, as Dennis Foster's essay on Burroughs's *Cities of the Red Night* argues, far from serving as a reliable political tool, dissolves the social ties on which political action depends. Where many contemporary historicist accounts stake their claims to political relevance on a reductive conception of the power of presymbolic enjoyment to undo the normative strictures of ideological interpellation, Foster's properly political analysis exposes as fantasy the idea that access to unmediated drives—to untrammeled enjoyment—releases us from ideo-

logical repression. As he shows, Burroughs fatally undermines the political dream of the subversive potential of perversion by interweaving
that fantasy with evidence that, in the West, the staging of enjoyment
itself serves as a primary means of social control.

Social systems themselves operate through a form of belief that has the
same structure as the fetishist's disavowal, as Octave Mannoni's essay
"I Know Well, but All the Same . . ." argues.[6] This deceptively simple
association provides a first step to understanding the limits of the politically subversive potential of perversion as well as perversion's constitutive functions at the limits of the social, for, as Mannoni points out,
disavowal is not repression. The demystification of ideology or authority
can serve to reinforce, at a next step, the split structure of disavowal:
"I see now that X was not true, but all the same, it is true in a way." In
effect, the demystification can serve as the springboard to consolidate
the status quo: As Mannoni puts it, "Belief, shedding its imaginary form,
is symbolized sufficiently to lead on to faith, that is, to a commitment,"
a commitment precisely to the ideological sociocultural world.

This connection between perversion and the "normal" world of social
order transpires overtly in the realm of religious belief, as in Mannoni's
example of the Hopi Katcina rituals. Nina Schwartz's essay, "Exotic
Rituals and Family Values in *Exotica*," gives us a deeper look into the
everyday staging of perverse rituals as a means of recovering from traumatic loss and reconstituting familial relations. In a brilliant reading of
Atom Egoyan's film, Schwartz shows how the film's promise of a pay-
off in jouissance lures the viewer into accepting an Imaginary version of
the law—the same version that emerges in the political register. At the
same time, the film obscures the actual devastation jouissance wreaks
on social ties by emphasizing the characters' static ritualized repetitions,
which makes the symbolic realm appear to be untouchable by the drive.
In effect, at the level of diegesis the film presents perversion as a repara-
tive repetition compulsion—that is, as a neurosis—while at the level of
enunciation, it instantiates a perverse relation to the law.

This imbrication of perversion and neurosis does not stem from a flaw
in the conception of this film but inheres in the relation between drive
and desire at the level of the subject. The losses that the individual undergoes in order to emerge as a social subject never "disappear" but continue to function as propulsions toward satisfactions, propulsions that

operate in both desire and in drive, understood in Lacanian terms. For the child enmeshed in the jouissance of the mOther has undergone some subjectivation (what Lacan calls separation) even if he has not become a subject of desire. In that first approach to subjectivation, the child's jouissance is directed toward ends established through the relation to the mOther. The child does not have unmediated access to jouissance: the drives are "cooked," as Miller puts it.[7] His drive satisfactions are not "his own": there is something in him "more than him." Like Burroughs's viruses, the drive persists alien to the self and, in essence, as a kind of defense against desire. In his essay on David Fincher's *Fight Club,* Slavoj Žižek explores the persistence of this "subjectless partial organ without a body" in order to unravel the dynamics of masochism in its social dimension and the political possibilities it offers. In Žižek's view, the assumption of a degraded subject position with full acknowledgment of the obscene pleasure in such degradation affords "genuine contact" with the "suffering other." This "politics of masochism," therefore, depends upon conceiving the pervert's access to jouissance as an access to something or someone other, not one's own.

Ironically, a similar strategy is adopted by that most infamous of perverts, the fifteenth-century French nobleman, Gilles de Rais—"'sodomite,' pederast, infanticidal criminal, and enthusiast of the black arts," as James Penney denominates him. Tried by the church for his lifelong habits of torturing and sexually molesting young boys, Gilles confessed in spectacular detail the horrific crimes he had committed. Even more spectacular, however, is the bond of sympathy that he forged between himself and the community whose children he had murdered. In his searching critique, Penney demonstrates how a historicist interpretation of Gilles, such as Georges Bataille's, fails to take into account the force of the social ties Gilles established with his victims' families. These "honest" villagers willingly turned over their children to serve as pages in Gilles's manor year after year, despite their knowledge of the disappearance of other children, a willingness that not only marks their complicity but also signals the disavowal underpinning their belief in religious and aristocratic authority. Gilles's theatrical recounting of his crimes works like Burroughs's staging of enjoyment to reinscribe the normative social order (represented in this case by the church), thereby allowing the pervert to present himself as the "object-cause of redemption" for the community as a whole while offering obscene enjoyment to the crowd. The pervert's standing in for *objet a*, the object-cause of the Other's desire, becomes the means by which an entire community, constituted through hysterical identification, mis-recognizes itself and Gilles de Rais as recuperable within the law when they are simply recuperable by the law of church authority.

The essay's implication of perversion with the law is consonant with the Lacanian reading of Kant's categorical imperative, but it leaves open the question as to whether perversion contaminates the law or is already part and parcel of its Imaginary status. If one retains the standard stigmatized connotation of perversion, then it might seem as though there could be forms of the law that evade jouissance, precisely the fantasy described above as "political." E. L. McCallum offers another suggestion for thinking about perversion and its import for sociality: take seriously perversion's "preference" for parts, dissemination, and detachment. From our point of view, this proposal helps lay due stress on the duality of the drive, both as *Trieb*, or propulsion, and as force for dissolution. The social relation requires both, for the social subject must seek connection with its objects (even if only as instruments of enjoyment) in order for any relation to obtain, but at the same time the links thus forged must be susceptible of delinkage in order for the subject to retain any separate identity. The tendency to emphasize the first at the expense of the second leads to a nostalgic utopianism, as Michael Bibler's discussion of William Styron's *The Confessions of Nat Turner* makes clear. Taking to task Leo Bersani's model of homo-relationality, Bibler shows that, in the context of the homosexual and pedophiliac characters of Styron's novel, the vision of community that Styron predicates on "homo-ness" participates in fascistic fantasies of social control precisely to the extent that it underestimates the disruptiveness and ungovernability of jouissance.

McCallum's essay takes the opposite tack. Offering readings of Don DeLillo's *White Noise* and Christa Wolf's *Accident: A Day's News*, she focuses on the types of social relations made possible by the diremptive properties of perversion, the self-separation into "particles," repetitions that do not consolidate but disperse. McCallum argues that this dispersal or "particle-ization" of the self runs counter to the "particularity" of individuals, and so can motivate a social relation not based on the individual or, by implication, on the capitalist mode of (self) possession. While this dissolution of individuality does not constitute a political position, it offers a possible alternative to the utopianism of a Bersani or a Kristeva, while respecting the forces of jouissance.

In his critique of the impulse toward communal, unified communities, Jean-Luc Nancy describes what he calls the "inoperative," "unworking," *désoeuvrée* in community: "that which, before or beyond the work, withdraws from the work, and which, no longer having to do either with production or with completion, encounters interruption, fragmentation, suspension."[8] In this model, we live together of necessity, but there remains something separate in each mortal body that is resistant to the dissolving of differences. Nancy refers to skin, the organ by which we touch, as the marker of our otherness: "A singular being *appears*, as finitude itself: at the end (or at the beginning), with the contact of the skin (or the heart) of another singular being, at the confines of the *same* singularity that is, as such, always *other*, always shared, always exposed."[9] Skin divides us, and we are finally alone, despite any illusions that might be generated by the symbolic systems we share. As the essays in this volume demonstrate, we too are skeptical about any political movement that claims or aspires to overcome the distance that separates us as individuals, whether that movement, in the name of a greater cause, exploits the perverse structure of its followers as a means of social control, or whether it seeks to subvert the Law of the Father through stagings of perverse enjoyment. In the realm of the political, the uses of perversion are almost always profoundly conservative, bound to repetition in their fixation on a lost past.

In social relations, however, where what is singular about each of us is "always shared, always exposed," it may be no bad thing to admit to the perverse fantasies that allow us to disavow separation. No matter that the psychic history determining the precise nature of each one's fantasy is different: in the polymorphous opening to enjoyment we expose how deeply we share a bodily origin, nursed into life by someone whose skin touched ours. This is, of course, no panacea for social or sexual relations, for one can no more live permanently within that disavowal than one can live happily within the primal circuit of the mother's demand. But in failing to recognize that the perverse retains its power to sustain social relations, we not only risk missing the jouissance that binds us to others, but we also risk falling prey to the far more dangerous political injunction that we lose ourselves in the cause.

Notes

1   Bruce Fink, *A Clinical Introduction to Lacanian Psychoanalysis* (Cambridge, Mass.: Harvard University Press, 1997), 168.
2   This double existence of the fetish, as positivity and as negation, is related to Freud's notion of the splitting of the ego in *Verleugnung;* see Bruce Fink, "Perversion," in this volume.
3   Jacques Lacan, "Kant with Sade," trans. James B. Swenson Jr., *October* 51 (1989): 55–104.
4   Richard Rorty, "Ethics without Principles," in *Philosophy and Social Hope* (New York, N.Y.: Penguin, 1999), 75.
5   Even the most "radical" political theorists in contemporary cultural studies make this error, but it is particularly common among the utopian theorists of the "subversion" of gender and sexuality, such as Butler, Bersani, and Dean.
6   As Foster points out in his essay, Peter Sloterdijk has used this formulation to analyze the functioning of cynical reasoning, and Slavoj Žižek's work is well-known for its elaboration of the proposition.
7   Jacques-Alain Miller, "On Perversion," in *Reading Seminars I and II: Lacan's Return to Freud,* eds. Richard Feldstein, Bruce Fink, and Maire Jaanus (Albany: SUNY Press, 1996), 310.
8   Jean-Luc Nancy, *The Inoperative Community,* ed. Peter Connor, trans. Peter Connor, Lisa Garbus, Michael Holland, and Simona Sawhney (Minneapolis: University of Minnesota Press, 1991), 31.
9   Ibid., 28.

Fatal West:

W. S. Burroughs's

Dennis Foster   **Perverse Destiny**

Shortly before the suicide of Kurt Cobain, lead singer for the group Nirvana, I heard a cultural commentator say that if you find a kid who listens to Cobain and reads W. S. Burroughs, chances are he also uses heroin. A recent television advertisement for workout shoes featured Burroughs extolling the virtues of technology, his familiar image (black suit and hat, gaunt face) on a micro TV that lies like junk in a wet alley while a high tech-shod urban youth runs past. In the film *Drugstore Cowboy* (1989), Burroughs appears briefly as the priest-turned-junky who had introduced the protagonist (Matt Dillon) to drugs and who unrepentantly explains that only squares do not understand that the pleasures of drugs are necessary in a world devoid of delight. Burroughs has become an icon that illuminates the obsessions of American culture where the hopes for ageless bodies and technological fixes are inseparable from the self-destructive fixes of drugs and despair. Whatever Burroughs's conscious critique of the Western world might be, his position as a switchpoint between fixations of perverse longing and healthy aspiration provides a way of examining the currents that underlie the westward path, the American destiny.

Burroughs's writing, with its mockery and disparagement of almost all Western values, looks as if it aims at some subversion of those values, perhaps even at some alternative vision. We might, that is, see him as a political writer aspiring to produce social change, an aspiration like those that animate much post-structuralist writing. But if we do, we are certain to find his critique to be at best secretly conservative, at worst suicidal, which would make him no worse than most ostensible subversives.[1] The failure of subversion seems to be built into most modern political critiques. Baudrillard, for example, shows that Marx's categories of exchange and use value imply his already accepting a capitalist understanding of value (1975: 22–25), freeing Baudrillard himself to pursue a love affair with the very mechanisms of consumption he critiques. Roberto Calasso hears "Marx's secret heart beating" with a pervert's excitement over the possibilities of the "total dominion" of his ideas over the world (227). Kristeva brilliantly demonstrates the ways in which patriarchal forces create a structural cage for women, but is unable to articulate a non-paradoxical alternative to the psychosis that comes with any rejection of the symbolic law.[2] Foucault thoroughly explores the institutional forces that constitute the individual within every social context, a critique that has the disadvantage of being unable to suggest methods of resistance beyond the "micro" (1980: 95–96). Butler in *Gender Trouble* attempts to provide a subversive alternative to complement her Foucauldian analysis of gender and produces an ethic of "drag," something unlikely either to worry the repressive forces of gender or to console those most deeply troubled by gender; meanwhile, drag becomes fashion (137). These examples stand for a theme in critical discourses, both of "subversives" who fail to subvert, and of critics who point these failures out.

The reason for failure, however, remains constant throughout the range of texts. Frederick Dolan, arguing Burroughs's entanglement with the culture he attacks, puts Burroughs's argument this way: Burroughs's "central quarrel with Western civilization" is the inaccuracy of the "Aristotelian construct":

> "Reality" just *is* synchronous and unpredictable, whereas the declarative sentence moving ahead determinably through time makes it appear as if one event follows another in an orderly manner. Burroughs might attempt to write in ways that undermine the Aristotelian construct, but not without declaring *something*, and finally, as we have seen, not without becoming inveigled in this construct's seductive images of lucidity, order, control, and a plenitude beyond mere writing as fiction. (549)

Like Poe's perverse universe in *Eureka,* Burroughs's universe does not function according to the rules of logical discourse, cause and effect. But criticizing Aristotelian reason is easier than escaping it, perhaps because the structure of rational thought always steps in as the judge, converting every voice into its own. Any voice that is not complicit with reason becomes, inevitably, unreasonable. As in capitalism, every challenge to the market (the "green" revolution, for example) becomes a marketing opportunity, the challenger just one more player on the field. The subversive assumes that once the foundations have been exposed to be fictive, have been deconstructed, the structure can be reshaped or replaced to function according to new rules, even rules that ignore the Aristotelian construct. The process of exposure itself, however, seems to transform the subversives, drawing them into the ancient dialectic that ties systematic thinkers to their detractors, that ties "abnormal" sexuality to the "normal," to use Rorty's Freudian metaphor for the relation between Derrida and post-Kantian philosophers (1982: 106).

To view Burroughs as part of this failure to subvert the dominance of reason is, at best, to find him to be one more symptom of a general malady, another sad example of Marcuse's one dimensional man, caught up in "sweeping rationality, which propels efficiency and growth, [that] is itself irrational" (xii). But the readiness to which Burroughs's work opens itself to the charge of failure should be a warning. His contradictions, his reversals of sign and referent (is space conceived of as timeless synchronicity a metaphor for outer space or vice versa?), his general longing for a beyond, and other refusals of logical form betray less a failure within symbolic mastery than an excessive purposeless delight in manipulating the very forms of mastery. Certainly, he feels a deep hatred for what he refers to in his later writings as the "Ugly Spirit." His biographer Barry Miles defines this spirit as "the Ugly American, [driven by] forces of greed and corruption, selfishness and stupidity, of *Homo sapiens* [sic] arrogance" (253–54). And though Burroughs derides the manifestations of this spirit, what remains compelling about him is how he represents the sources of control and how he evokes a sublime dimension to life, a real not subject to symbolic strictures.

Rather than reading Burroughs the symptom, then, I want to read Burroughs the *sinthome,* whose writing stages enjoyment.[3] If Burroughs's iconic doubleness does serve as the switch between health and perver-

sity, it is because the world he represents also stages sublime enjoyment within the contradictions and inverted metaphors of social nor-
malcy. Burroughs fascinates, despite his failures of rational criticism and
his at times repellent aesthetics, because he so clearly delights in the
violence, sexuality, and bodily luxuriances of disease, beauty, intoxica-
tion, and excess that attend the ugly spirit. His subscriptions to *Gun
World, American Survival Guide,* and *Soldier of Fortune* (Miles 2–3), for
example, flaunt an enjoyment of violent technologies that finds its expression in the various gun-toting figures of his fiction and in his own
love of weapons. His misogyny includes an appreciation of homosexual
eroticism so boisterous that it leaves no room for women. We might ask
with Dolan whether Burroughs's ultimate love of narrative inevitably en-
tangles him in the longings and delusions of the Aristotelian construct,
but the political question is whether such conformity with the ugly spirit
of the West implies his unwitting accord with that spirit.

When Slavoj Žižek adopts the term "cynical reasoning" to describe
much contemporary thought, both popular and professional, he moves
a step beyond the stoical position of "suspicion," the resistance of those
who would not be duped by delusions of authority.[4] The cynic, by contrast, while not duped, lives as if he were: "I know very well, but all
the same. . . ." He stops doubting and resigns himself to living under
demands he can never hope to fulfill.[5] He sees the cultural superego's
injunctions to be honest, generous, and dutiful as a fool's game, but one
he continues to play without being tormented by an awareness of its
falsity. As discouraging as it is to deal with such cynics in daily life—
it is futile to argue with someone holding this view—an avowed cynicism has the advantage of clarifying the subject's motives: just follow
the stupid rules as if they were real, and you get real rewards. Women's
magazines have long given a version of such advice to women, telling
them that men care only for the appearance of virtue. Marabel Morgan
goes so far as to suggest to women that if they merely *tell* their men that
they admire them (even though they do not deserve admiration), they
can make their husbands love them (64). Cynical reasoning has been
easily adopted by popular culture for men as well: "My father always
said, 'buy the best and you'll never be disappointed,'" says the son of
wealth in an advertisement for high end commodities, repeating a claim
that is effective despite its obvious fraudulence: "I know very well that

cost is no reliable guarantee of quality, nevertheless, when I spend more I feel as if I have the best." Although the consumer is bound to be disappointed (since consumption never removes desire), the advertisement helps transform the commodity into a fetish, that is, into a thing that can provide a perverse enjoyment, despite the lack of satisfaction.

Cynical reason returns the reasoner, surprisingly, to the Cartesian position of stupid obedience: in the absence of certainty, it is better to follow the rules. However, where Descartes gave his obedience to the laws of the kingdom, contemporary ideology dictates that reason guide one to pursue wealth and self-interest. The tremendous appeal of such a position is that merely by following duty, reason, and common sense, one incidentally accrues not only wealth and position but the special rewards that come to those who adhere most strictly to duty. Those fortunate enough to escape poverty, for example, often find themselves, as a matter of civic duty, in the position of disciplining the poor. Their methods may be doomed to fail (choosing not to feed the children of the poor does not usually make such children into productive members of society), but the experience of inflicting suffering on others can still make the job rewarding. It is difficult to subvert those systems (such as the prison system or the campaigns against imported drugs) that seem to accept as a working principle that they will be ineffective. Burroughs's work seems, rather, to celebrate aspects of modern culture that are often acknowledged (sadly, hostilely, sardonically) to fail. However, he takes as the motive of cultural activity not its intentions to improve life, but its capacity to produce enjoyment. The evil of the ugly spirit does not lie in its capacity to produce perverse enjoyment but in its failure to recognize that perversity is what sustains it. Burroughs's achievement is to invert the terms of Western history, imagining a culture developing not out of its impulses toward spirit or wealth, but out of the impulse toward enjoyment and a denial of the legitimacy of all authority.

Retrospective Utopia

Cities of the Red Night imagines an alternative history of the Western world from one hundred thousand years ago, developing out of the Eurasian plains and reaching into the Americas. This history gives no sense of a utopian past, however, no moment when life was sweet and from which humankind has fallen. The distant past of the Cities of the Red Night was as corrupt as any modern time in its greed, racism, and violence. Nor, on the level of individual history, is childhood a place of innocence: at the conclusion of *Cities*, the narrator recalls a dream: "I remember a dream of my childhood. I am in a beautiful garden. As I reach out to touch the flowers they wither under my hands. A nightmare feeling of foreboding and desolation comes over me as a great mushroom-shaped cloud darkens the earth. A few may get through the gate in time. Like Spain, I am bound to the past" (332). An ambiguity in the first line leaves us uncertain whether he dreamed *about* his childhood or *during* his childhood, diminishing the difference between ordinary time and the timeless space of dreams. Within this dream he dreams a second dream, a nightmare of the future. Something happened, we feel, to cast us from the garden into the realm of time and death, into reality. Dreams "[blow] a hole in time" (332), leading us to imagine when we awaken that a timeless, deathless realm must once have existed, before or beyond the trauma, the fall from infant bliss, that marks all historical life. But at no time, even in the dream of a garden, can we touch the flower.

Sublime America, the edenic garden, was from the beginning a denial of every constraint of European history. This founding fantasy imagined America as a land without difference, "a fresh, green breast of the new world," as the final page of *The Great Gatsby* describes it, where every child is whole and not riven by fantasies of race, religion, wealth, and class. False from the start, the fantasy has nevertheless found embodiment in numerous icons of American life. The astonishing thing about the people of this land is how readily an image of ourselves as uncorrupted can be evoked in us. Despite the venal motives behind almost all of America's founding adventures that led to the decimation of native populations and the importation of African slaves, we repeatedly affirm our commitment to the propositions of non-difference: that Americans aspire to a color-blind, classless, pluralistic society with many religions, but one god.

Burroughs opens *Cities* with a version of the American story, wherein piracy is neither the nascent form of early capitalism nor, in a perversion of big business, the eventual outcome of wild capital's pillaging every weak spot in the financial field. Rather, it is an originating impulse of liberty. Piracy, rejecting the cover of a national flag, declares the absence of limiting, castrating authority, claiming the right to take all wealth for its own.[6] It expresses, that is, the dream that it is possible to win absolute, stable command of the world's wealth. But wealth under capital is wealth only when it is fluid, endlessly circulated and allowed to function as a signifier. All modern capitalists must, consequently, work with a double consciousness: they recognize that capital, as a signifier, is empty despite its profound effects; at the same time they derive the meaningless enjoyment from money that only a fetish can command, even though the fetishized object is often no more than a fleeting electronic transaction. Piracy, then, embodies the enjoyment of a monetary fetish that legitimate capitalism takes as the incidental consequence of its enterprise, but which is in fact a primary inducement for its labors.

Don C. Seitz, whose story of the pirate Captain Mission Burroughs quotes, recognizes an ambiguity of motivations in idealists: Mission's "career was based upon an initial desire to better adjust the affairs of mankind, which ended as is quite usual in the more liberal adjustment of his own fortunes" (xi). The problem with such a desire to elevate others, as Conrad displayed in *Heart of Darkness*'s fortune-hunting "gang of virtue," is that in remaining ignorant of where they derive their enjoyment, the "benefactors" of mankind need not question what they attain merely in passing. In saving the less fortunate peoples of the world, the powerful stage master-servant/sado-masochist fantasies that "incidentally" exploit and destroy those who come in contact with them. Burroughs seizes this story of the pirate Mission for its sublime potential, seeing in it an American liberty that might have effectively put an end to the history of industry and capitalism by eliminating need, wealth, and class. But unlike the young Marx who imagines that the elimination of "exchange value" will produce some authentic existence, Burroughs's imagined community evades the tyranny of authenticity by producing a deliberately and literally staged enjoyment.

Burroughs's characters parody our activities, showing how social, economic, and political motives conceal some more fundamental need. Farnsworth, for example, is the District Health Officer, but he is uninterested in typical ideas of health: he has "very little use for doctors" because they interfere with the function of his office, which is to alleviate suffering, whether it arises from illness or desire: "The treatment for cholera was simple: each patient was assigned to a straw pallet on arrival and given a gallon of rice water and a half a gram of opium. If he was still alive twelve hours later, the dose of opium was repeated. The survival rate was about twenty percent" (4). The opium cure also works well to relieve Farnsworth of his erections. The conventional medical professionals' fight against the enemy Death all too frequently works counter to their aspirations to relieve suffering. We suffer, quite literally, from life and its ally, desire, both of which project us into a future where we will have evaded death. The wealth we accumulate, like the children we have ("money in the bank," one new parent said of her recent deposit), stands as a symbolic screen against the Real, an investment in the promise that with time we will increase and not simply waste away. But of course, in the long run, the survival rate is zero percent, a point worth forgetting. Farnsworth's goal is to find what gives pleasure to the body independent of the anxieties of the individual subject about death and failure: he tries to relieve the patient of the fantasy that anyone is capable of any action that will evade death, that consciousness might transcend the body. Opium is, in part at least, sometimes the mechanism, sometimes the metaphor for this condition—sometimes it is merely a drug to suppress desire, sometimes it represents a state free of time and hence of desire. Through Farnsworth, Burroughs both mocks the medical establishment and suggests an alternative orientation for the practice.

At the heart of all social practices in this book is the stage. When Farnsworth's opium is gone and he is recovering with his boy Ali, this other alternative to conventional reality appears. In this theatrical performance, he becomes aroused in a sexual "dream tension," during which he smells "a strange smell unlike anything he had ever smelled before, but familiar as smell itself" (11). He awakes to find that he is becoming an alligator whose head is "squeezing the smell out from inside." Burroughs alludes here to the idea that the human brain contains the "reptile brain," a formation that recalls and preserves our reptilian origins. The reptile brain is rich in serotonin, opiate receptors, and dopamine, "a neural sap of vital importance for bringing the total energies of the organism into play" (MacLean 406). For Farnsworth, this brain emerges as a smell connected to some ancient, reptilian sense of the Real that displaces all human consciousness. Farnsworth the alligator, whose body pops, boils, and scalds, ejaculates in an agony of enjoyment. But this apparent metamorphosis and literalization of the lizard brain turns out in the next paragraph to have been merely a theatrical production, the alligator a costume and the jungle a backdrop on stage. So, we are left asking, *is* there actually some access to the lizard brain, and, through it, some immediate access to total bodily enjoyment, or is the passage only a metaphor for a kind of experience Burroughs *hopes* might be possible? We seem to be caught in a familiar Burroughs contradiction, such as we just saw with the opium, where the literal and the metaphoric are interchangeable. However, the enjoyment is real (Farnsworth is fucked by Ali in both situations, though we might ask whether fucking is literal or metaphoric), and Farnsworth's enjoyment connects the two worlds, acting as a switchpoint between reality and the stage. The Real question—both the question I want to pursue and the question of the Real—is what might squeeze the "smell," so intimately strange, out of your own brain and thereby give you access to that ancient sense?

Perhaps the contradiction is more accurately an opposition between delusion and illusion, hallucination and artifice (what we mistake as truth versus what we recognize as constructed), and not between what is real and what is merely staged. The *Real* by definition is not open to perception, not directly available to the mind operating in the symbolic realm. We respond to representations, whether we understand them to be true or fictive. Although enjoyment may once have been evoked by the direct experience of stimulation that presumably floods the infant body, for the speaking person it is mediated by repetition: each subject is constructed by events that must be symbolically restaged as fantasy in order to create enjoyment.[7] Reality, in this context, refers merely to those experiences of the world that we fail to notice as staged. That is, we hallucinate a Real based on the images we perceive, as the suckling child hallucinates "milk" at the sight of a breast. Those who would kick a stone and say "there is reality" betray a desire for a Real as immediate as a rock.

When we seek some experience of sublimity, we look to extremity, whether outward to the grandeur of the natural world or inward to the raw passion of, say, sexuality; but neither the Grand Canyon nor the most intimate sexual acts occur for us unconditioned by previous expectation, images, stories—by theater. If we still derive the sublime thrill, it is because we forget the staging or because, like perverts, we give ourselves over to the fantasy. Too much or too little, that is always the problem of pleasure. The Aristotelian construct may stand like a fire wall between the subject and enjoyment, but the perverse subject can use it as a backdrop against which to stage a fantasy.

Virus and Vampire

Viruses and vampires exert a fascination in contemporary imagination for similar, but opposing reasons. Viruses, intruding invisibly on the level of DNA, remind us as their progeny emerge within our own cells that our bodies are not our own.[8] These secret guests arouse in us an abjection that holds the consumer's attention through popular magazines, books, television, and film, as demonstrated by the wealth of stories about ebola, a virus exotic in America, that liquefies the internal organs so that they pour out of any orifice. Viruses illuminate the silent interior of the body, a flesh that is close, vital, and familiarly strange as only our mothers' has been to us. The vampire's appeal, however, is sublime: flesh that refutes time and mortality, that limits its knowledge of the body's interior to blood sucked from another as a baby sucks the breast, preserving beauty, longing, and passion.

At the heart of our interest in both viruses and vampires, however, is the recognition that "life" does not favor the living organic body, but the "undead" core of memory. Bodies live to reproduce DNA, which is itself non-organic and immortal and which would happily have us bite off the heads of our mates during intercourse if that would favor successful reproduction. Viruses are simple replicating nucleic acids, DNA packages that appropriate the liquid interior of cells for their own ends. In the virus we see the hopeless insufficiency of our bodily selves, our submission to an inhuman process even when that process is our own DNA's survival. The vampire, however, although it also appropriates our liquid interior, represents a fantasy through which we can identify with the inorganic force of replication. The appeal and the horror of both are related to their disregard for the rational subject and its autonomy: something in you exceeds the limits of you, something you do not identify with as *you* and which follows a path that is not yours. Burroughs's well-established hatred of "control"—the insidious compulsions of sex and drugs as they are tied to corporate interests—finds its expression in the ways the viral/vampiric human can be appropriated by social forces and turned to other ends.

Burroughs does not suggest, however, that we might evade such so-cial subjection by "curing" the virus: as one character suggests, " 'any attempts to contain Virus B-23 will turn out to be ineffectual because we carry this virus with us. . . . Because it is the *human virus*' " (25). The virus's symptoms (such as uncontrollable sexual desire) are those of "love": the human virus ("known as 'the other half' ") constitutes our knowledge of our inadequacy, our mortality. We are double, and yet that part of ourselves with which we identify will vanish while the undead within us continues.[9] Conventionally, we deny this knowledge when we speak of the soul as the immortal part of each person. The idea of the soul inverts the relation between body and mind, claiming that the physical vanishes while the soul, a representation of consciousness as unembodied spirit, lives on, untouched by time. In fact, the opposite is more likely true, since consciousness is usually the first thing to go. The account of the Cities of the Red Night retells the story of the immor-tal soul, stripping it of its sublime dimension and linking it to a history of social power, a practice by which the strong reproduce their kind at the expense of the weak.

The Cities' most distinctive practice involves their refusal of sexual reproduction, of bodies and mortality. The chapter entitled "Cities of the Red Night" lays out the system of "transmigration" of spirit, dis-playing the interdependence of two classes, Transmigrants and Recep-tacles: "To show the system in operation: Here is an old Transmigrant on his deathbed. He has selected his future Receptacle parents, who are summoned to the death chamber. The parents then copulate, achieving orgasm just as the old Transmigrant dies so that his spirit enters the womb to be reborn" (154). The denial of death by elite Transmigrants—those who consider the perpetuation of their spirits more valuable than their mere bodies—leads them to appropriate not just the sexuality of others, but the orgasm itself, the males' at least, for the purpose of cul-tural reproduction. This system leads inevitably to "mutters of revolt" by the women, who see most directly how their enjoyment has been chan-neled for social designs: women produce children for the pleasure of others (155). In addition, the practice produces "a basic conflict of inter-est between host child and Transmigrant" (158) since the point of being born is to serve for a few years as the vessel for another's spirit, at the end of which the host submits his body to orgasmic death, again all in the interest of maintaining the Cities' power structure. The solution to this conflict is to "reduce the Receptacle class to a condition of virtual idiocy": that is, children must find their bodies' enjoyment only through service to the City. One of the inadvertent outcomes of this practice is that the Council of the Cities "produced . . . races of ravening vampire idiots" (157).

The denial of mortal limitation, as the story represents it, leads the elite to abuse power and turn away from the thought that derives from recognizing death. As sublime as the concept of soul may be, it is easily adapted to a system that perpetuates those who are spiritually deserving, which the powerful always consider themselves to be. Perhaps history could have developed otherwise. *Cities* locates the "basic error of the Transmigrants" in their desire to by-pass the "basic trauma" of conception. Conception, after all, requires the most fundamental loss of integrity in the splitting of DNA and a rejoining of sexually-halved chromosomes. The particular result of conception is fundamentally uncontrollable, subject to the chaotic slippage of dynamic systems and tending toward a purposeless complexity. Evolution—viable genetic mutation—proceeds for the good of neither the individual parent nor the species, but, like an artist of serendipity, will try anything, even though a stray "success" (it lives!) may destroy everything that came before.

The Transmigrants, then, are justified in fearing conception, as should all cultures that exalt stability over change. The ultimate collapse of the Cities during the radioactive period of the Red Night ("a time of great disorder and chaos") resulted from the introduction of mutation —change, complexity, and diversity—into a culture devoted to exact replication. Conception, that is, is at odds with "spirit," the reputed essence of an individual ego. Something else within you, something in-you-more-than-you, works silently toward a future. Call it DNA, the Drives, the Human Virus: components of the body work without regard for the spirit, soul, or individual body. But they are represented through the individual body as horrible and thrilling enjoyment, depicted in this story as orgasm; and enjoyment, unless it is channeled by culture, undermines all practices that depend on control—and what social practices do not?

Burroughs suggests that one way of distinguishing cultures is by the way they control enjoyment. In a series of statements about the relationship between what is true and what is permitted, the following claim is associated with America: "Everything is true and everything is permitted" (158). The genius of America is to pretend that despite the absence of limits, the structure of symbolic meaning remains intact, able to guarantee truth: enjoyment is not only possible and good, it is obligatory. The pretense is what enables large parts of American culture to channel enjoyment so effectively—through advertising, entrepreneurial business (as in pentecostal meetings of Mary Kay Cosmetics distributors), patriotism, and ecstatic religions—without the disillusionment that characterizes most other, older cultures. Everything is true!

Such is the interpretation the most American of the Cities of the Red Night gave the "last words of Hassan i Sabbah, Old Man of the Mountain": "Nothing is true. Everything is permitted" (158). The words are obscure, at best. It would take a culture such as that which introduced the zero into Western mathematics to recognize both that *nothing* is true (more true than *something*), and that everything is permitted ("whatever is, is," as Parmenides put it).[10] Each of the Cities gives its own interpretation of the sentences,[11] inserting its own fantasy into the tautological emptiness of the juxtaposed claims. In the statement "Everything is true," Burroughs suggests that in a contemplation of Nothing, the American fantasy is to see a hint of the sublime, of a totality beyond expression.

Many of the sequences in *Cities* parody conventional attempts to reach beyond the linguistic medium. In sexuality, for example, we imagine we move through ecstasy toward freedom: in sex, we seem to transgress the human realm of law, convention, and restraint and to approach a reality that is fully physical, bodily. For Burroughs, however, no activity is more clearly bound to the stage. We see this staging in the passages involving Port Roger, the pirate's home base. The port is itself a set that Burroughs compares to Prospero's enchanted island, and the pirate's main weapon for establishing an alternative society is magic, i.e., staged illusion: "It is our policy to encourage the practice of magic and to introduce alternative religious beliefs to break the Christian monopoly" (105). Christianity, in this vision, works by the same rules as other magical productions, so one has only to perform the part of a devout believer to undermine Christianity's status as truth: a ceremony is above all a performance, transcendence an effect.

Recognizing the family to be one of the fundamental institutions of

Christian control, the pirates exploit the performance aspect of family: they enlist members of their community to become "families to operate as intelligence agents in areas controlled by the enemy" (106). For families to operate, they must have children. To this end, the pirates gather all the young men and women for a mass dance and insemination: "Juanito announces: 'Rabbit men and rabbit women, prepare to meet your makers.' He leads the way into a locker room opening off the east wall. The boys strip off their clothes, giggling and comparing erections, and they dance out into the courtyard in a naked snake-line. The women are also naked now. What follows is not an unconstrained orgy but rather a series of theatrical performances" (108). The more orgiastic and unconstrained sex appears to be, the more it requires the careful preparation and control of the governors. What Burroughs displays is not a more authentic vision of family and sexuality than exists in conventional life, of course, but a parody that reveals how readily sexuality can be turned to the service of a state, the pirates' state in this case. As Don DeLillo reveals in his account of the mass wedding staged by the Rev. Moon in Yankee Stadium, the most sublime, mystical events can derive from power and showmanship.

Unlike Marxist critics of such cultural issues, Burroughs is less interested in how institutional power shapes its subjects by instilling an ideology than in how the staging of enjoyment serves as a means of social control. Even when Burroughs seems most intent on imagining a way to escape the forces of social control, for example, he tells us more about how those forces work than about possibilities for actual liberation. Dink Rivers, one pirate character, demonstrates the utility of staging enjoyment when he explains the way a "magical brotherhood" achieves total bodily control, the ultimate aim of which is to escape all unconscious symbolic determinants: "At the age of fourteen, when I began to have dreams that culminated in ejaculation, I decided to learn control of the sexual energy. If I could achieve orgasm at will in the waking state, I could do the same in dreams and control my dreams instead of being controlled by them" (127). The technique requires him deliberately to relive a wet dream. " 'I ran through a sex dream like reciting my ABCS' " (128). His model for "reliving" is the recitation of a child's rhyming lesson, by which he exploits a symbolic form to get at its presymbolic ground[12]: "I used the same method of projecting myself into a time when my mind seemed empty of words. . . . [producing] a vertiginous sensation of being sucked into a vast empty space where words do not exist" (128). In projecting himself backwards to that originating moment, he finds that his mind *seems* empty of words. However, that moment is always a *nachträglich* construction, an illusion of wordlessness constructed out of the limitations we experience within language, an illusion of freedom made from the constraints of subjectivity. The "dying feeling" Dink describes is a momentary lapse of subjectivity, a feeling many long for (and pursue in drugs, alcohol, sex, and religion) and one they misconstrue as death.

Dink's control of orgasm is based on Zen traditions of bodily control and tantric sexuality, practices that, despite the regular supply of sex manuals they inspire, remain exotic for Americans. However, American institutions employ recitations little more complex than the ABCs to bring crowds of people to this extremity of deathly, linguistic oblivion, a circumstance DeLillo dwells on in *The Names*. We see such practices in religion and political assembly, in action on the stock exchange floor, and in other events that are socially useful yet inspire a sublime thrill. But when someone stages such enjoyment for himself, we know him to be perverse rather than admirable.

The difference between the pervert and a futures trader sweating and screaming like any Pentecostal is that the pervert *knows* what he wants while the other comes to it inadvertently in the course of his duties. This power of the word to produce ecstasy finds expression in one of Burroughs's dream images: the dreamer sees a body spattered with "a shower of red sparks" that create "burning erogenous zones that twist and writhe into diseased lips whispering the sweet rotten fever words" (277). In Burroughs's imagination, every part of the body can be eroticized by a tongue of flame, but the forms those parts take are likely to be abject. The vampire's kiss may look like love, but its aim is blood. The vampire, the ad man, and the evangelical fundraiser on television will, if they know their jobs as well as Poe's diddler, drain you and leave you wanting to give more. The most reasonable language carries something ancient within it that can give speech an elemental power.

The One God Universe Con

Dolan points out that Burroughs's valuing of space over time, of an escape from time's compulsion, allies him with a romantic strain, a gnosticism in American thought, as Bloom refers to it.[13] His writing implies a desire to evade the constraints of the individual psyche in favor of something larger and more persistent. We see this impulse played out repeatedly: in the preference Burroughs shows for polytheism, over the "OGU," the soul mastering, thermodynamically fading One God Universe (1987: 113); in his disregard for chronology in *Cities,* which allows the same character to appear anywhere within a three-hundred-year period; in his preference for the cut-in in the investigative work of Clem Snide and in his own writing.[14] In a world so insistently governed by the ideals of progress and accumulation that make a capitalist economy possible, such a dream of timelessness inevitably looks like nostalgia. The desire that drives capitalism depends on notions of a need that can be remedied through production and consumption. The resulting velocity of cultural change produces a "complexity" that we come to depend on for survival, and it cannot be undone. But as Burroughs implies, the past persists, encrypted in complexity, and we would be as foolish to ignore it as we would be to attempt to return to it. Within the progress of civilization and the entropic waste of time lie generative, productive patterns that endure and return.

The model of memory that Freud presents in *Civilization and Its Discontents* places memory outside of time, with the implication that past events are never recovered as separable, independently standing moments but are imbricated in foundational patterns of mind. Philip Kuberski's *The Persistence of Memory* draws out the correspondences between Freud's layered cities, our timeless unconscious, and the compacted history of life contained in DNA. We achieve our sense of linear movement through time only by denying the evidence that time is less an arrow than a tangled vine. The temporal development of dynamic systems tends not to produce unique forms but spatially transformed replications of the same. One implication of this view of temporal development is that the production of constantly varying elements leads not to wholly original forms but to the same on a different scale.

Although he is working from a different model, Burroughs seems to take the implication literally: he disregards the idea that character is located in a unique and perishable individual, seeing instead that a character can arise repeatedly from given circumstances. Consequently, he "reincarnates" characters from century to century as easily as he carries his characters from book to book. Vampires create the vampire anew over generations; viruses transform diverse organisms into replications of the same disease; and language, for all its subtlety, transforms lumps of human infancy into subjects as alike as a patch of cats. But while the human subject develops out of a specific linguistic culture, the body is nearly eternal and governed even more strongly by ancient patterns. Over 90 percent of all human DNA is identical. If an individual wished to evade the determinations of cultural power, the trick would be to get at that common flesh that links one to the eternal, to something older than this culture.

In Burroughs, one of those tricks, "sex magic," employs a ritual that divorces sex from its functioning within a social practice and provokes something ancient and non-individualized in the body. Preparing for a performance, one character says, "According to psychic dogma, sex itself is incidental and should be subordinated to the intent of the ritual. But I don't believe in rules. What happens, happens" (1981: 76). And what happens is that "pictures and tapes swirl in my brain" as the many gods appear and The Smell (that primordial essence of the lizard brain) surrounds the performers (77). Sex magic, it seems, provides access to knowledge and power that does not derive from the individual subject's reasoning intelligence or talents. Clearly, most sex is not magic: the magic requires one to turn over evolution's gift of orgasm to the proper staging. The ritual requires the performer to submit to the pleasure of some Other, foregoing his or her own desires in order to approach the ancient, the Real: earth knowledge. But in Burroughs's world, the ritual is important because there is no alternative source of power and knowledge.

Elsewhere, I have considered what happens when authority fails, and the father, the state, the phallus, or whatever we would call the figure that holds the symbolic world in place is unable to promise enjoyment at the end of a long life of repression and self-denial.[15] Burroughs addresses a world in which all authority has revealed itself to be a con game, where the Aristotelian construct to which Dolan refers has shown its hand. But since you cannot, apparently, ignore or directly challenge the construct, you beat a con with another con. Burroughs's image of one con that can resist authority is the NO: "Natural outlaws dedicated to breaking the so-called natural laws of the universe foisted upon us by physicists, chemists, mathematicians, biologists and, above all, the monumental fraud of cause and effect, to be replaced by the more pregnant concept of synchronicity" (1987: 30). Burroughs connects this NO figure in *The Western Lands* to Poe's diddler (31), the grinning figure who takes his pleasure in providing people with the illusion they desire, and who also takes their money. This con, like others, depends on the illusion that the diddler can deny limits, deny death. That is, the NO's breaking of natural laws mimics the perverse wish implicit in phallic authority—enjoyment will one day be yours—only it offers the reward now. The NO challenges two biologic laws: against crossbreeding between unrelated species and against evolutionary reversibility. Both say that each individual's pleasure is limited, that each of us is on a narrow track to personal extinction, a mere tool of evolution. And what is the God of the OGU, the One God Universe, but a promise that despite the inevitability of thermodynamic decline, despite "sickness, famine, war, old age and Death" (113), you personally, are immortal. The NO plays the same con, offering the perverse where the sad mortal longs for the sublime.

The contradictions that mark Burroughs's writings as argument are demonstrated nowhere more clearly than in the doubling that occurs between the outlaws he values and the figures he most despises. For example, Burroughs seems to promise that those with courage and dedication might travel to the Western Lands, a trip "beyond Death, beyond the basic God standard of fear and danger" where one gains access to "Immortality" (124). But every guide to the lands, from those of the Egyptians and Tibetans to the Messiah, is simply working a con on those desiring eternal life: "Messiahs on every street corner transfix one with a confront (sic) stare: 'Your life is a ruin.' 'We have the only road to personal immortality'" (126). If you turn over your life, they will provide you with a way of evading the biologic imperative of death. It is an unlikely story, but Burroughs does not provide the true pilgrim with an alternative, a true road. These obvious cons, however, mimic the offers made by legitimate religions, advertisers, and the other operators that inhabit our real Western lands. Burroughs cannot subvert these assurances of future happiness except by pointing out the way rational culture has *always been perverted,* has always linked reason to an unreasonable expectation of enjoyment.

We should not be surprised that Burroughs's attention to divine vampires has coincided with an explosion of popular interest in this figure, ranging from Anne Rice's soft-porn romances to Hollywood's productions. One big budget film, for example, seems to have been written by a Burroughs fan. *Stargate* explicitly links the Egyptian origins of monotheism to an intergalactic, time-traveling vampire who passes himself off as the One God to ensure a steady supply of victims. What is particularly surprising is that the utterly blasphemous nature of this film went unnoticed: its claim that the bloody God of Judeo-Christian religions is merely a cover story for the vampire has, apparently, already been too fully accepted by popular culture to be worth mentioning. Burroughs, the pop icon, may be so readily accepted by youth because he comes out of the perverse yet familiar heart of the West.

The sustaining delusion in the Western world is what Burroughs calls the "fixed image," which he associates with the "basic mortality error" (158). This fixed image—God, Truth, the Phallus, or any other figure that says, like Parmenides, whatever is, is; whatever is not, is not—is behind the monotheistic promise of the individual soul's survival. It suggests permanence—even beyond death—when there is always change. The error allows us easily to link sexuality to reproduction: our longings for immortality are so strong that we have no trouble taking sexual appetite to imply a drive to make copies of ourselves, as if the vast liquidity of the bodily Real manifested an unchanging purpose. The romance of the fixed image is allied to perverse fixations, but it provides the perverse the guise of an economic, social, and spiritual good. Economically, this romance implies the reproduction of the means of production by means of an infinitely replicating ideology; biologically, the immortal extension of oneself through children; spiritually, the immortality of one's double, the soul. The fantasy of the fixed image denies temporality—at least when time is conceived of as the wasting stream of entropic decay—by positing a self not subject to degeneration. Burroughs's undermining of this "mortality error" also helps explain his attack on "sex" ("Sex is the basis of fear, how we got caught in the first place and reduced to the almost hopeless human condition" [201]), as well as his rejection of the female (The god Ka "is the only defender against the female goddesses of sexual destruction and orgasm death" [103]). These attacks represent his refusal of the tendencies to use sex and women as defenses against human mortality. The "human covenant" (180) that keeps humans bound to the fixed image is a version of the oedipal contract that we make with the One God: limit your desire, and you will be immortal.

The fixed image, of course, is incompatible with the reality of reproduction. After all, in reproduction the image is subject to chaotic fluctuation as genes err, language slips, and time and accident happen. The "biologic revolution" Burroughs imagines would cause "unimaginable chaos, horror, joy and terror, unknown fears and ecstasies, wild vertigos of extreme experience, immeasurable gain and loss, hideous dead ends" (112). Sounding like Nietzsche here, Burroughs mixes perspectives, giving us both the danger such a step would pose to the rational world as well as the ecstasy it could bring. But the chaos he describes is no longer just a paradoxical problem leading to a cultural impasse; rather, it has emerged as a solution within contemporary chaos theory. The apparently romantic step that Burroughs proposes—"from word into silence. From Time into Space" (115)—gestures toward the sublime ("awakened pilgrims catch hungry flashes of vast areas beyond Death to be created and discovered and charted"). But it also suggests that one might let go of the commitment the West holds to linear trajectories of meaning and motion that culminate in the presence of Voice and Truth. Burroughs writes, "Imagine you are dead and see your whole life spread out in a spatial panorama, a vast maze of rooms, streets, landscapes, not sequential but arranged in shifting associational patterns" (138). That is, to imagine your "self" dead means to imagine that the parts of your life are not fixed by sequence, but by shifting patterns of connection: "This happens in dreams of course." Dreams tell us something about a condition of our lives that we call being dead or, rather, beyond dead. By comparison with the linear path of life, this image of death is vividly dynamic. Chaos does not refute the necessity of temporality—dynamic change, whether in physical systems or in dreams, is irreversible—but the fixed intention, the target of time's arrow, vanishes. In "chaos," one loses the delusion of individual purpose, direction, control, which was why the One God put an end to it. The image that chaos and the theory of complexity substitute for control is the dynamic order of the developing image, of the fractal patterns generated by non-linear equations, where scale replaces time as complex development replaces purposeful growth.

Burroughs's curious preoccupation with the figure of Hassan i Sabbah, Imam of the Assassins, corresponds to his disregard for the significance of the individual subject: not only do his effective assassins kill
individual political figures without remorse, but they willingly accept
their own deaths. If one's enjoyment is in submission, the persistence of
a personal soul or image might be less important than it would be to one
committed to individuality. Burroughs quotes Hassan i Sabbah: " 'It is
fleeting: if you see something beautiful, don't cling to it; if you see something horrible, don't shrink from it, counsels the Tantric sage. However
obtained, the glimpses are rare, so how do we live through the dreary
years of deadwood, lumbering our aging flesh from here to there? By
knowing that you are *my agent*, not the doorman, gardener, shopkeeper,
carpenter, pharmacist, doctor you seem to be.' . . . So acting out a banal
role becomes an exquisite pleasure" (200). In his identification with the
figure of HIS, as he calls him, Burroughs finds a way of placing himself
outside of any political or economic order, precisely because the "concept of salvation through assassination" (202) is ultimately a parody of
the social forces he detests, made perverse in his case by its deliberate
exploitation of the enjoyment one can derive from being the agent of
another.

The idea of the Western Lands reaches back to Egypt and into a version of America, to the land of the dead and beyond death, to the dream
of Hassan i Sabbah and that of Captain Mission. There is a fatality in
Burroughs's vision of history, and consequently his critique never develops a clearly external position, never offers an alternative that does
not fall into the same history he mocks. This mockery, this con, this
clowning queer vision shows that the American sublime shares its soul
with the perverse. But I would hesitate to call this writing subversive.
Burroughs comments on the Arab world's having led civilization to become what it is, in part, by "introducing such essential factors as distilla-
tion for drunkenness, and the zero for business. What would Burroughs
and IBM do without it?" (198). Alcohol, pathway to both the sublime
and the abject. The zero that enables us to signify the Nothing, the Real
that defines us, and that made double entry bookkeeping possible; the
zero that made the Burroughs Adding Machine Company and IBM, but
that also made W. S. Burroughs. The inseparability of the two aspects of
transcendence—below and beyond—suggests less subversion than contamination. Burroughs with his black suit and his dead, knowing eyes

brings both the vampire's glamorous seduction and the virus's infection to our vision of American culture, adding a touch of abject enjoyment to the icons of the West.

Can anyone doubt that Burroughs did the athletic shoe commercial for any reason other than money? But given that motive, could anyone who has read Burroughs, who has seen Burroughs in *Drugstore Cowboy,* who even got a good look at the pale face and hooded eyes on the tiny TV screen, watch the commercial without deriving a peculiar enjoyment inappropriate to simple consumption? What kinds of enjoyment does Burroughs add to the enactment of a ritual purchase that improves the body and drives the economy?

Notes

This essay originally appeared as chapter 7 of my *Sublime Enjoyment* (Cambridge: Cambridge University Press, 1997), 130–52. It is reprinted here with the permission of Cambridge University Press.

1   Frederick Dolan convincingly demolishes any hope that Burroughs would lead us out of the wilderness, demonstrating how clearly he remains within a romantic metaphysics.

2   See, for example, "Women's Time," 187–213. Kristeva argues that a rejection of the symbolic is "lived as the rejection of the paternal function and ultimately generat[es] psychoses" (199), but by the end of even this early essay, she is proposing the highly suspect category of "guiltless maternity" (206) as a way of evading the impasse of the law. If there is a solution to the problem of patriarchy here, she does not find it through the Aristotelian construct.

3   For a discussion of *sinthome,* see my discussion in chapter 1 of *Sublime Enjoyment.*

4   "Stoicism" is a position Hegel describes dialectically, wherein one has moved beyond a slavish belief in authority, but has achieved freedom by becoming "*indifferent* to natural existence . . . , lacking the fullness of life" (122). For Lacan, this faith in the power of the individual mind, the *cogito,* to think itself to the truth becomes the delusion of those whose faith in the "name of the father," the "*nom du père,*" displays how the "non-duped err." The cynical reasoner accepts the contradictions implicit in his position and yet still continues to assert its validity.

5   See Slavoj Žižek (1989), 29–33. Žižek develops this formulation out of Peter Sloterdijk's book *Critique of Cynical Reason* (1983).

6   Chomsky recounts St. Augustine's story of a pirate, putting it in the context of international terrorism by the democratic Western nations: "[A] pirate [was] captured by Alexander the Great, who asked him 'how he dares molest the sea.' 'How dare you molest the whole world?' the pirate replied: 'Because I do it with a little ship only, I am called a thief; you, doing it with a great navy, are called an Emperor'" (1).

7   For a good summary of the relation of fantasy to sexuality, see Teresa de Lauretis, 81–85.

8   Philip Kuberski's "Hard Copy" has developed the metaphor of viral information in the late 20th century to speculate on the relation between computers, ideology, and subjectivity. Commenting on the film *Blade Runner,* he notes the murderous rage of one replicant who destroys his creator: "This scene dramatizes the film's major concern: what precisely does a man do when he learns, as has postmodern man, that his subjectivity is an artefact of society, and that his body is the accidental product of mutation and the manifestation, like a computer or a television, of Information" (70). The dilemma is that this man, constituted of information, should be both superior to "natural" men and yet inhumanly, abjectly inferior.

9   Lacan introduces the "lamella" to identify "the relation between the living subject and that which he loses by having to pass, for his reproduction, through the sexual cycle" (1978: 199). Sexual reproduction means that there is something in us that is not us, that is unconcerned with the fate of the individual subject. The mortal subject lives with the undead of replication.

10   Compare with Wallace Stevens's "Snowman," who "nothing himself, beholds/ Nothing that is not there, and the nothing that is." See also Brian Rotman's brilliant analysis of nothing, *Signifying Nothing: The Semiotics of Zero.* In this book, he traces various ways in which *nothing* has served both a productive and disturbing function in the Western world.

11   The interpretations other Cities of the Red Night gave to the words are:

The city of partisans: "Here, everything is as true as you think it is and everything you can get away with is permitted."

The university city: "Complete permission derives from complete understanding."

The cities of illusion: "Nothing is true and *therefore* everything is permitted." (158–59)

12   This is an idea I develop in chapter 5 of my *Sublime Enjoyment.*

13   See "Introduction" of my *Sublime Enjoyment.*

14   The "cut-in" or "cut-up" in Burroughs's own work and in that of his character Clem Snide involves assembling information (taped sounds, news clippings, etc.) cut at random from some source. Burroughs describes it:

The cut-up method brings to writers the collage, which has been used by painters for fifty years. And used by the moving and still camera. In fact all street shots from movie or still cameras are by the unpredictable factors of passersby and juxtaposition cut-ups. And photographers will tell you that often their best shots are accidents . . . writers will tell you the same. The best writing seems to be done almost by accident but writers until the cut-up method was made explicit—all writing is in fact cut-ups . . .—had no way to produce the accident of spontaneity. You cannot *will* spontaneity. But you can introduce the unpredictable spontaneous factor with a pair of scissors. (1982: 35)

15   See other chapters of my *Sublime Enjoyment,* especially chapter 1.

Bruce Fink | **Perversion**

Desire is a defense, a defense against going beyond a limit in jouissance.
—Jacques Lacan, *Écrits*

Modern psychiatry, for its part, has not in any way expanded our understanding of perversion. Doing what Freud tells us it does best, giving
new "names to different [behaviors] but saying nothing further about
them" (SE XVI, 260),[1] psychiatry has simply provided a panoply of new
terms to describe the particular objects that turn people on: pedophilia,
frotteurism, toucherism, transvestic fetishism, and so on.[2]

Lacan in contrast, is able to help us better understand the nature of
perversion with his crucial distinctions between the imaginary, the symbolic, and the real, and between desire and *jouissance*. If neurosis can
be understood as a set of strategies by which people protest against a
"definitive" sacrifice of jouissance—castration—imposed upon them by
their parents (attempting to recover some modicum of jouissance) and
come to desire in relation to the law, *perversion involves the attempt to
prop up the law so that limits can be set to jouissance* (what Lacan calls
"the will to jouissance"). Whereas we see an utter and complete absence
of the law in psychosis, and a definitive instatement of the law in neurosis (overcome only in fantasy), in perversion the subject struggles to
bring the law into being—in a word, to make the Other exist. As usual,
Lacan's work here grows out of Freud's, and thus I shall begin my discussion of perversion here by taking up some of Freud's distinctions.

The Core of Human Sexuality

If we begin with Freud's early assertion that any sexual activity engaged in for a purpose other than that of reproduction is perverse, then we have to accept the fact that the vast majority of human sexual behavior is perverse. Indeed, perversion lies at the very core of human sexuality, as we all begin life "polymorphously perverse"—that is, as pleasure-seeking beings who know nothing of higher purposes or appropriate objects or orifices—and continue throughout our lives to seek pleasure for its own sake in forms other than those required for the reproduction of the species.

If we begin with the notion that "normal" sexual activity is directed toward a "total person," a partner who is desired for him- or her-"self," not for any particular attribute he or she may embody, then we once again must accept the fact that the vast majority of human sexual behavior is perverse. The obsessive reduces his partner to object *a*, neutralizing the partner's Otherness, and the hysteric does not so much desire her partner as desire *via* her partner and wish to be the object he is lacking. The sexual partner is not considered as "an end in himself or herself"—in the Kantian sense of something pursued for its own sake, instead of for some other "selfish" purpose like achieving pleasure, feeling loved, or the like—but is pursued because he or she *has* something (even if it is but a lack that engenders desire) that does something for us. Indeed, as Lacan says, object *a* has something inherently fetishistic about it.[3] The object that elicits love from us is not necessarily the same as the object that elicits desire or that can bring us jouissance.

If we begin with either or both of these notions (or notions similar in kind), we are ineluctably led to qualify virtually all human sexuality as perverse. Given the way in which the terms "pervert," "perverse," and "perversion" are used by certain people to stigmatize those whose sexuality seems different from their own, it will no doubt seem politically expedient to certain readers to simply affirm that *all human sexuality is essentially perverse in nature,* and leave it at that. Indeed, Lacanian psychoanalysts view the perverse nature of sexuality as a given, as something to be taken for granted—in other words, as "normal."

What Lacanian analysts are concerned with, however, is a specific mechanism of negation—"disavowal" (Freud's *Verleugnung*)—characteristic of very few of the people considered in the popular mind and by most contemporary psychologists to be perverse, a mechanism that can be clearly distinguished from repression (at least, that is what I hope to show in this chapter). It is evidence of the functioning of this mechanism—not this or that sexual behavior in and of itself—that leads the analyst to diagnose someone as perverse. Thus, in psychoanalysis "perversion" is not a derogatory term, used to stigmatize people for engaging in sexual behaviors different from the "norm." Rather, it designates a highly specific clinical structure, with features that sharply distinguish it from neurosis and psychosis. The analyst can agree that *all* human desire is essentially perverse or fetishistic in nature, but nevertheless maintain an important theoretical and clinical distinction between neurotic structure, say, and perverse structure. In psychoanalysis, perversion is not to be viewed as a stigma but rather as a structural category.

Disavowal

In a number of different texts, Freud describes a process that he refers to as *Verleugnung,* a term that has been rendered in English as "disavowal," though in many ways the English term "denial" is closer to the German (indeed, the French have preferred the term *déni,* close in meaning and use to "denial").[4] Freud develops the notion to account for a curious attitude he detects in certain young boys who, when confronted with a girl's genitals, deny that the girl does not have a penis and claim that they in fact see one. Little Hans, for example, watching his seven-day-old sister being given a bath, says: "Her widdler's still quite small. When she grows up it'll get bigger all right."[5]

 Freud formulates this by saying that, in such cases, the perception or sight of the female genitals is disavowed. He notes that in certain older male patients, one finds a twofold attitude regarding the fact that women do not have penises: they disavow the perception, maintaining a belief in what Freud terms the "maternal phallus," but develop symptoms which seem to indicate that this perception has nevertheless been registered at some level. It is not as if the memory of a specific perception had simply been "scotomized"[6] or in some way excised from the men's minds (as we might very loosely think of foreclosure); we know it is still *there* because it has effects—it generates symptoms—but it is nevertheless denied. In his article "Splitting of the Ego in the Process of Defence," Freud mentions two examples of such symptoms: a man's fear that his father will punish him (for continued masturbation), and "an anxious susceptibility against either of his little toes being touched" (SE XXIII, 277–78).

Described in this way, disavowal seems very similar to repression: the pushing of a memory out of consciousness, and the return of this memory in the form of symptoms. Indeed, Freud at first tries to devise a clearer distinction between repression and disavowal by proposing that what is repressed is affect, whereas the idea or thought related to it is disavowed (SE XXI, 153). Yet this first attempt contradicts Freud's more rigorous and oft-repeated assertion that only an idea or thought can be repressed. In neurosis, an affect and the thought related to it (its "ideational representative," as Strachey translates Freud's term *Vorstellungs-repräsentanz*)[7] become dissociated; for example, the thought representing a sexual impulse that the ego or superego considers incompatible or unacceptable is repressed, while the affect associated with it is set free to be displaced. In the description Freud provides in "Splitting of the Ego," disavowal and repression seem to collapse into one and the same process.

In an article from 1938, Freud makes a second attempt to distinguish repression from disavowal by saying that in repression one of the patient's own sexual impulses ("an instinctual demand from the internal world") disappears, whereas in disavowal it is "a portion of the real external world" (SE XXIII, 204) that disappears. To state this more rigorously: in repression, the *thought* associated with one of the patient's own drives[8] is put out of mind (the quantum of libido or affect associated with the drive being set free to drift or be displaced), while in disavowal a perception of the "real external world" is put out of mind.

This only makes matters worse, however, because the "portion of the real external world" in question is, Freud says, the "lack of a penis."[9] It should be clear that, strictly speaking, one never *sees* or *perceives* the lack of anything: one sees what is there to be seen, not what is absent. The lack of a penis (or of anything else for that matter) is not a question of perception: there is no lack at the perceptual level—there the world is full.[10] One "sees" nothing only if one is expecting something in particular and mentally notes its absence. Except in a totally dark room, one always sees something; there are always photons striking the rods and cones of the eye. "Nothing" exists only at the level of thought.

Thus, what is involved here is not perception per se—as Freud says, it is not as if there were a scotoma or black spot on the retina, impeding the fetishist from seeing what is there to be seen, stopping him from receiving certain photons—but a thought related to a particular perception. Seeing is not believing.

Freud's 1938 distinction between repression as related to the internal world and disavowal as related to the external world is reminiscent of his 1924 distinction between "neurotic anxiety" and "realistic anxiety." Neurotic anxiety stems from an internal danger—that is, an impulse within the patient that is considered inappropriate by the patient's own ego or superego—whereas realistic anxiety (which Freud also refers to as "fear") stems from a real external danger (SE XXII, 81–89). Insofar, however, as disavowal clearly involves a thought related to a perception—that is, something generally considered to be inside the subject, part of his or her psychical reality—not a perception alone,[11] the internal-versus-external distinction breaks down.[12] Both repression and disavowal involve thoughts, not perceptions.

Having discussed the overriding importance of psychical reality and the social/linguistic constitution of reality compared to some sort of objectivist view of reality, I will restate Freud's distinction as follows: in repression, the thought associated with one of the patient's own drives is put out of mind, whereas in disavowal a thought, or complex of thoughts —related to a perception of the female genitals, to the father's supposed castration threat (issued to keep the boy away from his mother and to keep him from masturbating), and to the patient's narcissistic attachment to his penis—is put out of mind.

A first symbolization

One of the important things to note here is that, if what is put out of mind is a thought, then at least a first symbolization has taken place: in perversion, something related to the father and his will to separate his son from the mother is symbolized, and thus, in contrast to psychosis, an initial acceptance or admission (*Bejahung*) of the father as symbolic separator takes place. Basing our theorization on Freud's clinical observations about the perverse patients he treated, we can assert that the father is symbolized to at least some extent because of the castration-related symptoms that form.[13] Yet this symbolization is not as complete as that achieved in neurosis.

Since my goal here is not to exhaustively critique Freud's inconclusive definitions of disavowal as a mechanism that clearly differs from repression, I will first indicate what I think we *can* take disavowal to refer to in the context of Lacan's thought (though to the best of my knowledge Lacan never formulates it as I am going to) and then I will try to translate some of Freud's discussions into Lacanian terms, that is, in terms of the Other and the sacrifice of jouissance. My claim here is that disavowal is a mechanism that *can* be clearly distinguished from repression.

Like foreclosure and primal repression, *disavowal concerns the father*: the father's desire, the father's name, and the father's law. *The three mechanisms that constitute the three essential psychoanalytic categories—* neurosis, psychosis, and perversion—*all concern the paternal function* (typically fulfilled by a child's father in our society). This point is not nearly as clear in Freud's work as it is in Lacan's, and thus Lacan can be seen to have systematized Freud's work in this respect.[14]

As we saw in chapter 7, while Freud maintains that paranoia (one of the psychoses) results from a defense against homosexual urges (SE XVI, 308), Lacan says that homosexuality is not irrelevant to the understanding of psychosis but rather a *consequence* of the foreclosure of the Name of the Father. The defense against homosexuality turns out to be a *byproduct* of foreclosure, not the cause of psychosis. Similarly, Freud's notion that the fetish object is related in the fetishist's mind to the so-called maternal phallus is not irrelevant from a Lacanian perspective, but is, rather, understandable in terms of the father, his desire, and his law. Belief in the maternal phallus suggests, as we shall see, that the mother's desire-engendering lack has not been canceled out or named by the father as it is in neurosis.[15] In other words, Lacan does not consider Freud's observation irrelevant but subsumes it within a larger theoretical framework.

From a Lacanian perspective, the apparent contradiction inherent in disavowal can, it seems to me, be described as follows: "I know full well that my father hasn't forced me to give up my mother and the jouissance I take in her presence (real and/or imagined in fantasy) hasn't exacted the 'pound of flesh,'[16] but I'm going to stage such an exaction or forcing with someone who stands in for him; I'll make that person pronounce the law." This particular formulation applies better to the masochist than to the sadist or fetishist, as we shall see, but suffices to indicate that disavowal implies a certain *staging or making believe regarding the paternal function*.

Refusing the sacrifice

The notion of sacrifice or exaction is certainly not absent from Freud's work on perversion, and one of the places we see it most clearly is in Freud's discussions of the "splitting of the ego." A splitting of the ego, Freud postulates, occurs in perversion, not in neurosis. In neurosis, contradictory thoughts are situated at different levels, in different agencies. For example, "I want to sleep with my sister-in-law" is repressed and persists in the unconscious, while the idea "I *don't* want to sleep with my sister-in-law" is what becomes conscious.[17] In perversion, on the other hand, the ego itself splits (SE XXIII, 204), and contradictory ideas—a woman both does and does not have a penis—are maintained side by side in the same agency.[18] Freud refers to this as a partial "turning away from reality" (SE XXIII, 277) by the ego, a procedure he would prefer to reserve for psychosis. Yet the description he provides of the case on which he bases his notion of splitting (SE XXIII, 276–78) differs little from cases of repression; for, in the former, the repressed returns in the guise of two symptoms (the man's fear that his father will punish him for continued masturbation, and "an anxious susceptibility against either of his little toes being touched"). Symptom formation requires, as Freud himself teaches us (SE XVI, 358–59), two different agencies that are at odds—ego and id, or conscious and unconscious—and we seem to have neither more nor less than the conditions of neurosis here: the splitting of the "I" (*Ich*) into conscious and unconscious due to repression.

But let's take a closer look at this supposed case of splitting to see where renunciation comes in ("instinctual renunciation," as it is translated in the *Standard Edition*, though it is a question of renouncing the pleasure provided by the drives). A young boy, early "acquainted with the female genitals through being seduced by an older girl," takes pleasure in touching his own genitals after relations with the older girl are broken off. One day his nurse catches him doing it and tells him his father will "cut it off" if he does not stop. Freud tells us: "The usual result of the fright of castration, the result that passes as the normal [neurotic] one, is that, either immediately or after some considerable struggle, the boy gives way to the threat and obeys the prohibition either wholly or at least in part (that is, by no longer touching his genitals with his hand). In other words, he gives up, in whole or in part, the satisfaction of the drive" (SE XXIII, 277). This boy, however, continued to masturbate as if no threat had been issued. He refused to give up that jouissance *in the name of the father.* His nurse demanded that he give it up for his father's sake (otherwise his father would castrate him, Freud tells us), because his father would not approve, but the boy refused.

Faced with the possible loss of jouissance, the pervert and the obsessive react in different ways, Freud suggests. The obsessive submits to the loss, however reluctantly, however half-heartedly, and even if he never stops trying to get some of that jouissance back later.[19] He gives up that jouissance in the hope of gaining esteem, recognition, and approval — a symbolic equivalent. He loses one thing to gain another: we might say that he is induced to give up his narcissistic (imaginary) attachment to his penis — which Lacan later refers to as the imaginary phallus, ϕ, the penis as invested narcissistically — and the autoerotic pleasure it gives him, to win something at the social, symbolic level. He gives up ϕ for Φ, the phallus as signifier, as the socially recognized signifier of value and desire. As Lacan says regarding little Hans, a boy must, in some sense, hand over his little penis to get a bigger and better one from his father (Seminar IV). Often the latter is not considered bigger and better enough, in the end. Often it is considered totally inadequate, and the boy may feel he got a raw deal and hold it against his father forever. But some autoerotic pleasure is nevertheless yielded, given up, or handed over by the obsessive.[20]

The pervert, on the other hand, does not hand that pleasure over, does not surrender his pleasure to the Other. Freud insists again and again that the pervert *refuses* to give up his pleasure, that is, the masturbatory pleasure related (in his fantasies) to his mother or mother substitute.[21] Why does one boy surrender it and another refuse? Freud sometimes appeals here to constitutional factors in explaining this refusal: perhaps the pervert's drives are stronger than the neurotic's, and cannot be subjected and tamed the way the neurotic's can.[22] It seems, however, that a number of different explanations are possible. Consider the following:

Clinical work and everyday observation show that mothers are often

dissatisfied with their husbands and look for satisfaction in their lives
from their relationships with their children. It is also clinically at-
tested that mothers are more inclined to take a male child as their all-
encompassing complement in life than a female child, and we can only
assume that that is due to the child's sex (and its social meanings, of
course).[23] Now a mother's interest in her son's penis always contributes
to the localization of jouissance in the male sexual organ; and in cases in
which a mother places great value on her son's penis, he may become extremely attached to it, narcissistically speaking, his whole erotic relation
to his mother revolving around it. Such a son is likely to energetically
resist any kind of perceived demand that he stay away from his mother,
and the struggle is likely to center around his penis, even if no direct
threat is made to it (though such direct threats still are made more often
than many think).[24]

Insofar as mothers do not often take their daughters as their complement to the same extent, look to them for such intense satisfaction in
life, or take such great interest in their genitals, the mother-daughter
relationship is rarely eroticized to the same degree,[25] jouissance is not
usually symbolically localized for females in the same way, and the
struggle with the father over separation from the mother generally does
not come to a head in the same way or focus on a specific organ.[26] The
father often has an easier time separating his daughter from her mother
(though he may not find it as important to do so, not feeling that he is
in competition with his daughter as he is with his son); nevertheless, the
result is likely to be either hysteria with traits of perversion when the
father is not forceful, or psychosis when the father refuses to intervene
at all.

This explains, in part, my use of masculine pronouns alone here when
talking about perverts. In psychoanalytic terms, perversion is virtually
an exclusively male diagnosis. Indeed, Lacan goes so far as to say that
"female masochism is a male fantasy,"[27] and qualifies lesbianism, not as
a perversion, but as *"hetero*sexuality": love for the Other sex, that is,
women ("homosexuality"—*hommosexualité,* which includes the two m's
from *homme,* "man"—being love for men [Seminar XX, 78–79]).[28] The
fact that males are "the weaker sex with respect to perversion" (*Écrits,*
823; 320) should certainly give us pause for thought, and warrants more
explanation than I can provide here.[29]

To return to the question of why one boy might agree to give up pleasure while another might refuse, we see that in cases in which there is a
very close bond between mother and son, a father has to be very forceful
in his threats to bring about a separation and/or convincing in his promises of esteem and recognition. But the very fact that such a close bond
has been able to form suggests that the father either is incapable of fulfilling the paternal function or does not care to interfere (perhaps happy
to be left alone by his wife who is now preoccupied with her son). It may
also be that the boy's mother is perhaps overly indulgent and undercuts
the father's authority. The father, while avoiding the rivalrous ferocity
of certain psychotics' fathers, does not forcefully put himself in the position of symbolic separator (the one who says this is mine and that is
yours, that is, the one who gives the child a symbolic space). And even
if he does try to do so, he may be undermined by the boy's mother who,
the moment the father's back is turned, winks at the boy, letting him
know that their special relationship will secretly remain unperturbed.

It seems to me that we have to shift our focus from the kind of father
Freud often seems to have *presumed* to exist—that is, the father who
forcefully enunciates his will to separate his son from the boy's mother
(the pervert being the son who obstinately refuses)—to the all-too-
common contemporary father who is a much weaker figure and is often
confused about his role.[30] In cases where there is a strong mother-son
bond and a weak or indifferent father, the paternal function, while not
altogether absent, may well stand in need of a boost. In an early childhood phobia such as little Hans's, appearing around age four, the object that becomes central in the phobia Hans develops (the horse) serves
as *a* name of the father that contributes to the separation of mother
from child. Perversion, like early childhood phobia, results from a partial failure of the paternal function, the latter requiring supplementation
in order to bring about separation. Rather than emphasizing, as Freud
does, the pervert's refusal to sacrifice jouissance, and his attempt to
maintain the jouissance he obtains from the relationship with his mother
or mother substitute (a fetish, for example), we need, it seems to me, to
stress *the inadequacy of the paternal function.*

While disavowal could be described as a defense mechanism, a defense against the father's demand that the child sacrifice jouissance, we
could instead view it, like Hans's phobia, as not simply evasive, but as an

attempt to prop up the paternal function (expressed in the father's law) —to make the Other *pronounce* the law, or to indicate oneself the place of the law—so that the anxiety-relieving separation can come about. In a Lacanian perspective, separation from the mOther may be anxiety producing in certain respects (the object becomes lost or falls away at the moment of separation), but is generally relieving at a more profound level, that is, at the level of being. Hans, for example, is "afraid" at the conscious level that his mother will go away, but unconsciously wishes she *would* go away and allow him to have desires that do not involve her. His "separation anxiety" reflects a wish to continue to "coax" with his mother—in other words, to obtain certain pleasures with her—but a simultaneous wish for an end to be put to that "coaxing," to that jouissance, for the latter engulfs him and stops him from coming into being as a desiring subject.[31] Thus his "separation anxiety" is a wish for separation—separation from his mother.

Jouissance is simply overrated. It is not so wonderful that everyone really wants it, the pervert supposedly being the only one who refuses to give it up and who is able to go out and get it.[32] The psychotic suffers due to an uncontrollable invasion of jouissance in his or her body, and neurosis is a strategy with respect to jouissance—above all, its avoidance. Perversion too is a strategy with respect to jouissance: it involves the attempt to set limits thereto.

Being and having, alienation and separation

The whole problem of the perversions consists in conceiving how the child, in its relationship with its mother—a relationship constituted in analysis not by the child's biological [*vitale*] dependence, but by its dependence on her love, that is, by its desire for her desire— identifies with the imaginary object of her desire.—Jacques Lacan, *Écrits*

Freud reveals to us that it is thanks to the Name-of-the-Father that man does not remain bound to the sexual service of his mother.—Jacques Lacan, *Écrits*

One way to describe my essential thesis regarding perversion here is to say that *the pervert has undergone alienation*—that is, primal repression, a splitting into conscious and unconscious, an acceptance or admission of the Name of the Father that sets the stage for a true coming-to-be of the subject in language (unlike the psychotic)—*but has not undergone separation*.[33] How can we characterize the pervert's alienation here? As

Lacan tells us, we come into the world offering ourselves up as partial objects to the Other's desire (*Écrits*, 582; 225), hoping to be the object of the Other's desire, to win the Other's desire; and the pervert— whose father's desire is not terribly pronounced it would seem—"identifies with the imaginary object of [his mother's] desire, insofar as she herself symbolizes it in the phallus" (*Écrits*, 554; 198). In other words, the imaginary object of the mother's desire here is the phallus—not as a displaceable symbol, in the sense that the mother might desire, say, all the trappings of status, all socially valorized objects, or a husband (or boyfriend or whatever) who resembles socially accepted images of "real men," sometime "possessors" of the phallus, but as an unsymbolized, nonfungible, undisplaceable object—and the child attempts to become it for her. He attempts to be her little prized possession, her little substitute penis, as Freud might have put it, and the father often does not care to interfere (perhaps preferring to be left alone) or is ineffectual in his attempts to interfere.

We can represent the pervert's situation as shown in Figure 1.

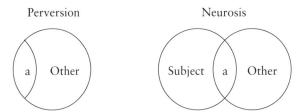

When we compare this configuration with that of neurosis, we see that the pervert's "subject position" does not entail something outside or beyond the Other. Instead the pervert, as subject, plays the role of object: the object that fills the void in the mOther. A first division in the Other has occurred for the pervert, graphically speaking: the Other is not whole; his mOther is lacking in something, wants for something. To the question, "What am I?" the pervert responds, "I am that," that something she is lacking. Thus, for the pervert, there is no persistent question of being—in other words, no persistent question regarding his raison d'être.

To separate the boy from his mother here would entail forcing him to stop *being the phallus* so he can have it, stop being the imaginary phallus in order to obtain a symbolic one (through the father's recognition and esteem, through social, symbolic channels). If he *is* the phallus for his mother, he will never accede to a symbolic position—that associated with symbolic castration. Rather than becoming someone the mother can be proud of, he remains someone she cuddles with, strokes, and perhaps even reaches sexual climax with. He cannot go off to "make a name for himself" in the world, for it is not symbolic stature that he is able to seek.[34] He remains stuck at the level of serving as his mother's be-all and end-all.

Primal repression allows the subject to come into being, but the child is then left to ask, "What *am* I? What am I to my parents?" The pervert constitutes himself as what is lacking in the mOther; making himself into the object of her desire, he constitutes himself as her object *a*. He becomes what she is missing (her penis/phallus) and what she wants. He plugs up her lack with himself. The Other's desire/lack is anxiety producing, insofar as it is not named; the pervert's solution to this anxiety is to become the object that can stop up the desire by providing the Other with jouissance, with the kind of satisfaction that squelches desire (albeit temporarily).[35]

This explains why it is so difficult to do analytic work with perverts: the pervert casts himself in the role of object *a*, expecting to play the part of the object that can satisfy (plug up) the analyst's desire. The analyst may be hard pressed to maneuver the transference in such a way as to become the cause of the perverse analysand's desire, when the latter works so hard to occupy the position of cause of desire. The pervert would rather serve as the cause of the analyst's anxiety and desire than let the analyst become the cause of his own musings. It is thus quite difficult to do genuinely analytic work with perverts, to get them intrigued by unconscious formations and by what the analyst underscores in them, and to get their desire in motion. As Lacan says, object *a* must be situated by the subject in the Other, the Other as analyst here, in order for transference to be possible (Seminar X, July 3, 1963).[36]

In order to articulate the pervert's position more rigorously, however, it must be emphasized that *the pervert deals not so much with the mOther's desire as with her demand*. As long as the desire/lack a child's mOther "has" is not named, the child is confronted with her demand alone. Strictly speaking, we cannot even say that he is confronted with her lack or desire since lack does not exist outside of a symbolic system. Lacan's often-repeated illustration of what constitutes lack is the example of a book that is *not present* on a library bookshelf. From the perspective of perception, we cannot say that the book is missing because we see only what is there, what is present, not what is not there. It is only because of a symbolic grid—for example, the Dewey decimal system or the Library of Congress book classification system—that provides the book with a designation or name (such as "BF 173, F23, 1899, v. 2") that we can say that the volume is not in its place or is missing (volumes 1 and 3 being there, with no space between them). Nothing can be thought of as missing except when there is a signifying system in which certain spaces or places are laid out or ordained. We cannot think of something as missing without language, without some kind of symbolic order.

What this implies is that *we cannot even speak of the mother as lacking* (so far as her child is concerned) *until she is* said *to be wanting in some respect*—until she herself verbalizes a longing for something or someone or a desire for something or someone other than her child, or until someone else (typically the father) pronounces something about her desire (for example, she is envious of so and so, she wants a fur coat, she wants to be promoted, she would like the father to act like this instead of like that) or about her shortcomings. The child cannot be said to understand his mother to be lacking or to desire until her desire or lack has been articulated, formulated, verbalized, put into words. Once it has been named, the weight of her demands (her real, physically unavoidable demands regarding the child's bodily functions, for example) lifts, and a space of desire opens up—a space in which her desire is articulated and moves, and in which her child can model his desire on hers.

Until "it" is named, there is no lack; the child is submerged in the mOther as demand and cannot adopt a stance of his own (a desire that constitutes a stance with respect to jouissance, a defense against jouissance).[37] The child here is confronted with what we can refer to as a *lack of lack*. Only the mOther's demand exists; she is lacking in nothing "to speak of," nothing that is symbolizable for the child.[38] Once named, however, the "real lack" (the lack in the mother's life—for example, the dissatisfaction with her husband, her career, her whole life—that she has been attempting to make good through her son, even though it has never been spoken) is neutralized to some extent. As Lacan says, the word is the death of the thing; the thing (the "real lack"), once named, comes into being as a word that can be linked up with other words, joked about, and so on. The word is far less dangerous than the thing it supposedly signifies or designates, for it actually annihilates the thing, drains away some of its oppressive force.

Once that which the mOther is missing is named, the *object* the child was for his mOther can no longer be. For once desire is articulated in words, it does not sit still, but displaces, drifting metonymically from one thing to the next. Desire is a product of language and cannot be satisfied with an object. The naming of the mOther's desire forces the child out of his position as object, and propels him into the quest for the elusive key to her desire. What does she want? Something ineffable that seems to characterize the endless series of things her desire alights upon—what in Western society is known as the phallus. No longer the real object (the real organ) required to complete her, the child can go on to seek to possess what her desire points to, connotes as desirable, as phallic.

The mother's lack has to be named or symbolized for the child to come into being as a full-fledged subject. In perversion, this does not occur: no signifier is provided that can make that lack *come into being at the level of thought*, easing its real weight. Neither the mother nor the father provides the articulation necessary for symbolization. As we see in Freud's work, the question of the mOther's lack often centers, in perversion, around the mOther's genitalia, her sexual difference from her son.

There are two moments of the paternal metaphor. This naming of the mOther's desire/lack is the second (logical) moment. If the first moment of the paternal metaphor is the father's *prohibition* of the child's pleasurable contact with its mother (prohibition of jouissance), *le Nom du Père* taking the form of the father's "No!," the second moment involves the symbolization of the mOther's lack—that is, *its constitution as lack* due to the fact that it is given a name (here we see le Nom du Père as the name provided by the father, or the father himself as the name of the mOther's desire).

The two substitutive moments can be represented schematically as follows:

Father's "No!"	Father's name
Mother as jouissance	Mother as desire

Only the second moment can be considered genuinely metaphorical, since it is only in the second that language operates in a full-fledged manner by naming. These two moments correspond precisely to the two schemas provided in Figure 1: the first moment leads to a division within the mOther, whereby the child comes into being as the object with which the Other obtains satisfaction, while the second leads to the advent of a desiring subject (separate from the Other as source of jouissance). The first corresponds to what Lacan calls alienation, the second to separation. The first may also be fruitfully associated with what Freud calls primal repression, the second with secondary repression.

As I said earlier, my essential thesis here is that, although the pervert has undergone alienation, he has not undergone separation. The psychotic has undergone neither, while the neurotic has undergone both. This can be schematically represented as follows:

	Alienation		Separation	
Psychosis	Father's "No!"	Perversion	Father's name	Neurosis
	Mother as jouissance		Mother as desire	
	Primary repression		Secondary repression	
	Prohibition of jouissance		Naming of lack	
	ϕ		Φ	
	Demand		Desire	

If psychosis can be understood as owing to the absence or failure of paternal prohibition, perversion can be understood as owing to the absence or failure of symbolization.[39]

From jouissance to separation

In discussing perversion, Freud almost always emphasizes the subject's refusal of the law, his obstinate refusal to give up satisfaction; thus, in a sense, he considers perversion almost exclusively from the perspective of the satisfaction the pervert continues to obtain.[40] Lacan examines perversion in what might be qualified as a more classically Freudian manner: perversion, like every other activity, must be considered in terms of the satisfaction it brings (however indirect or unintuitive), but it also must be considered in terms of the function it serves in relation to the law and separation. A neurotic symptom provides the patient with a certain substitute satisfaction, but it also forms, in certain instances, *in order to bind anxiety;* so too the pervert's activities serve a purpose that is not simply that of achieving direct sexual satisfaction.[41] Many neurotics think perverts must be getting an awful lot more satisfaction in life than they are—indeed many analysts fall into the same trap. This stops them from seeing what it is that the apparent "will to jouissance," as Lacan calls it, in perversion is designed to do, is in the service of, and is covering over.

Turning our attention from the kind of father Freud often seems to have assumed to exist—that is, the father who has no reservations about separating his son from the boy's mother (the pervert being the son who obstinately refuses to let that happen)—to the all-too-common contemporary father who never worked out his own problems with authority, does not believe fathers should wield authority over their children, believes children are rational creatures and can understand adult explanations, prefers to let his wife discipline the children, wants to be loved not feared, and who (perhaps to boot) allows his wife to undercut his authority, we can begin to understand perversion from a rather different perspective.[42]

Perversion and the law

One of the paradoxical claims Lacan makes about perversion is that while it may sometimes present itself as a no-holds-barred, jouissance-seeking activity, its less apparent aim is to bring the law into being: to make the Other as law (or law-giving Other) exist. The masochist's goal, for example, is to bring the partner or witness to the point of enunciating a law and perhaps pronouncing a sentence (often by generating anxiety in the partner). While the pervert seems to be able to obtain a kind of "primal satisfaction"—transcending his own subjective division as a subject of language (who like the rest of us speaking beings is not supposed to be able to obtain more than a mere pittance of jouissance: as Lacan tells us, "jouissance is prohibited to whoever speaks" [*Écrits*, 821; 319]), and finding a kind of wholeness or completeness neurotics can only dream of or fantasize about—anxiety in fact dominates the pervert's sexuality. The pervert's conscious fantasies may involve a kind of unending jouissance (consider the Marquis de Sade's numerous scenarios where the male sexual organ never manifests any limit in its ability to recommence sexual activity), but we must not confuse conscious fantasies with concrete activity, and *the latter is designed to place limits on jouissance*.[43]

Desire is always a defense, "a defense against going beyond a [certain] limit in jouissance" (*Écrits*, 825; 322), and the pervert's desire is no exception. The masochist, for example, in fantasy, seems to do everything for the Other and nothing for himself: "Let the Other get off on me, use me as he or she sees fit!" he seems to say. Beyond this fantasy, however, his aim is somewhat different: beyond this apparent altruism—"Nothing for me, everything for the Other!"—there is something in it for him. Desire as a defense appears in the pervert's fundamental fantasy that manifests his position with respect to the law.

The neurotic desires in relation to the law: the father says the child cannot have its mother, and the child thus unconsciously desires her. The pervert, on the other hand, does not desire as a function of the law—that is, does not desire what is prohibited. Instead, *he has to make the law come into being*. Lacan plays on the French term, *perversion*, writing it as *père-version*, to emphasize the sense in which the pervert calls upon or appeals to the father, hoping to make the father fulfill the paternal function.

Jouissance and the moral law

Jouissance . . . is indecently admitted to its very wording.—Jacques Lacan, *Écrits*

Certain moralists and ethical philosophers like Kant would have us believe that moral principles are "rational" and objective, and that we can accept living by them "rationally" just because they are "true." Freud suggests, however, that a principle is nothing in someone's psychical reality until a quantum of libido has been attached to it; in other words, a moral principle, like any other thought (*Vorstellung*), has to be *cathected* before it can play a role in someone's psychical economy. And the psychical agency in which Freud situates moral principles is the superego which, as Freud himself teaches us, takes pleasure in criticizing the ego—not simply reminding the ego of the law, but getting off on berating the ego for its failure to execute the law and enjoying a kind of vicious enunciation of the law. The superego, as the internalization of the criticism we receive from our parents, is a repository not merely of the moral principles our parents hand down to us, but also of the kind of harshness we sense in their voices when they lecture, scold, and punish us. The superego can be ferocious in certain cases, obviously taking a good deal of pleasure in badgering, berating, and bludgeoning the ego, but the important point here is that it is impossible—except in philosophical treatises—to divorce the statement of a moral principle from the libido or jouissance attached to its enunciation; it is impossible to divorce a precept taught us by our parents (for example, "Do unto others as you would have others do unto you") from the tone of voice in which it was pronounced.

The moral law, as it plays a role in our psychical lives, is *not* an abstract proposition, principle, or statement with universal or quasi-universal application: it is an enunciation, announcement, proclamation, or kerygma. The moral law—whether it goes by the name of the "voice within," the voice of conscience, or the superego—originates in parental voices, most typically in the voice of the father.[44] It is experienced by children as *an expression of the Other's desire.* The father who "lays down the law" for his children expresses, announces, and proclaims his desire for things to be a certain way and not another.[45]

The moral law is thus inextricably associated with expressions of the Other's desire and jouissance, and the masochist seeks to elicit that jouissance in lieu of the law. Since he cannot obtain the symbolic law as such, he seeks that which he somehow understands to be associated with it. The Other's desire or will is accepted by the masochist instead of the law, in the place of the law, in the absence of the law. As Lacan mentions, the Marquis de Sade (better known as a sadist, but here manifesting decidedly masochistic tendencies) pushes his mother-in-law, Madame de Montreuil, to the point where she expresses her will that Sade be punished. It is her desire or will that has to serve Sade as a law. Not *the* law, but *a* law.

The neurotic tends to be upset when the enunciation of the law is accompanied by jouissance on the part of the enunciator. The neurotic senses that there has been some kind of miscarriage of justice or abuse of power when a judge allows him or herself to make certain kinds of comments or adopts a certain tone in sentencing a criminal: "and if it were up to me, Mr. Jones, given your heinous crimes, your sentences would run consecutively and you would be unable to even apply for parole until you were 140!"[46] For here "justice" becomes vindictive, exceeding its mandated role to act objectively and dispassionately. The neurotic implicitly grasps the notion and even clings to the *ideal* of the symbolic father who is fair, impartial, and disinterested, and who simply applies rules that govern everyone equally. "That symbolic Father, insofar as he signifies the Law, is clearly the dead Father" (*Écrits*, 556; 199), that is, the father who can experience no jouissance, who cannot derive some sort of "perverse" pleasure from the enunciation of the law.

The pervert seems to be cognizant, at some level, of the fact that there is always some jouissance related to the enunciation of the moral law. The neurotic would prefer not to see it, as it strikes him or her as indecent, obscene. The symbolic law is supposed to be free of invocations of this kind. Indeed, it would seem that the pervert accepts the invocations in lieu of the symbolic law itself, unable as he is to obtain the latter. The criminal justice system, with its often vicious guards and wardens, certainly provides perverts who are subjected to it confirmation that vindictiveness and cruelty constitute the hidden face of the law.

Incarceration nevertheless continues to serve as an often sought-after form of punishment for the masochist, seeking some sort of substitute symbolic castration, as he does. As Lacan says, "Recourse to the very image of castration can come as a relieving, salutary solution to [*issue à*] anxiety for the masochist" (Seminar X, March 26, 1963). The subject in need of separation turns and returns for relief to whatever substitute castration can be had.[47]

Meta-Considerations

Freud's whole investigation comes down to this: "What does it mean to be a father?"
—Jacques Lacan, Seminar IV

Psychoanalysis has not, with Lacan, completely moved beyond the stage of cosmology, of mythological thinking; indeed, at certain points, Lacan deliberately provides his own myths.[48] But his work on the relationship between words and the world (signifiers and "reality"), and on the movements and displacements within language itself (metaphor and metonymy), provide the necessary linguistic basis for understanding the crucial role of the Freudian father. The paternal function served by the latter is grounded in linguistics: his function is a symbolic one. His crucial role is not to provide love—as the popular mind is so likely to sustain—but to represent, embody, and name something about the mother's desire and her sexual difference: to metaphorize it.[49] Serving a symbolic function, he need not be the biological father, or even perhaps a man. It is the symbolic function itself that is essential.

The Paternal Metaphor as Explanatory Principle

Understood as involving two distinct logical moments, and as instating the symbolic order as such, the paternal metaphor can be usefully understood as providing a subject with an "explanatory principle," an explanation of the why and wherefore of its having been brought into the world, an interpretation of the constellation of its parents' desire (and oftentimes grandparents' desire, as well) that led to its being born.

For the neurotic, there is always some sort of explanatory principle; there is always a little story, vague and confusing as it may be, about why our parents wanted us, or perhaps didn't want us at first but grew to love us. This little story tells us something about the place we occupy in their desire—not the place we occupy in the universe as a whole, science seeming to provide us with such insignificant places in it (the universe contains, as Carl Sagan says, "billyuns and billyuns of galaxies")—and this space in their desire, however small, is our foothold in life.

But what are we wanted for? That is the question.[50] If we are wanted only as an extension of one parent, and expected to devote ourselves to that parent's "sexual service," trouble ensues. We must be wanted for something else, something perhaps extremely obscure: "We just want you to be happy," "We want you to achieve something important," "We want you to make us proud." As anxiety producing as such parental desires often are to the neurotic, they are part of the price that must be paid to stave off the "worst."

The delusional metaphor constructed by a psychotic serves to make up for the lack of just such an explanatory principle. The psychotic's delusions—when allowed to pursue their own course—move toward creating a world in which the psychotic is assigned an important place, a critical role. The psychotic's delusional cosmology serves to explain the why and wherefore of the psychotic's birth, and the purpose of his or her life on Earth. Thus, it too attempts to tie word to meaning, like the paternal metaphor.

Consider the case of a very young boy I know whose mother had destroyed the boy's father, demanded complete loyalty from her son (never tiring of telling him that he would have trouble finding a wife later because of his special relationship with his mother), put him in her bed every night, and never revealed her genitals to him or said anything to correct his belief that both men and women had what he called "a ball" (his term for a penis). In order to have him, his mother had decided to get pregnant without consulting the father, a man she had just begun dating; she later told the boy his father had abandoned him because he didn't love him (when she had actually driven the father to suicide).

A therapist has a number of options in such a case. He or she can wait, and hope the child articulates something that will transform the mother's unbearable presence and demands (the mother as real) into a speakable, bearable reality (the mother's desire as named), but the therapist then runs the risk of abandoning the child to psychosis or perversion. Or the therapist can invent an explanation: "Your father very much wanted a little boy like you, and asked your mother to have his child. Since your father's death, your mother has been very scared and upset, and holds onto you as a reminder of her lost husband."[51]

This is not merely a construction—it is a calculated lie. But with such a lie, if it is introduced after a strong relationship has been established between therapist and child, and does not blatantly contradict too much of what the child has heard about the absent father, the therapist creates an important place for the father in the mother's world and thereby names her desire. In other words, if the therapist is successful in making this construction stick (and I have seen it work), the therapist transforms the mother's demand for the child to give her all of her satisfaction in life with the whole of himself—transforms it into a desire, a desire for something else, for the father or something about the father that the boy can then try to fathom.

This construction will contradict certain things the mother says, but the child will set about trying to understand what the mother says in the context of the construction: "She won't let go of me because she misses my father"; "She complains of his abandoning us because she is lonely." The contradictions do not uproot the construction or anchor the therapist has provided, but rather serve as the point from which everything else is interpreted. So although the mother's behavior and presence have not necessarily changed a whit, the therapist has enabled the child to *read* them differently. The child's experience of his mother has been radically transformed by the construction.

Later in life, the child may come to reject virtually all facets of the therapist's construction, coming to believe instead that the mother's motives were mostly malicious and self-serving, but *he will reject the construction from the standpoint of the construction.* In other words, he will have a point on which to stand that remains unshakable, a vantage point from which to cast doubt upon the accuracy of the construction. Prior to the construction, there was no place to stand, no ground, and thus no possibility of questioning or wondering. After the construction, the child can call everything into question without ever cutting out the ground from beneath his feet. He may, at the extreme, come to wish he had never been born, but at least there will be a place from which he can formulate that wish! That place is the subject, the Lacanian subject.

Notes

This essay originally appeared in *A Clinical Introduction to Lacanian Psychoanalysis* by Bruce Fink (Cambridge, Mass.: Harvard University Press), 165–202, copyright 1997 by the President and Fellows of Harvard College. It is reprinted here in abridged form with the permission of Harvard University Press.

1   Sigmund Freud, *The Standard Edition of the Complete Psychological Works of Sigmund Freud,* ed. and trans. James Strachey et al. (London: The Hogarth Press and The Institute of Psycho-Analysis, 1961). Subsequent references to *The Standard Edition* both in the text and in the notes will use the abbreviation SE followed by volume number and page number or lecture number.

2   These "fine" diagnostic distinctions are included under the general category of the "paraphilias" in the *Diagnostic and Statistical Manual of Mental Disorders* [DSM-III-R] (Washington: American Psychiatric Association, 1987). The psychiatric authors of this all-too-widely used manual seem to adopt the more scientific sounding term "paraphilias" in order to avoid the seemingly less politically correct term "perversions." However, they go on to use the most crassly political and moralistic language

in their detailed discussions of the paraphilias—for example, "The imagery in a Paraphilia . . . may be relatively harmless" (279); "*Normal* sexual activity includes sexual excitement from touching or fondling one's sexual partner" (283, emphasis added); and so on.

3   See *Écrits*, 610; 248, where Lacan speaks of the "fundamental fetish of every perversion qua object glimpsed in the signifier's cut," implying thereby that the object as fetish is crucial in every perversion. The object as isolated by the signifier (as "cut out" of an undifferentiated ground, simultaneously creating both foreground and background) will be discussed later in this chapter.

4   See the fine discussion of *Verleugnung* in J. Laplanche and J.-B. Pontalis, *The Language of Psychoanalysis*, trans. D. Nicholson-Smith (New York: Norton, 1973), an indispensable book that provides encyclopedic analysis of Freud's most central and complex concepts. Note that, in translating *Verleugnung*, the French also sometimes use the term *démenti*—from *démentir*, meaning "to belie" or "to give the lie (to something)."

5   SE X, 11; see also SE XXIII, 276.

6   See Freud's reference to this term in SE XXI, 153.

7   See the discussions of this term in Bruce Fink, *The Lacanian Subject: Between Language and Jouissance* (Princeton: Princeton University Press, 1995). It should be understood in relation to Freud's related term, *Triebrepräsentanz*—the representative, at the level of thought, of a drive (for example, the thought "I want to sleep with my sister-in-law").

8   Or "representative of the drive" (*Triebrepräsentanz*)—that is, the drive's representative at the level of thought. Strachey translates *Triebrepräsentanz* as "instinctual representative."

9   Freud sometimes seems to suggest that it is castration itself that is repudiated—in other words, the *idea* that the mother's penis was cut off and that one's own penis could thus be cut off. In this case it would seem that one idea remains in consciousness—"Every human being has a penis"—while a diametrically opposed idea is put out of mind, and this is tantamount to Freud's own definition of repression.

10   As Lacan says, "By definition, the Real is full" (Seminar IV, *La relation d'objet, 1956-1957*, ed. Jacques-Alain Miller, Paris: Seuil, 1994, 218)—that is, nothing is lacking in the Real. See also Seminar VI, April 29, 1959 (*Le désir et son interprétation, 1958-1959*, privately published by and for the members of L'Association freudienne internationale, Paris: I.S.I., 1994, 364), where Lacan says "The Real as such is defined as always full." The same general idea is repeated again and again in Lacan's work. In Seminar X (*L'Angoisse, 1962-1963*, unpublished) Lacan suggests that what he means by this is not so much that there are no holes or rips in the Real, but rather that there is nothing *missing* in the Real, nothing absent or lacking.

   Subsequent references to each seminar in the text and notes will appear as Seminar followed by volume number and page number.

11   Indeed, as the hysteric teaches us, perception itself is not an "innocent" or scientifically objective process, giving us a "true view" of the "real external world." Each

culture "perceives" differently, as a function of the distinctions its language engenders.

12 Consider how Lacan problematizes any attempt to draw clear lines between inside and outside in his use of surfaces such as the Klein bottle and the cross-cap in Seminar IX (*L'identification, 1961–1962*, unpublished). See also Fink, *The Lacanian Subject*, end of ch. 8.

13 In other words, some repression has occurred. Note that if something is put "out of mind," it first had to be "in mind"—it first had to be a thought, had to be symbolized.

14 Theorists and practitioners who place little emphasis on the importance of language, law, and the symbolic are likely to think Lacan has systematized Freud in an infelicitous way, leaving out the importance of the mother. It should be clear, however, to anyone who reads Freud carefully that throughout his work the father is of capital importance. Lacan simply provides Freudians with the wherewithal to refute Freud's critics who stress the importance of the pre-Oedipal: with the advent of language and the law, the pre-Oedipal is rewritten or overwritten. "The pregenital stages . . . are organized in the retroactive effect of the Oedipus complex" (*Écrits*, 554; 197). The Oedipus complex has a retroactive effect on that which preceded it temporally, implying that it is a symbolic operation; for in the signifying process, the addition of a new signifier to a series (say, of the term "father's 'No!'" to the series "name of the father," "father's name," and "name given by the father") transforms the meaning of what was said before. Since speech is the only tool at our disposal in psychoanalysis, what we deal with as analysts are the retroactively constituted meanings, not the pre-Oedipal relations that preceded them.

15 This is one instance in which Freud's terminology needs to be clarified by using Lacan's categories: the fetishist believes his mother has a penis—that is, a real, biological organ, not a phallus; for a phallus is a symbol—in other words, part and parcel of the symbolic order. Lacan sometimes loosely refers to the organ the child believes in as the imaginary phallus, but that should generally be understood to imply the penis (the real organ) the child imagines the mother has.

16 This expression is used in Shakespeare's *The Merchant of Venice*.

17 Freud says one thought persists in the id and the other in the ego (SE XXIII, 204), a formulation that leads to further problems in his own metapsychology.

18 Freud encourages us to understand this split in the ego in terms of knowledge. According to Freud, the perception of the female genitals is put out of mind because it implies that the father means business when he threatens to cut off the boy's penis (indeed, the boy believes that the father has already done it to the boy's mother); this newly realized possibility of losing the highly invested organ leads to considerable anxiety. The anxiety is dealt with, not as in neurosis where a symptom forms to bind or alleviate anxiety, but by the formation of a kind of split (*Spaltung*). The split is such that two bits of "knowledge" are maintained side by side in a kind of punctual suspension of the law of non-contradiction: "Women don't have penises" and "All humans have penises." There may be abstract, rote knowledge where the pervert simply repeats what those around him say ("Women don't have penises"), and yet

simultaneously a recognition at some level that that is true, as the thought generates anxiety in the pervert. Alongside this, however, there is a kind of subjective necessity leading to a belief beyond all proofs, a disavowal of that intolerable knowledge ("It's small now, but it will grow"). The pervert knows full well that women do not have penises, but cannot help feeling that they do anyway ("Je le sais très bien, mais quand même").

Whereas neurosis consists in a defense against an incompatible idea involving sexuality—leading to a denial taking the classic form, "The person in my dream was *not* my mother," the idea coming to consciousness only thanks to the addition of the "not"—perversion involves a kind of split, according to Freud: the pervert says yes and no simultaneously.

19 Consider the importance in American culture—intuitively understood by every successful merchandiser—of getting something for nothing, of getting things for free. Consider too the eminent popularity of movies, books, and stories about bank robbers (e.g., *A Fish Called Wanda*), jewel thieves (e.g., *The Pink Panther*), and so on where the audience is led to identify with criminals and enjoy their exploits leading to free millions.

20 At the very least, the obsessive's autoerotic behavior is transformed: if he continues to masturbate, it is in defiance of the paternal prohibition and thus this prohibition becomes part and parcel of the masturbatory activity. The Other becomes included in the fantasies that accompany it (not necessarily consciously, of course). One of my female analysands, for example, continued to masturbate while fantasizing about being watched by a powerful man.

This yielding of pleasure to the Other can also be understood in terms of sublimation, as Freud conceptualizes it.

21 According to Freud, a young boy's masturbatory behavior generally involves fantasies about the boy's mother, which implies that it is already alloerotic—in other words, that it involves another person. I would even go so far as to claim that, beyond an extremely tender age, *there is no such thing as autoeroticism*. Even an infant's masturbatory touching already includes its parents insofar as they first stimulated certain zones, showed interest in them, paid attention to them, lavished care on them, and so on. The connection to other people—which is so evident in the adult's fantasies that invariably accompany "autoerotic behavior"—is so fundamental that there seems to be no *eroticism*, as such, without it. All eroticism is alloeroticism.

22 For example, SE XVI, Lectures 21-22.

23 Consider, for example, the behavior of little Hans's mother: whereas she beats her daughter Hanna, she takes her son into her bed, into the bathroom with her, and so on.

24 This is how I think we can understand what Freud means when he talks about the pervert's great narcissistic attachment to his penis, and his "excessive" drives. For drives are not constitutional or biological in origin, but come into being as a function of the Other's demands (the anal drive, for example, comes into being due to the parents' demands that the child become toilet trained, that it learn to control its ex-

cretory functions). It is the mOther's interest in and demands related to the pervert's penis that are responsible for the intensity of the pervert's drives.

25 Though in cases of psychosis, this might well be the case.

26 Fetishism, which holds an important theoretical place among the perversions, involves the localization of a great deal of libido on a kind of substitute sexual organ (as we shall see in the case study discussed below), and this occurs to a much lesser extent in girls than in boys.

27 Similarly, Lacan defines Don Juan as a feminine dream, a dream of a man who is lacking nothing ("qui ne manque rien"; Seminar X, March 20, 1963); he also refers to Don Juan as a feminine myth (Seminar XX, *Encore. On feminine sexuality: The limits of love and knowledge, 1972–1873*, ed. Jacques-Alain Miller, trans. Bruce Fink [New York and London: W. W. Norton & Company, 1998], 10). It should be noted that Lacan is not necessarily saying that there is absolutely no such thing as female masochism, but rather that men tend to see it in women because they want to see it in them, and that it is thus certainly far rarer than men would like to believe.

28 "Let us, by definition, call 'heterosexual' those who, regardless of their sex, love women" (Lacan, "L'Étourdit," *Scilicet* 4 [1973]: 23).

29 Jacques Lacan, *Écrits*, 823; 320. Subsequent references to *Écrits* appear parenthetically and include the page number of the original edition followed by the page number of the English translation.

See Jacques-Alain Miller, "On Perversion," in *Reading Seminars I and II: Lacan's Return to Freud*, ed. Bruce Fink, Richard Feldstein, and Maire Jaanus (Albany: SUNY Press, 1996). On page 319, Miller says of female perversion:

You have to look for female perversion where it is invisible. Female narcissism may be taken as a perversion, as an extension of the concept. It is because Woman is Otherness as such or the Other that she spends so much time in front of the mirror—just to recognize herself, or perhaps to recognize herself as Other. Even if it is a myth, it is very important. You may find female perversion in narcissism, at the core of one's own image, or as Freud proposed, in the child—the child used as an object of satisfaction.

In the latter case, we have the mother and the imaginary object, the phallus. The mother here is responsible for the perversion of the male child, but at the same time uses the child as an instrument of jouissance. According to the preceding formula, you could call that perversion. Was the first perverse couple mother and child? Lacan, in the fifties, suggests that it is in the connection between the mother's own body and the child that you may find a concealed expression of female perversion.

Insofar as female homosexuality eliminates the male organ, there is some difficulty placing it in the register of perversion proper.

It is not clear to me whether or not Lacan would have equated the "perverse" nature of the mother-child relationship with perverse structure, strictly speaking.

30 It should be kept in mind that such weak fathers are well documented in literature dating back at least to the time of ancient Rome, and that the argument that fathers have lost tremendous power since the last century seems a bit under-demonstrated.

31   Consider, in the following exchange (from SE X, 17), the way in which his mother
     tries to prevent him from having a desire for a woman other than herself by guilt-
     tripping him when he manifests such a desire:
       Hans: "Oh, then I'll just go downstairs and sleep with Mariedl."
       Mother: "You really want to go away from Mummy and sleep downstairs?"
       Hans: "Oh, I'll come up again in the morning to have breakfast and do num-
     ber one."
       Mother: "Well, if you really want to go away from Daddy and Mummy, then take
     your coat and knickers and—good-bye!"

32   Indeed, as Freud tells us, the pleasure principle would have us achieve the lowest
     possible level of tension or excitation.

33   In this book, my comments on the two operations Lacan terms "alienation" and
     "separation" are fairly basic, as I have discussed them at length in chapters 5 and 6
     of my *The Lacanian Subject*. Note here that while the subject comes into being in
     language through alienation, s/he comes into being as a mere place-holder or lack
     (*manque-à-être*). It is separation that provides something more along the lines of
     being.

34   The father fails here to provide the "phallic signifier"—to "unscrew," for example,
     Hans's imaginary phallus (in one of the boy's dreams, the faucet in the bathtub, a
     symbol for his penis, is to be replaced by the plumber) and replace it with a sym-
     bolic one.

35   A subject position, like a symptom, is fundamentally a solution to a problem. The
     schema I have provided in Figure 1 of the pervert's solution bears a certain affinity to
     the hysteric's solution (though in the former the subject side is altogether missing).
     There is, nevertheless, an important difference in register between the two: whereas
     the hysteric tries to be the object that causes the Other's *desire* (symbolic), the per-
     vert becomes the object that causes the Other's *jouissance* (real), that is, the object
     by means of which the Other obtains satisfaction. The hysteric refuses to be the real,
     physical object by means of which the Other obtains satisfaction.

36   The analyst occupies the place of the analysand's question or lack of satisfaction:
     when there is no question—whether it involves one's reason for being or one's con-
     fusion over what gives one sexual satisfaction—or lack, the analyst cannot play his
     or her role. As Jacques-Alain Miller says, "You need a certain void or deficit in the
     place of sexual enjoyment for the subject supposed to know to arise" ("On Perver-
     sion," 310).

37   Here, the first libidinal object (that is, the object that provides the child jouissance)
     is the mother.

38   Lacan brings up the question of the lack of lack in a somewhat different context: It
     is most commonly believed that a child becomes anxious when its mother is absent,
     when she is not there with the child; Lacan suggests, on the other hand, that anxiety
     actually arises owing to a lack of lack, when the mOther is present all the time. "What
     provokes anxiety? Contrary to what people say, it is neither the rhythm nor the alter-
     nation of the mother's presence-absence. What proves this is that the child indulges

in repeating presence-absence games: security of presence is found in the possibility of absence. What is most anxiety producing for the child is when the relationship through which he comes to be—on the basis of lack which makes him desire—is most perturbed: when there is no possibility of lack, when his mother is constantly on his back" (Seminar X, December 5, 1962). What this suggests in the case of the pervert is that, given the overly close mother-child relationship, not only is the mother not perceived as lacking, seeming to desire nothing beyond her child (whom she "has"), but the child himself cannot sense a lack in his own life and thus cannot desire, strictly speaking—cannot come into being as a desiring subject. Desire, Lacan teaches us, is a cover, but also a remedy for anxiety.

39   In perversion, there seems to be both a backward-looking and a forward-looking gesture: the former involves the attempt to give the Other satisfaction; the latter, as we shall see below, seeks to prop up or supplement the father's act of naming. In neurosis, too, there are both backward- and forward-looking gestures: the former involves the attempt to become what the Other desires—in obsession, to perfectly incarnate the signifier of the Other's desire (Φ), in hysteria to perfectly incarnate the cause of the Other's desire (a)—while the latter involves the attempt to shake free of one's fixation on the Other's desire, this being the analysand's path.

40   Consider his comments about the advantages of fetishism: "We can now see what the fetish achieves and what it is that maintains it. It remains a token of triumph over the threat of castration and a protection against it. It also saves the fetishist from becoming a homosexual, by endowing women with the characteristic which makes them tolerable as sexual objects. In later life, the fetishist feels that he enjoys yet another advantage from his substitute for a genital. The meaning of the fetish is not known to other people, so the fetish is not withheld from him: it is easily accessible and he can readily obtain the sexual satisfaction attached to it. What other men have to woo and make exertions for can be had by the fetishist with no trouble at all" (SE XXI, 154).

41   Binding anxiety is, obviously, something that can also be understood in terms of satisfaction, for it lowers the level of tension as required by the pleasure principle; similarly, the pervert's enactment of separation can be understood in terms of satisfaction, as we shall see.

42   If we take le désir de la mère (the mother's desire for the child or the child's desire for the mother) as a given, the onus very often falls upon the father to bring about triangulation and separation.

43   A person's concrete actions often give us a far better sense of his or her fundamental fantasy than the fantasies of which he or she is aware, especially at the beginning of an analysis.

44   In the Old Testament, it is the voice of God that commands. In Judaism, it is the shofar sounded on Yom Kippur that recalls/re-presents the voice of God. Lacan discusses this at length in Seminar X (May 22, 1963).

45   Kant, for example, attempts to eradicate desire from a moral law that leaves no room for human feelings, attachments, and desires in its pursuit of universality (applicable

to all cases); but morality is never detached from its medium: the parental voice that expresses desire and/or anger (passion or jouissance) even as it expresses a moral principle.

46   A comment made recently by a Pittsburgh judge.

47   Lacan draws many a link between castration and the sexual act for men. See in particular his discussions in the second half of Seminar X—above all the class given on June 19, 1963.

48   For example, the myth of the libido as the "lamella" in "Position of the Unconscious" in *Écrits,* trans. Bruce Fink, in *Reading Seminar XI: Lacan's Four Fundamental Concepts of Psychoanalysis,* ed. Bruce Fink, Richard Feldstein, and Maire Jaanus (Albany: SUNY Press, 1995), 273–76.

49   A recognition, however small, by psychoanalysts of the importance of language and of the paternal function will hopefully lay to rest the kind of approach to perversion taken by an object relations theorist like Sheldon Bach who, regarding sadomasochists, proffers the following banality: "One might say that these patients have to some degree failed to adequately integrate the mother of nurturance and the mother of frustration, or the mother of pleasure and the mother of pain" (Bach, *The Language of Perversion and the Language of Love* [Northvale, N.J.: Aronson, 1994], 17).

50   The answer is provided in the fundamental fantasy.

51   The therapist would likewise do well to explain sexual difference, with pictures if need be. And in a case such as this one, the therapist would be advised to tell the boy that, since his mother does not have a penis, she tries to get one from a man, and failing that, from her son. The point is to indicate that there is something a man has that she wants: she desires something outside herself, for she is lacking in something, something that can be named. Nothing is more anxiety provoking than a lack of lack.

"I Know Well, but All the Same . . ."

Octave Mannoni
Translated by G. M. Goshgarian

As soon as we begin to attend to the psychological problems thrown up by beliefs, we discover that they cover a very broad range of experience and display rather close similarities across the most widely divergent domains. Because these problems remain unsolved, we are not only unable to say with certainty what a sixteenth-century humanist—Rabelais, for instance—did or did not believe, but are not much better off when it comes to assessing our contemporaries' ambivalent belief in superstitions. The ethnographers cite astonishing statements by their informants, who assure them that people *used* to believe in masks *in the old days;* but these ethnographers do not always clearly tell us just what has changed since, as if the change in question could be chalked up, as it were, to the steady spread of enlightenment. It is a fairly safe bet that a belief of this sort has *always* been associated with the old days; but we would like to know why. A person watching a magician perform does not for an instant believe that his tricks are magic, yet she insists that the illusion be "perfect." We would be hard put to say who is supposed to be fooled. Something similar occurs in the theater—is, indeed, so much a part of the theater that playwrights have devised "induction scenes," as in *The Taming of the Shrew*, or imagined little fables about naive, gullible spectators who take what happens on the stage for real life. These are run-of-the-mill examples of the problem of belief; others, as we shall see, are more surprising.

Psychoanalysis, which encounters problems of belief every day, has not made much effort to elucidate them. Freud has suggested how it might, but he makes the suggestion obliquely and unexpectedly, which doubtless explains why virtually no one has explored the path he has opened up. It may be noted that neither the word "belief" nor any of its equivalents in other languages appears in the index to any edition of his works.

The problem of belief necessarily arose very early for Freud, and he never lost sight of it. It forms the subject of one of his last writings (left unfinished in 1938),[1] which approaches the question as something both quite familiar and altogether new. But it is in a very short 1927 paper on the problem of fetishism that Freud opens up the problematic of belief, in the course of defining *Verleugnung* with all the precision the concept requires. This German term may be rendered by the French *désaveu* or *répudiation* [or the English disavowal or repudiation]. It occurs in Freud as early as 1923, always in passages that turn, implicitly or explicitly, on the question of belief. This is so consistently the case that, to locate the passages in question despite the lacuna in the indexes, one need only look up the term *Verleugnung*.

It is well known how *Verleugnung* comes into play in the constitution of fetishism, according to Freud's 1927 essay. When a child first becomes aware of the anatomy of the female body, he discovers, in reality, the absence of a penis; but, so as to preserve his belief in the existence of the maternal phallus, he disavows or repudiates the refutation of his belief that is imposed by reality. Yet he can retain this belief only at the price of a radical transformation (which Freud tends to treat, first and foremost, as a modification of the ego). "It is not true," says Freud, "that, after the child has made his observation of the woman, he has preserved unaltered his belief that women have a phallus. He has retained that belief, but he has also given it up. . . . a compromise has been reached, as is only possible under the dominance of the . . . primary processes. The child has maintained a divided attitude towards that belief."[2] This "divided attitude" becomes, in the 1938 text, the *splitting* of the ego.

Belief is transformed under the influence of the primary processes; in other words, it is subject, in the final analysis, to the effects of the repressed, especially of unconscious desire. In this sense, it obeys the basic laws. However, *Verleugnung* itself has nothing in common with repression, as Freud expressly states and as we shall explain in a moment. It may be understood as a simple *disavowal* of reality (although it must also be distinguished from scotomization). Laplanche and Pontalis have accordingly translated *Verleugnung* as *déni de la réalité* [disavowal of reality] in their (unpublished) *Vocabulaire de la Psychanalyse,* which they are writing under Daniel Lagache's direction.[3] This is, to be sure, the first meaning of the term; what is initially disavowed is the refutation, imposed by reality, of a belief. But the phenomenon is more complicated, as we have already seen, for the reality that is observed does not remain without effect. The fetishist has disavowed the experience that proves to him that women do not have a phallus, but he does not cultivate the belief that they have one; he cultivates a fetish because they *do not* have one. Not only is the experience not eradicated, it is ineradicable. It leaves an *indelible mark* on the fetishist, one he bears forever. What is eradicated is the *memory* of the experience.

We shall see that Freud's 1927 paper is far from elucidating the problem of fetishism, although it is generally only cited in discussions of that perversion. In fact, the paper examines a precondition for elucidating this problem, by showing how a belief can be abandoned and preserved at the same time. The obstacles that we run into if we go down the path that Freud thus points out—they probably explain why no one has taken it after him—are of a rather special kind, as the reader will discover soon enough: one finds oneself torn between an impression of extreme banality and a powerful feeling of strangeness. The matter that requires explanation also seems to be plain as day. This was Freud's own experience in 1938; his paper begins with the words, "I find myself for a moment in the interesting position of not knowing whether what I have to say should be regarded as something long familiar and obvious or as something entirely new and puzzling."[4] This impression is rooted in the very nature of the subject: we have to do here, at any rate, with phenomena we encounter at every turn, in daily life as well as in our psychoanalyses. In analysis, they take a —indeed, virtually stereotypical— form: the patient, ill at ease in some cases and quite relaxed in others, employs the phrase, "I know well, but all the same. . . ." Of course, the fetishist does not use a phrase of this sort to describe his perversion: *he knows well* that women do not have a phallus, yet he cannot add a "but all the same," since his "but all the same" is his fetish. The neurotic spends her life saying "but all the same," yet she cannot, any more than the fetishist, declare that women have one after all; she spends her life stating this in other ways. However, like everyone else, by virtue of a sort of displacement, she utilizes the mechanism of *Verleugnung* in connection with other beliefs, as if the *Verleugnung* of the maternal phallus furnished the paradigm for all other disavowals of reality and was at the origin of all other beliefs that manage to survive their refutation by experience. Thus fetishism obliges us to consider, in a "puzzling" form, a class of phenomena that can easily escape our attention when they wear a familiar, everyday aspect.

As everyone knows, Freud once had a patient who was told by a fortune-teller that his brother-in-law would die of shellfish poisoning that summer. After the summer had passed, the patient said to Freud, in sum, "I know well that my brother-in-law hasn't died, but, all the same, that prediction was wonderful."[5] Freud was amazed by this comment, but he was preoccupied by a very different problem at the time and did not pause over the form of belief that his patient's statement implied. Something on the order of belief had to have subsisted, with the fortune-teller's help, in order to be recognizable, despite its transformation, in this feeling of satisfaction, which was patently absurd. Yet it is neither more nor less absurd than the construction of a fetish, although it is a phenomenon of a very different order.

We are so used to hearing the phrase "I know well, but all the same" that it does not always seem as surprising to us as it does here. In a certain sense, indeed, it is constitutive of the analytic situation. It might be said that, before the invention of psychoanalysis, psychology had focused exclusively on the "I know well," while striving to banish the "but all the same." Since St. Paul, at least, people had been quite familiar with a certain duplicity, a vague prefiguration of the splitting of the ego; but all they could see in it was a scandalous violation of their unitary, moralistic conceptions of the self. Even those psychoanalysts who (a bit like St. Paul) held that it was necessary to strike up an alliance with the healthy half of the subject never imagined that, by privileging the "I know well," they would, once and for all, gain the upper hand over the "but all the same," since that is no longer possible once the analytic situation has been established. Evidently, the sole reason for the "but all the same" is the "I know well." For example, the sole reason for the existence of the fetish is that the fetishist *knows* that women have no phallus. Precisely this relationship might serve to define *Verleugnung*, for it makes it obvious that *Verleugnung* cannot be confused with denial [*négation*]. The statement "I am quite sure that it is not my mother" does not at all require a "but all the same." For the "it is my mother" continues to be repressed—in the way in which, precisely, repression subsists after denial. In such cases, we speak of *knowledge*, not belief; in other words, there is no reality more or less directly at stake here.

Whenever an analyst fails to recognize an act of *Verleugnung* in the analytic situation—as sometimes happens, since *Verleugnung* is often obscure or disguised—the patient, fortunately, immediately calls her attention to it by replying, "I know that, of course; but all the same. . . ." The analyst may then conclude that what is involved is repression; for instance, she may content herself with the idea that her interpretation has reached the patient's conscious without penetrating his unconscious. This somewhat simplistic topographical explanation has one flaw: it does not help us see what to do. The unconscious is too remote, or the patient is, so to speak, too thick; his consciousness and his unconscious are separated by too dense a barrier. Yet the "but all the same" is not unconscious. It finds its explanation in the fact that desire or fantasy operates, as it were, at a distance. Plainly, that is the point at which we must ultimately arrive. But we cannot do so directly, nor does this justify oversimplifications. After all, we cannot respond to someone who has asked us about the tides by telling him to "consider the moon"; we would be responsible for too many drownings. In other words, although repression is in the final analysis the key to the problem, as always, we must begin by examining *Verleugnung* as such.

No repression is involved where beliefs are concerned. That is one of the founding axioms of psychoanalysis (it dates from May 25, 1897). It is of small importance here that every representation initially appears as a reality; that is a question of a different order, and has to do with hallucination, not belief. It is another aspect of the problem—indeed, *the* other aspect of the problem. Freud himself notes how far we would be from fetishism if the subject opted for the solution of *hallucinating* the phallus.

Problems connected with religious faith have to be put aside at the outset; they are of a different nature, even if it is a fact that faith is always mingled with belief. So as not to create the impression of contenting myself with stating a paradox, I would like to say a word about the matter.

The true nature of religious faith has no doubt been concealed from us by borrowings from Greek ontology. At some point, faith began to concern itself with the *existence* of God—so, at any rate, it would seem. One need only read the Bible to see that the Jews believed in the existence of all the gods; they even waged war on them. Yet they maintained their *faith* in just one. Faith meant their unconditional commitment. The subject to hand is belief: the belief that, for example, allowed the Jews to believe in the existence of Baal, although they had no faith in him. At the limit, a reduction can be effected in this case as well; the stuff of both faith and belief is the word [*la parole*] of others. That, however, does not warrant confounding them at the level on which I am placing myself here.

We will need examples to make this clearer, and they will have to be of a rather massive cast, for the question is, by its nature, an elusive one. I will take the first of them from ethnography: ethnographic literature abounds in them. I have already mentioned the phrase that is constantly on informants' lips: "In the old days, people believed in masks." It raises a hidden problem involving the informants' beliefs—and also, if more subtly, the ethnographers'. Yet it is easy to bring out what is at stake, and even to transform it into an apparent banality.

The French reading public knows Don Talayesva's *Sun Chief.*[6] The book makes it rather easy to see what the belief in masks consists in and how it is transformed. Hopi masked dancers are known as Katcinas. At a certain season of the year, the Katcinas appear in the pueblos, much as Santa Claus appears in our culture; and, again like Santa, they take a strong interest in children. They also resemble Santa Claus in that they conspire with parents to deceive them. The imposture is very strictly maintained, and no one would dare to expose it. Unlike the ambiguous but easygoing Santa Claus, however, the Katcinas are terrifying figures, for, if they are interested in children, it is because they want to eat them. The children's mothers save their terrorized progeny, of course, appeasing the Katcinas with pieces of meat. In return, the Katcinas give the children little balls of corn meal, known as *piki,* which, though usually yellow, are colored red for the occasion. The error of too simple a psychoanalysis would be to assume that these rites should be interpreted in terms of stages, fantasies, or symbols. Their real interest lies elsewhere, as will soon appear.

"Once," Talayesva tells us, "when there was to be a Katcina dance

within two days, I found my mother in a nearby house, baking piki. I
had entered unexpectedly and discovered that she was making red piki.
When I saw that it was red piki . . . I was upset. . . . That evening at
supper . . . I ate almost nothing. . . . The next day when the Katcinas
were distributing their gifts to us I did not want any of their . . . piki.
But to my surprise they gave me not red but yellow piki. . . . Then I was
happy" (75–6).[7]

This time, then, Talayesva has managed to avoid giving up his belief,
thanks to his clever mother's ploy. As to the other judgment, "Mama
is fooling me," it is hard to say what becomes of it. It must be present
somewhere. It can be seen that what we might call a first test of disavowal causes anxiety, and is not far from being a traumatic ordeal; our
young Hopi is relieved to escape it. This crisis is akin to the one that
Freud assumes the future fetishist undergoes, and, as it is not directly
accessible, proceeds to reconstruct: it is an *unheimliche*, traumatic moment, that of the discovery of reality. Beyond the shadow of a doubt,
the crisis of belief in the Katcinas reproduces, as its model, the structure
of the crisis of belief in the phallus. Similarly, Freud saw in the crisis
linked to castration the model for the kinds of panic that erupt later in
life, when people are suddenly overwhelmed by the feeling that "Throne
and Altar are in danger." We will already have recognized castration in
the emotion that overcomes the young Hopi when he is confronted with
the red piki. The alarm soon passes; it is a mere foretaste of what will
occur when the boy reaches the age of ten or so, the age of initiation.
Yet it is not a matter of indifference, in my view, that things should thus
transpire in two distinct periods. This makes an "it was true after all"
possible, and this repetition certainly plays an important role.

When the children are initiated—in the course of ceremonies that are
intended to be as impressive as possible, and that *directly* evoke castration—the adults who are known as fathers and uncles in the Hopi kinship system reveal, by removing their masks, that they were the ones
who played the Katcinas. How do the initiated react when they learn
the truth?

"When the Katcinas entered the kiva without masks," Talayesva
writes, "I had a great surprise. They were not spirits. . . . I recognized
all of them, and I felt very unhappy, because I had been told all my life
that Katcinas were gods. I was especially shocked and angry when I saw

that all my clan fathers and uncles were dancing as Katcinas. I felt the worst when I saw my own father" (84).[8]

Indeed, what can one believe if authority is deception [*mystification*]?

What is truly puzzling here is the fact that this ceremony of demystification and the blow it deals to the children's belief in the Katcinas provide the institutional foundation for the new belief in them that forms the heart of Hopi religion. Reality—the fact that the Katcinas are the initiates' fathers and uncles—has to be disavowed by way of a transformation of belief. Yet is this so puzzling after all? Do we not tend to find it natural? "Now you know," the children are told, "that the *real* Katcinas do not come to dance in the pueblos *the way they did in the old days.* Now they only come invisibly, and, on the days of the dance, they dwell in their masks in mystical fashion." A Hopi Voltaire would doubtless reply that, having been fooled once, he won't be fooled again! But the Hopis distinguish and contrast the way the children are deceived and the mystical truth into which they are initiated. A Hopi can say in all good faith, in a way that is manifestly not quite identical to the formulation we meet with in psychoanalysis, "*I know well* that the Katcinas are not spirits; they are my fathers and uncles. *But, after all,* the Katcinas are present when my fathers and uncles dance masked."[9] The formula "in the old days, people believed in masks" is not as simple as it seems. I shall come back to the relationship between belief and imposture.

Thus, after this trying experience, in which infantile beliefs are refuted, these beliefs can continue to exist in adult form: something has, as it were, gone over to the other side (the definition of initiation). When Talayesva later falls ill and is saved by a tutelary spirit, the spirit appears to him in the guise of a Katcina. At another point, Talayesva takes pleasure in the thought that he will come back to dance as a Katcina in his pueblo after his death. But he also says something else: that all of this has been a lesson to him, and that, from now on, he will take care to do what is right. We have here a reaction that recalls the establishment of the superego; but it also and all but indiscernibly recalls the moment when belief, shedding its imaginary form, is symbolized sufficiently to lead on to faith, that is, to a commitment.

Since some might ask, though the answer is obvious, about the question of castration, it should be pointed out that this question arises for Talayesva too, both apparently and explicitly; but it arises elsewhere, without ever intersecting the question of belief in the Katcinas or even the symbolic castration rites that are part of initiation. This is a general phenomenon that will not surprise us any more than the fact that the fetishist does not associate his worship of the fetish with his castration fantasies. What we have already glimpsed will be confirmed as we go along: namely, that belief in the presence of the maternal phallus is the first belief that one disavows and the paradigm for all other acts of disavowal. Let us also note how difficult it would be to rewrite Talayesva's history in terms of repression or fantasy. The concept of the splitting of the ego does not appear to be of much service here; it is not, at any rate, indispensable, probably because we no longer conceive of the ego as a synthetic apparatus.

Talayesva's story is everybody's story, whether she is normal or neurotic, Hopi or not. After all, it is plain that we have installed God in the heavens, although we have found no trace of him in the sky, by dint of a transformation comparable to the one carried out by the Hopis. But, obviously, this story cannot be the same as the fetishist's; if we examine the matter more closely, we shall see that there are major differences among the effects of disavowal, whether they are acknowledged or ignored. Because these differences are hard to define, we shall have to try to rough out, for better or for worse, a classificatory schema. Talayesva would provide a good model for the simplest, most straightforward class in this schema.

I have so far left aside a very important point, the fact that there always remain non-initiated children who continue to be taken in by the imposture. A crucial feature of every initiation is that the initiated make a solemn vow to keep the secret. They will take part in perpetuating the imposture in their turn; one might say that the children are a kind of prop for the adults' belief. In some societies, the women too are among the credulous; but, in all societies, beliefs are based, first and foremost, on the credulity of the children.

Here I am repeating an idea that forcefully impressed itself on me when I asked myself, while doing other research, what sustained the belief of theatergoers;[10] I wondered where the imaginary credulous spectator was. I will add that I do not think we have paid enough attention to the question as to exactly what transpires when, in our societies, an adult feels the need to deceive a child — about Santa Claus, the stork, and so on—to the point that she sometimes fears that Throne and Altar, to use Freud's expression, will be endangered if someone suggests disabusing the victim. Because of our geneticist preconceptions, we make childhood a means of diachronic explanation. But, in synchronic perspective, the child can, as someone who is both present and an outsider, play a non-negligible role by assuming, as he does among the Hopis, the burden of our beliefs after disavowal. He is not privy to the adults' secrets. This may seem to go without saying; but we know well that, in the case of certain perverts, it is the normal adult who is assumed to be credulous and ignorant of the child's secrets. To put it differently, the situation is not as natural as it may seem; if psychoanalysis has delivered us of the myth of children's purity and innocence, it has not gone very far in analyzing the function of this myth. Dazzled by the resistance that the revelation of infantile sexuality initially provoked, analysts were persuaded that, by pointing to the repression (the amnesia) of adults, they were on the way to clearing everything up. But if we admit that invoking the ostensible innocence of children is only a way of talking about their credulity, the picture is considerably altered. As with the Hopis, if more confusedly, infantile credulity helps us disavow our own beliefs: needless to say, even if we have no direct contact with children, our mental representation of them suffices. Many adults would readily confess—they are sometimes struck by the absurdity of the situation—that they are religious not for their own sake, but for their progeny's. This reasonable concern for children's spiritual education is not the whole explanation for the large place that children hold in the organization of beliefs. Yet this concern alerts us to the interest that specialists in belief of all kinds take in children, in a way that is somewhat reminiscent of the Katcinas', even if the social institution that regulates *Verleugnung* is much less well organized in our societies.

This very clear-cut example is more a model than anything else: it quite plainly shows how a belief can, if transformed, survive even if it flies in the face of reality. It will be readily granted that the structure conforms to this model in those cases in which what occurs is rather well concealed from the consciousness of the subject; but, as will soon appear, we also have to admit the possibility of other kinds of structures, not all of which correspond to the same model. For the moment, let us content ourselves with noting that a belief may be retained without the subject's knowledge. In analysis, we often observe that unexpected reactions or effects reveal irrational beliefs or "superstitions" of which the subject is not conscious, although they are not repressed; we cannot make them manifest by overcoming a resistance. Rather, they are elusive, insubstantial, difficult to grasp. The reason is that they are attributed to others. Examples of this are to be found everywhere. Thus, in a recent book on Dien Bien Phu, Jules Roy notes that the code name of the *Groupement opérationnel du nord-ouest* [Northwest Operational Group] was "GONO." This was, he says, a name of ill-omen,[11] a circumstance the general should have taken into account. No doubt. But who believes in this sort of ill omen? Would Roy himself confess to a belief in divination based on the sounds of certain words? Surely not. Nobody believes in it—and everybody does. It is as if we live in a world in which certain beliefs are in the air, even if no one will admit to having them. *One* has such beliefs. There is nothing more common than the kind of remark Roy makes—and yet nothing more puzzling, if we stop to think about it.

Let us, then, put aside what others believe in order to observe how a belief may appear to the subject himself, and in what sense it more or less eludes his grasp. For reasons that are no doubt suspect, but hidden, I sometimes read the rather rudimentary horoscopes published in certain papers. It seems to me that I do not take much of an interest in them. I wonder how people can believe in them. I like to imagine the kind of tragedies that such predictions may occasionally provoke. Once, last year, my horoscope said that "tomorrow will be an extremely favorable day for tidying up the house." This was not a spectacular prediction, except that I had long been planning to move on the day in question. I burst out laughing at so funny a coincidence—and it was undeniably happy laughter. As I realized after thinking about it, the coincidence would have been just as funny if the horoscope had said that "tomorrow will be an extremely unfavorable day for moving," but it would have made me laugh differently. I could say that I am not superstitious because I pay no mind to such things. But, to be precise, I should rather say: I know well that coincidences of this kind are meaningless, but I take a certain amount of pleasure in them all the same. The banality of this remark does not relieve us of the obligation to pay attention to it.

Mobilizing a very different set of categories, Descartes had already observed that the operation by virtue of which one believes something is different from that by virtue of which one knows that one believes it; the remark comes in a passage in which he considers the question, precisely, of other people's beliefs. Naturally, he himself has no doubt that he knows what he believes, or even that he can believe whatever he wants. He thus exposes the essence of the nature of belief and, above all, the obstacles that his study puts in our way, obstacles that are not exactly of the order of resistance.

The "I know well, but all the same" may be said to crop up all the time in analytic sessions, if we extend it to cover beliefs that are inaccessible to the subject himself. Its frequency and banality by no means help us assess its significance, but there are cases that are more edifying than others. I would like to cite one that is rather typical.

I do not find it altogether agreeable to bring up this example because everything began with a mistake of mine. But nothing is more instructive than our mistakes, as everyone knows, especially in psychoanalysis. I have already mentioned the example in question to a number of analysts, but, no doubt because these questions are elusive ones, they failed to grasp its import; annoyingly enough, they only noticed my gaff. Now, in the light of all that has preceded, readers will appreciate the considerable importance of this incident.

I have no choice but to begin by telling the story of my mistake. It went back to a telephone conversation. Someone who had taken a call for me had distorted the caller's name, making it sound like that of a black poet from whom I had been expecting a friendly visit. I was busy, so I asked that the poet be given the message to come see me as soon as he could; we would have the time, I added, for a pre-dinner drink. The person who was to open the door was informed of all this. The doorbell rang, and, a bit surprised despite himself, he came to tell me, "Monsieur, it's not a Negro, it's a client of yours."

Of course, there was nothing particularly distressing about the situation, since it was clear enough how I should handle it. What I had to do was to usher the patient to the couch, as usual, and wait to hear what his first words would be. But I waited for these first words with more than the usual interest, after all. We shall see in a moment that that, precisely, was my mistake.

Naturally, I later remembered these first words verbatim, and am not in the least likely to alter them now. After a short silence, the patient declared, in a rather satisfied tone, "Yes, I knew that you were joking about that pre-dinner drink. But all the same, I'm terribly pleased." Almost in the same breath, he added, "especially because my wife thinks you meant it." A remark of this kind may well be called puzzling. At the time, I was very surprised to hear it; but, unfortunately, I too was quite pleased, if not for the same reasons as my patient. My uppermost concerns were technical, so that I was glad to see that he had slipped right back into the correct analytic situation, as his use of the formula "I know well, but all the same" sufficed to show. The fact that everything had so easily fallen back into place was, I realized, due to the state of the transference at the moment. I did not realize that my mistake had a deeper effect on me than on him; but, thanks to my curiosity to hear what would come next, my residual caution, and my satisfaction over the technical aspect of things, the rest of the session was satisfactory and ran smoothly. The incident was never spoken of again.

But it was late, well after the hour when I usually received patients, and I had time for reflection. The expression my patient had used now seemed odder than it had before; moreover, it reminded me of something—of the expression used by the patient of Freud's whose brother-in-law had not succumbed to shellfish poisoning. I had a rather hard time locating the passage. It occurs in a short paper on telepathy. (I do not think that this is mere happenstance; telepathy poses a problem of belief.) I saw that what Freud had singled out for attention was the fact that the fortune-teller had guessed her client's unconscious—or rather, in this case, conscious—wish. After all, we go to people who practice divination so that they can divine things about us. That, however, did not apply to the case at hand. True, it was quite as if I had guessed my patient's wish, even if I had not done so telepathically. But we cannot account for my patient's satisfaction in this way, or for Freud's, unless it is so pleasant to hear someone divine one's wishes that one cannot but be satisfied. No, the effect had not been called up by naming my patient's desire, but by reinforcing a belief of his, just as his wife had. No doubt belief ultimately finds its explanation in desire: this is a truism that we find even in La Fontaine's *Fables*, which, although it is a charming book, has never ranked as a very original one as far as psychology is concerned. Freud's discovery was rather that desire acts at a distance on conscious material, causing the laws of the primary process to manifest themselves there: *Verleugnung* (thanks to which belief survives disavowal) is explained by the persistence of desire and the laws of the primary process. One might deduce from this that my patient, for example, continued to desire that I ask him over for a drink, but the real point lies elsewhere: he continued to believe that, in a certain sense, I *had* asked him over, and he was expressing his gratitude for the invitation.

As I continued to peruse Freud's text, I came across a sentence that pulled me up short: "I myself," says Freud, "was so much struck—to tell the truth, so disagreeably affected—that I omitted to make any analytic use of [my patient's] tale."[12] I, for my part, had not been disagreeably affected by my patient's remarks, but I had not made any analytic use of them either. Moreover, rightly or wrongly, I did not much regret it. I thought I saw what had struck Freud: beliefs involving the sciences of the occult and predictions of death. In my case, the only thing that had been in question was a pre-dinner drink, which had nothing unsettling about it. But I understood that I had consented too readily to my patient's "I know well"; it gratified me, and I did not care to know anything about the "but all the same." I suppose that much the same held for Freud, given what we know about his somewhat superstitious attitude toward the predictability of the day of his death. I felt, for my part, that my patient's satisfaction was all too absurd from the moment that he "knew well." Thus I was relapsing into the position that psychologists and psychiatrists had occupied before the emergence of psychoanalysis. My mistake had left my patient in the position of the analyzed, but it had evicted *me* from my position of analyst! *He* had given up the belief that he had come as my guest, but he had a credulous wife who made the task easier for him, and he had preserved enough of his belief, in a different form, to be terribly pleased. *I*, occupying a position I ought not to have, would have preferred that nothing at all survive of his belief, for I had never believed that I had issued him an invitation. That taught me a great deal about the inner attitude to maintain after a mistake or unexpected turn of events: one needs to survey the consequences it has for the analyst, not the patient. If we were to put it superficially, we might say that the patient really had received an invitation, at least in his wife's eyes. But we would have to add that, as he said, "he knew well" that it was just a joke—which means that this superficial explanation is of no use at all. In a word, the belief must survive its refutation, even if it thereby becomes impossible to grasp and one can see nothing but its utterly paradoxical effects.

This example opens up paths of all sorts: the use of misinformation to propagandistic ends, even if it must later be admitted that the information given out was false; hollow promises; the psychology of the practical joke; and the psychology of impostors. There is no reason that someone who does magic tricks, however reasonable and lucid she may be, should not make a living from the transformed belief that she is a magician, or that that should not greatly enhance the pleasure that plying her trade gives her. Like the Hopi who admits that there are no real Katcinas left today, she holds a "but all the same" in reserve, one that is much harder to grasp than the Hopi's "but all the same," or even all but impossible to pin down, except in little details that require interpretation. Yet sometimes it is obvious that the belief that one might suppose had been abandoned has in fact been maintained. I shall give some examples of this; the first, which we owe to Claude Lévi-Strauss, is famous. It involves a shaman who, although he knows the tricks of his and his fellow shamans' trade inside out, one day finds himself fascinated by another shaman who uses the same tricks; he becomes capable of believing again, with all his former naiveté. I have summarized the story poorly, but everyone has read the essay in question and been more or less surprised by this paradox; as he describes it, Lévi-Strauss interprets it as proof that an impostor can be his own dupe and invent an excuse for himself in all good faith. As the preceding pages will have suggested, the real explanation is different, and, not surprisingly, at once more obvious and more puzzling. Voltaire's treatment of imposture, which comes down to repeating that two shamans or two Katcinas ought not to be able to look each other in the face without laughing, does not reflect the reality of the matter.

Pace Voltaire, we have already begun to glimpse that there are several ways of believing and not believing. There is some slight resemblance between the shaman and the Hopi: the shaman too must have believed naively before repudiating his belief, although we do not know anything about the crisis he may have undergone when he was initiated into the tricks of his trade. However, the positions that the two end up in are not identical: the shaman recovers his naiveté, but his faith is not reinforced.

He is, moreover, a medicine man by virtue of his personal powers, not, like the Katcinas, an officiant by virtue of something that transcends the group; thus these two cases are not reducible to each other. The reader will already have thought of the case of the con artist or the swindler who only needs a credulous victim in order to lend credence, in a certain sense, to his own fabrications. The con man knows, for instance, that everything will come out in the end, but all the same, etc. There is still a great deal left to explore here.

But what is still lacking, and what we need above all, is a means of classifying these various cases, or, still better, of establishing a sort of syntax or a system of permutations that would allow us to pass from one to the next, and, ultimately, to arrive at a precise formula for the fetishist's game of *Verleugnung*, which is plainly different from everything we have seen so far. Another example will help us make some progress here.

I take it from Casanova's *The History of My Life*. It is a lovely episode that covers the end of volume two and the beginning of volume three, which, I am afraid, suffers a bit when we reduce it to its essentials, as we must here. Casanova has been something of an embarrassment for psychoanalysts. His sexual behavior appears "normal," while exhibiting a streak of, as it were, counterphobic activism; Casanova poses as the champion of anti-castration. One hardly knows where to place him: Is he, first and foremost, a phobic neurotic who overcompensates? Is he a pervert of a peculiar kind? Does he illustrate a transition between phobic neurosis and perversion? In what follows, our interest will be focused on Casanova the impostor.

In 1748, Casanova, who is twenty-three, happens to be in Mantua. There he is accosted by a stranger who insists that Casanova come look at his natural history collection—a ridiculous accumulation of bric-à-brac, with nothing authentic in it. This collection contains, among other things, an old knife, ostensibly the one with which St. Peter struck off Malchus's ear. It is a knife of the kind to be found everywhere; Casanova has seen one in Venice. His reaction is immediate; without a moment's hesitation, he joins in the game. He has no doubt recognized the stranger for what he is at a single glance: an impostor or a gull, it makes no difference—or, better, an impostor *and* a gull. For Casanova, the game will consist in taking the impostor's role entirely for himself while leaving the stranger in the gull's. But in the end, as we shall see, it is Casanova who finds himself in the position of the gull, because what induces him to take part in this game are his disavowed beliefs.

His first words are a gambit: the knife, he says, is worthless, because the stranger does not own the sheath. Christ's words are "sheathe your sword," *gladium in vaginam.* Let us not pause to interpret this; it is not what matters here. What does Casanova plan to do? For the moment, this remains vague. He has made his first move the way one advances a pawn; the combinations will come later. Quite simply, because he has chanced upon a "fool"—that is the word he uses—he must take advantage of him.[13] He spends the night fabricating a sheath out of an old boot sole and making it look ancient. He presents this to himself and to the reader as a tremendous farce.

What happens next? In Cesena (near Rimini, about one hundred miles from Mantua), lives a peasant, another credulous sort, who imagines that there is a treasure buried beneath his cellar. I omit the impostures and maneuvers that follow: by the time they are over, Casanova has persuaded his dupe that, with the help of the magic in the knife (and the sheath), gnomes can be made to bring this buried treasure to the surface. For Casanova, there is nothing to be gained from all this beyond the pleasure, as he puts it, of unearthing, at the expense of one fool, a nonexistent treasure that another fool thinks he has in his cellar. The gain would seem meager if he did not add that he is dying to play the magician, a role he loves past all thinking. It is hardly stretching matters to translate this as follows: I know well that there is no treasure, but this is wonderful all the same.

Another credulous character makes her appearance in Cesena: Genoveffa, the daughter of a peasant. Casanova sees a potential conquest in her, of course, but not a romantic conquest; he wants to make her submit to him, unconditionally, with nothing but his magician's hocus-pocus. To explain this to himself, he comes up with reasons that are interesting in their absurdity: Genoveffa is a peasant girl, and it would take too long to educate her and awaken her sensibility for love! In fact, possessing Genoveffa will put the crowning touch on his triumph as a magician. This sheds a first ray of light on the reason that our hero loves the magician's role to excess. Genoveffa is a virgin, and Casanova declares that her virginity is essential to the success of his magic spell. (A study might well be made of Casanova and the taboo of virginity, but I can only note that in passing.)

Casanova prepares everything very carefully. He has special garb made for himself, as well as a huge circle of sheets of paper that he bedecks with cabalistic signs. He has read a good many books on the occult; the critics note that he invents nothing, but simply follows the usual procedures. Simultaneously, he pursues his design on Genoveffa: for magic reasons, they bathe together, each washing the other. This is a wise precaution, since Genoveffa is a peasant girl from Cesena; at the same time, it ensures that Casanova will be able to seduce her later—the more so as the virgin sleeps in his bed, where, for the time being, he respects her virginity. The farce continues.

When the time is ripe, Casanova goes outside at night, and, wearing a magic surplice, takes his place inside his paper circle. At precisely this moment, a storm comes up. This is enough, as will appear in a moment, to throw our hero into a state of panic. Just before telling us that he stepped into the circle, he utters a sentence that has an odd ring for an analyst: he says that he knew that his operation would fail. Impossible, and he knew it! Implicit in a sentence of this sort is an unspoken "but all the same." I think that it would be a mistake to evoke the notion of doubt here, in whatever form, and to say that Casanova was not all that sure he would fail. In fact, he has no doubts about the inevitable failure of a magic operation that he himself calls a farce; he is as certain as we are. *Verleugnung* has nothing to do with doubt. The belief in magic is disavowed and very conveniently assigned to the credulous. But we shall now see what happens to our magician when, at the worst possible moment, he has to manage with no one credulous on hand.

Indeed, when the storm breaks, his first thought is cast in the form of an eloquent regret: "How I should have been admired," he exclaims, "if I had dared to predict it!" (3: 4). His assessment of the situation is right on the mark: if he had predicted the storm, the farce could have gone on amid the thunder and lightning. Superficially, one might say that Casanova would have had the storm on his side and remained master of the situation, in a position of superiority. But this explanation explains nothing: no one has contested his mastery of the situation, and he is still in a position to run the show as he likes. The reversal precipitated by the absence of a gull takes place within Casanova himself. The role assigned to the credulous has to fall to *someone*, after all. We shall have occasion to examine this idea when we discuss the position of the fetishist.

"As all this was perfectly natural [*I know well*], I had no reason to be surprised at it; nevertheless [*but all the same*], a beginning of terror made me wish I were in my room." Here we see the last of Casanova's defenses before panic takes over, and the most futile: common sense. We know enough now to explain why it should be futile: common sense is always allied with the "I know well," never with the "but all the same." The "I know well" is blown away like a wisp of straw amid Casanova's utter panic. Magic has its revenge: "In the terror which overtook me I persuaded myself that if the flashes of lightning I saw did not strike me down it was because they could not enter the circle. . . . But for my false belief . . . I should not have remained in the circle for as long as a minute" (3: 4–5). Thus the circle was magic . . . all the same.

Because of this false belief, then, Casanova stays put until the storm blows itself out, returning to his room in a very sorry state. Genoveffa is waiting for him there, but *she frightens him*. All he wants to do is sleep, and he sleeps for eight hours. The next morning, he says, "Genoveffa . . . seemed a different person." Here is how he explains this to himself: "She no longer seemed to be of a different sex from mine, *since I no longer felt that mine was different from hers*. At the moment an idea whose superstitiousness took nothing from its power made me believe that the girl's innocence was protected and that I should be struck dead if I dared to assail it" (3: 6). One would be hard pressed to come up with a better description of the discomfiture—the utter decomposition [*débandade*]—of our hero of anti-castration, as I called him a moment ago.

A great deal might be said about so rich an example. I shall leave aside the non-negligible but secondary role that the taboo of virginity plays here, although anyone who sets out to study Casanova in the light of psychoanalysis would do well to start with this powerful superstition and appeal to the concept of *Verleugnung*, which is always pertinent where superstition is involved. The focus here must above all be on what happens as soon as the gull disappears and her role falls to Casanova, or, rather, as soon as Casanova falls into the slot vacated by the missing term. At that moment, the storm takes the part of the Other (with a capital O, to use Lacan's terminology). Casanova knows this well; he exclaims, "I recognized an avenging God who had lain in wait for me there to punish me for all my misdeeds and thus end my unbelief by death" (3: 5). He expresses himself poorly, yet, after all, well enough; it is the image of the big Other that appears amid, appropriately, thunder and lightning. We understand that Casanova had not intended to take the place of the magician in his own eyes—for he says he didn't believe in it (in other words, that he was not mad!)—but in the eyes of the gull, the other with a small *o*. He adds, "My philosophical system, which I thought was proof against assault, was gone" (3: 5). Unfortunately, just like the fetishist, he is altogether incapable of telling us exactly what that system consists of.

As everyone knows, there is no reason to worry about what the future holds in store for this twenty-three-year-old young man after his cruel ordeal: he makes amends to one and all by performing certain ceremonies that might be called expiatory, relinquishes Genoveffa, and finds himself back where he started from, as full of life as before, and more the magician than ever. There is nothing surprising about this. But we rather frequently encounter similar moments of panic among perverts in analysis; they do not necessarily have a therapeutic effect. Once the panic subsides, there is a return to the status quo. Yet we saw early on that *Verleugnung,* here as in the case of the fetishist, is part of a system of protection (I would not say a system of defense) against castration. We can also see that there is a certain relationship between magic and the problem of castration.

We psychoanalysts have taken up the notion of magical thinking in too simplistic a fashion. We have assumed, first, that the animism of the primitives was the projection of their own drives, and second, that it provided the model for magical thinking. We have more or less implicitly accepted a rather dubious notion of development: the idea, for example, that people once believed in magic, that ontogenesis repeats phylogenesis, and therefore that children . . . and so on. But nothing warrants regarding magical thinking as infantile; as children, in their "ignorance," can serve as a support for the disavowed beliefs of adults, we have to approach it more cautiously. The young Hopi who still believes that the Katcinas are gods is not engaged in magical thinking any more than, say, a child who encounters Santa Claus in the street, since her belief in him is underwritten by people she trusts. It is not the young Hopi who is responsible for the fact that he has been deceived, but the adults. He is objectively deceived; his subjectivity does not yet take any part in the matter. The magic obviously can only begin once his belief in the Katcinas has undergone a transformation after disavowal, once it has taken the form of belief in the mystical, invisible presence of the true Katcinas, their presence *all the same,* notwithstanding the evidence of the real. There can be no doubt that *Verleugnung* suffices to create this magic. After all, what is more profoundly magical than the fetish? Giving it this name was itself a way of acknowledging this. To put it in a striking (perhaps too striking) phrase, I would say that what comes first is not a belief in magic, but a magic of belief. Only by making this correction can we explain the patent links between the presence or absence of the phallus (castration) and magic; for the first magical belief is the belief that the maternal phallus exists all the same, and it remains the model for all subsequent transformations of beliefs.

We come now to the hardest and riskiest aspect of matters. The examples cited above were chosen to illustrate various types of structures; we ought to be able to provide a coherent account of them. The young Hopi, sure of the (non-magical) existence of the Katcinas, flies into a panic at the thought that it might be refuted by reality. He recovers by preserving his belief at the cost of a transformation that makes it "magical"; his people's institutions help him do so. For a psychoanalyst, this crisis is, without any doubt, the repetition of another, that connected with castration. In question here is the loss of something that will subsequently be recovered after undergoing transformation, in a process underwritten by the authorities. The role played by the children's credulity is just as obvious; the deception is institutionalized. But Talayesva can tell us the whole story in his autobiography, for nothing has been wiped out by amnesia. *Verleugnung* continues to be irrational, but everything takes place out in the open.

This particularly simple schema or model is not applicable to Casanova. Children's credulity no longer interests him, but the world is full of credulous people, of "fools"; they make it possible for him to escape the "idea whose superstitiousness took nothing from its power," in which we recognize a refusal of castration. Because of this refusal, magical belief by itself fails to protect him. Quite the contrary: when he finds himself in its grip for lack of a credulous victim—when his belief in magic, as it were, collapses back onto itself—he is overwhelmed by anguish; his system, as he puts it, "goes," and he is left defenseless. The structures of his belief and Talayesva's do not coincide, they cannot be superposed; there is a gap or lag between them.

In the case of the Hopi, we were able to describe the very process of formation of magical thinking. All indications are that Casanova has gone through a similar period, but has forgotten it, as the fetishist too has. This is the period of the first *Verleugnung*, of the disavowal of anatomical reality, and of the constitution of the phallus as something magic. I am speaking of structures, for in Talayesva's case too, of course, whatever transpired at the moment he discovered female anatomy, the first *Verleugnung*, remains obscure; the crisis of initiation, however, faithfully reproduces the same structure, as is readily seen. With Casanova, however, we have to assume the existence of a second period of which the Hopi model presents not the slightest trace, a period in which magical belief itself is attributed to the credulous, so that it is no longer by magic, but, literally, thanks to an imposture that Casanova possesses the phallus. However, just like the shaman, this impostor is a magician *all the same;* magic itself survives as a "memorial to castration," in Freud's phrase. Thus Casanova continues to be exposed to the threat of what can perfectly well be called magical castration. The impostor does not really have access to reality: Casanova knows well, as he says twice, that his operation will fail, but this is of no importance to him. What *is* of importance to him is that the "but all the same" seems to be realized: he wants rejection of the imposture to lead back, not to the truth—which would doubtless save him, if he were capable of being saved—but to credulity. That is, he wants to be thrown back from his "system" to the "idea whose superstitiousness took nothing from its power."

Constructions of this sort would only seem rash if we offered them with a view to reconstituting a real sequence of events, but they are indispensable if we are to get beyond mere description and specify differences in structure. To date, we have not had much success in treating magic in anything other than general terms; we are reduced to making contrastive descriptions of its most pronounced features, without being able to say exactly how an obsessional neurotic's rituals compare and contrast with, say, a "primitive" tribe's. When we try to chart the various effects of the original *Verleugnung* and the way in which they are taken up again and organized, we are led to make finer distinctions.

The logical sequel to the present essay would be an attempt to discover what the magic of the fetish consists of. Here, however, everything is shrouded in darkness; the path we have followed so far does not lead to further knowledge. If *Verleugnung* and the transformations of belief explain the point the fetishist sets out from, they do not throw any light on his point of arrival.

Along with his description of the period constitutive of magic, Freud also accounts for the origins of the fetish: it represents the last thing seen before the shock of the discovery of the female body. The memory of this discovery is blotted out by an act of forgetting that Freud quite simply likens to traumatic amnesia. What thus comes into being is, however, only a screen memory; it is not yet a fetish. But a belief in the phallus that is preserved in magical form, on the one hand, and, on the other, a screen memory associated with the anatomical discovery and tied to it in various ways, can very easily exist side by side—this is extremely common—in subjects who are not fetishists.

The future fetishist must necessarily undergo this first experience, but we do not know how things work out for him thereafter. Does he briefly or even only fleetingly adopt an attitude of defiance and imposture, like Casanova's, but without managing to sustain it, unlike Casanova, who rather astonishingly managed to sustain his all his life? However that might be, we should note that instituting the fetish banishes the problem of belief, magical or otherwise, at least in the terms in which we have posed it here. The fetishist needs no gull; as far as he is concerned, other people are in the dark, and that is where he prefers to leave them. The point is no longer to make others believe; consequently, the point no longer is to believe.

Plainly, the place of the gull, the place of the other, is now occupied by the fetish itself. If it is lacking, there arise problems comparable to those that beset Casanova when there is no gull on hand. But Casanova imagines that he knows who believes and who does not. Even if he is in fact mistaken, he can continue to frame the question in terms of belief. Once a fetish has been constructed, the sphere of belief disappears from view; we do not know what becomes of this question. Indications are that the fetishist's goal is to elude it. In the case of *Verleugnung*, the field of belief stretches to take in the whole world; but those who become fetishists fall outside its ambit, at least as far as their perversion goes.

Research of the kind pursued here cannot be conclusive. One should perhaps try to find out what becomes of belief in the fetishist's case, or one should perhaps drop the idea of belief in examining fetishism. And there remain other spheres in which one might, if one were to trace the avatars of belief, be led to make remarks of a different sort. For example,

Freud invites us to explore what becomes of such beliefs when death and mourning are involved. Again, we know that there are cases in which the subject has serious problems because of his fear of losing what he "knows well" that he doesn't have.

We should add a word about the method utilized in this study, for it was not the result of a deliberate choice: it seemed to be dictated by the nature of the subject. We had a few ideas at our disposal in setting out. Freud had provided *Verleugnung*. We had the topography that Lacan has elaborated. This furnished us with two axioms: that there is no unconscious belief, and that belief presupposes the Other as its support.

That, however, did not point us in the direction of theoretical work, work of the kind meant to develop or test the abstract, coherent apparatus known as a theory. Furthermore, there is virtually no clinical dimension to our discussion; nothing in it resembles a case study.

But there exists something that might be called a Freudian *phenomenology*; it differs from the phenomenology of the philosophers, and tends rather to have something of the meaning the term had before Hegel made use of it. Freud does not often employ the word (it figures, for example, in *The Rat-Man*), but he assigns the method a considerable role in his writings. It is (chapter 7 aside) virtually the only method used in *The Interpretation of Dreams*, where it consists in trying to present examples, without regard for chronological order and without appealing to principles, in such a way that these examples interpret each other, as it were. Many of Freud's texts are similar. In *The Rat-Man*, he confronts examples of different obsessive phenomena, without being able to formulate a theory. The passage that seems to be devoted to the clinic in fact consists of examples of transferential phenomena.

To be sure, the support provided by a theory and illustrations drawn from clinical practice are present throughout; but, in the absence of the phenomenological dimension, which plays a mediating role, theory and clinical experience would each be applied to the other non-productively, with clinical experience illustrating the theory except on the rare occasions on which, in accordance with the methodology of the empirical sciences, the clinic contradicts the theory and invites us to formulate new hypotheses. This would bring us back to Claude Bernard. Freud does at times proceed in that fashion, or, at any rate, seems to, but he does not produce anything new when he does, and that is not the method that we recognize as being typically his. Careful consideration shows that the Freudian method rests on the premise that the phenomenological dimension (in Freud's sense of the word) is always present, even if it is sometimes occulted, in all authentic psychoanalytic research.

Notes

Octave Mannoni's essay, "I Know Well, but All the Same . . ." is translated and reprinted by permission from Editions du Seuil. It is from "Je sais bien, mais quand même . . . ," in his *Clés pour l'Imaginaire, ou l'Autre Scène* (Paris: Points, Editions du Seuil, 1969), 9–33. [Note that comments by the translator appear in brackets in the text and in the notes.]

1   [All references to Freud's work are from *The Standard Edition of the Complete Psychological Works of Sigmund Freud*, ed. and trans. James Strachey et al. (London: The Hogarth Press and The Institute of Psycho-Analysis), hereinafter referred to as SE. The volumes referred to below were published in 1955 (vol. XVIII), 1961 (vol. XXI), and 1964 (vol. XXIII). Freud, "Splitting of the Ego in the Process of Defense," SE XXIII, 275–78.]

2   [Freud, "Fetishism," SE XXI, 154. I have inserted the ellipses. Mannoni presents the whole of the last sentence as if it were Freud's, whereas it is in fact a paraphrase.]

3   The book has now been published (Paris, Presses Universitaires de France, 1967). [Jean Laplanche and Jean-Baptiste Pontalis, *The Language of Psychoanalysis*, trans. Donald Nicholson-Smith (London: Karnac Books and The Institute of Psycho-Analysis, 1988), 118.]

4   [Freud, "Splitting of the Ego," SE XXIII, 275.]

5   [Freud, "Psycho-Analysis and Telepathy," SE XVIII, 183.]

6   [Don C. Talayesva, *Sun Chief: The Autobiography of a Hopi Indian*, ed. Leo W. Simmons (New Haven: Yale University Press, 1942). Mannoni quotes loosely from the French translation of *Sun Chief* (*Soleil Hopi*, trans. Geneviève Mayoux [Paris: Plon, 1959]), 63–64.]

7   [I have inserted the ellipses.]

8   [I have inserted the ellipses. Mannoni quotes loosely, substituting, for example, "I recognized all of them" for Geneviève Mayoux's accurate translation of Talayesva's/Simmons's "I recognized nearly every one of them" (75).]

9   Blaise Pascal, *Pensées de Blaise Pascal* (Paris: J. Vrin, 1942), "When the word of God, which is true, is false literally, it is true spiritually." (*But all the same*, it is true.)

10 Octave Mannoni, "Le Théâtre du point de vue de l'Imaginaire," *La Psychanalyse* 5 (1960): 164.

11 [Jules Roy, *La Bataille de Dien Bien Phu* (Paris: René Julliard, 1963), 95.]

12 [Freud, "Psycho-Analysis and Telepathy," SE XVIII, 183.]

13 [Giacomo Casanova, *History of My Life*, trans. Willard R. Trask (Baltimore: Johns Hopkins University Press, 1997), 2: 297.]

Exotic Rituals and Family Values in *Exotica*

Nina Schwartz

We know that there are cases in which the subject has serious problems because of his fear of losing what he "knows well" that he doesn't have.—Octave Mannoni, "I Know Well, but All the Same" [1]

Atom Egoyan's 1994 *Exotica* explores an apparently accidental community of people whose lives seem only arbitrarily to have overlapped at a strip and lap dance club, Exotica. The course of the film, however, reveals that what actually links these figures to one another is a series of structurally if not literally similar losses or failures of family stability and order. The film thus also exposes how the most "exotic" or perverse behaviors originate in and reproduce familiar domestic settings.

By now, following Jonathan Dollimore's work on the perverse, such a claim may have the status of a commonplace. In his essentially deconstructive analysis of texts ranging from Augustine to Freud to Foucault, Dollimore demonstrates how the perverse inheres in and originates the conventional energies of normative culture that it ostensibly contradicts or threatens. [2] Jacques-Alain Miller arrives at a similar conclusion about the perverse: "According to Freud, children are naturally polymorphously perverse. Thus for Freud, perversion is natural, that is, primary. Perversion is more primal than the norm, that norm being secondary or even cultural for Freud—though not for Lacan." [3] But, Miller continues: "In classical psychoanalysis, perversion is not a raw instinctual drive; it is cooked, so to speak, not raw. It is a highly complex structure which is as sophisticated and full of intricacies as a neurosis." [4]

Miller concedes, then, that much of what we call "perverse," belonging to the original energies of human sexuality, "throws into question the very notion of normal human sexuality,"[5] but further claims that this definition doesn't take us very far in our thinking about the particular structure of subjectivity that belongs to the pervert, a subjectivity that is as much an effect of living in the world as that of the neurotic. He thus seeks to begin his own analysis where Dollimore effectively concludes.

In the Freudian definition of fetishism, the pervert copes with the threat of castration—the sight of the female's genitalia—by disavowing what he sees and replacing the woman's missing penis with a nearby object, the fetish: the male child repudiates what he "knows" to be true—that the mother is castrated—and persists in his belief in the maternal phallus. And yet, Freud says, "He has retained that belief, but he has also given it up."[6] Perversion here is thus one among other strategies for coping with castration specifically and, perhaps, with loss more generally. According to Bruce Fink's interpretation of Lacan, however, the pervert does not so much disavow the mother's castration (and thereby protect himself from the threat of his own), but rather works to stage through his rituals the emergence of the law that would place a limit on his own (and his mother's) *jouissance*: "The aim [of perversion] is to bring the law into being: to make the Other as law (or law-giving Other) exist."[7] The pervert's experience has failed to provide for him the crucial naming of the mother's lack, and the child therefore perceives himself as the real object of the mother's desire: "The pervert constitutes himself as what is lacking in the mOther; making himself into the object of her desire, he constitutes himself as her object *a*."[8] The failure of the paternal function to bring the child fully into the symbolic order and its facilitation of desire's displaceability subject the pervert to overwhelming anxiety at the mOther's demand, and the perverse ritual is his response to the demand.

This characterization of perversion seems consistent with Miller's claim that "perversion is when you do not ask for permission."[9] Desire, always presuming and predicated upon the experience of absence, *asks*, struggles with the question of what satisfaction may be, where it may lie; perversion in contrast seems to bypass the purpose of such questioning in its assumption that jouissance is directly available. Perversion is "a particular way of negating castration, or rejecting the necessary sacrifice of satisfaction. What Lacan is saying isn't very different when he qualifies the perverse operation as bringing jouissance back to the Other, restoring object *a*—which represents the sacrifice of satisfaction—to the Other; we can represent the Other as the body from which satisfaction was evacuated."[10]

Such a reconceptualization of perversion may enable us to recognize perverse strategies at work in subjects who are not themselves necessarily structured as perverts. That is, in response to a particular trauma, an otherwise "normal" neurotic might cope with the failure or collapse of the symbolic order—the paternal function—by engaging in behaviors that seek to restage the law that has been rendered inoperative. In Octave Mannoni's words, "Freud saw in the crisis linked to castration the model for the kinds of panic that erupt later in life, when people are suddenly overwhelmed by the feeling that 'Throne and Altar are in danger'" (74).[11] I believe that *Exotica* demonstrates this process at work in a variety of otherwise unrelated characters. As the film unfolds, the relations and similarities between and among the characters and their mysteries begin to emerge, ultimately revealing a set of family resemblances among the people and the family traumas that impel them. In suggesting the relations among the characters by representing the familial origins of their losses, *Exotica* also suggests another connection operating in this strange and nontraditional community: each character, whether qualifying as a structural pervert or not, engages in apparently perverse conduct as a means of calling (back) into being a law that has previously failed him or her. The club thus becomes the not-quite-arbitrary site of their interaction because it facilitates the enactment of the various mutually reinforcing rituals.

These characters by and large eschew discourse—therapy or even conventional narrative—as a way of dealing with their traumas. Instead, they perform repetitions of activities and roles. Even the film's telling of their histories occurs in a fractured, fragmented, flashback-employing form that reflects the characters' repression of or lack of access to the straight story of their lives. Their performances include a certain amount of talk, but such speech is almost entirely ritualistic: rather than inviting any spontaneous or unscripted speech of the other that might challenge the staging, the characters' language seeks rather to protect the event being staged from any transfiguration, from the loss that would inevitably follow its entrance into a larger symbolic order.

The song to which the young stripper Christina performs her dance suggests the fetishistic structure that informs all the characters' strategies for dealing with their various losses and traumas. The song is Leonard Cohen's "Everybody Knows," which captures precisely the structure of the fetish as Freud and others describe it.[12] As something that stands in for the female's absent penis, the fetish both covers over that absence, thereby protecting the subject from the anxiety it would induce, and simultaneously testifies to the very absence that it is supposed to belie. In perversion, the subject holds two contradictory beliefs simultaneously without repressing either. Mannoni accounts for the specificity of disavowal as a response to castration: In this paradoxical form of belief that knows better, "desire acts at a distance on conscious material, causing the laws of the primary process to manifest themselves there: *Verleugnung* (thanks to which belief survives disavowal) is explained by the persistence of desire and the laws of the primary process" (80–81).[13]

In representing its characters to be both operating in accord with a disavowal of what they know to be true and attempting to bring a lost order into being, *Exotica* thus elucidates Lacan's theory of the perverse and also suggests both the efficacy and the limitations of a community organized around such repetitive restaging. Further, *Exotica* may also permit us to consider how films in general facilitate a similar repetition compulsion in mass audiences, staging the pleasurable violations that call up a comforting or retributive law with the reassuring implication that such a law can be trusted to exist in the world.

The film's first image initiates its consideration of how public and private spaces—and perverse and ordinary experiences—overlap with and infiltrate one another. The scene is either a static backdrop, such as might belong to Exotica the sex club, or a waiting area of an airport: it includes actual palm trees set against a painted background of the same; the images are accompanied by eastern-sounding music, clichéd signifier of the "exotic."[14] The ambiguity of the image's location results from a cut from the backdrop, against which the credits are screened, to the film's first diegetic moment in which two customs officers look through a one-way mirror at travelers recently returned to Canada. As one agent speaks to the other, his voice-over links the backdrop to the subsequent airport scene. That voice thus facilitates the bleeding of what might be the semi-private club into the official site of governmental surveillance, thereby linking to one another the various kinds of watching—official, pleasurable, obsessional—that take place throughout the film.[15]

In the film's first spoken words, the older agent waxes philosophical to the rookie: rather than provide the trainee with a list of material signs of guile to watch for, the seasoned agent raises an analytic question about history, causality, the derivation of the present from the past. As a means of determining who might be smuggling, he says, "You have to ask yourself what brought the person to this point. . . . You have to convince yourself that the person has something hidden that you have to find. You check his bags but it's his face, his gestures that you're really watching." In this remark, the deceptiveness of appearances, and the question of the past's determination of the present, become analytic challenges to the investigator, both the rookie agent and the film viewer. In fact, though the customs officers don't yet know it, the young man currently under surveillance, exotic pet store owner Thomas (Don McKellar), is at this moment smuggling rare birds' eggs, strapped to his torso in a mock pregnancy, into Canada. Thomas's examining his own face in a mirror behind which the young black customs officer observes him is the first of many occasions on which characters who imagine themselves to be enjoying a private viewing of self are in fact being observed by another.

In the next scene, an irritating young yuppie with whom Thomas has shared a cab from the airport avoids paying his share of the fare by giving Thomas some ballet tickets he's just learned he can't use anyway: it's an obviously uneven exchange, though the passive Thomas seems bemused rather than resentful. At the moment that the yuppie gets out of the cab across the street from a strip/dance club called Exotica, we see a young woman, Christina (Mia Kirschner), entering the club, followed by a scene in which the club's DJ, Eric (Elias Koteas), lasciviously introduces another dancer's act by promising that she will show the spectators "the mysteries of her world." The scene then cuts to Thomas at home, unwrapping the eggs from his body, exposing his own mystery. The following several scenes cut back and forth between shots of Thomas arriving at the ballet and picking up an attractive single man with his extra ticket, and Christina beginning her act at Exotica, dressed as a schoolgirl, while Francis (Bruce Greenwood), a morose-looking man in his forties, stares at her. Francis, we will much later learn, is a tax auditor soon to begin his investigation of Thomas for tax fraud.[16] Following Christina's dance and then his own private lap dance, Francis goes to the men's room, apparently sexually aroused, while Eric and Christina look ambiguously at each other, suggesting the existence of a complex relationship between the two.

The film's opening introduces most of its major characters in the context of sexuality mediated by either money and "art"—the ballet as a strategy for picking up men—or money and artifice—as in the repetitive staginess of the Exotica dancers' performances. In fact, it would be difficult to count the numbers of times money is passed from one character to another. Egoyan thus suggests the creepiest dimensions to these characters, who seem not just deceptive but sexually predatory (Thomas at the ballet; the men at the dance club) or sexually manipulative (the dancers and pregnant club owner, Zoë [Arsinee Khanjian, Egoyan's wife]), exploiting the spectators' frustrations for financial gain or some other kind of power. Such implications are intensified in a particularly disturbing way when we later see Francis dropping off a thirteen- or fourteen-year-old girl, Tracey (Sarah Polley), in front of a neon-lit storefront. When he then pays Tracey, we can't help but suspect that her services have been sexual, despite the fact that the scene includes banal dialogue in normative tones: "Are you free next Thursday?" "I think so."

The film, that is, chooses to introduce us to a world that seems not just tawdry but perhaps criminally exploitative with its suggestions of child porn (on one occasion, Eric introduces Christina as "a sassy bit of jailbait") and childhood sexual abuse (Francis and Tracey). What we will ultimately learn, however, is that these apparently conscienceless people engaged in various exploitations of others' weaknesses are themselves all mostly very nice, not particularly exploitative people working in not particularly successful ways to cope with loss. Some of these losses are conventional and not especially dramatic, and some are profoundly traumatic; some are clearly articulated in the film, and others are only hinted at.

One question the film raises, then, is why it should initially choose to display its figures in the most aggressively unflattering and disturbing possible light, only to frustrate the expectations that such a portrayal raises. Egoyan, that is, chooses to invert the strategy of David Lynch in his film *Blue Velvet* in which an apparently "normal" middle-class family life is disrupted first by illness—the father's heart attack—and then, in the early zoom shot, by the discovery of a human ear hidden in the suburban lawn of the heart attack victim. In *Blue Velvet*, the surface of the normal is revealed to conceal a variety of psychic, material, and sexual horrors including kidnapping, rape, torture, and so on. In *Exotica*, however, the surface of the ostensibly tawdry is peeled back to reveal decent, damaged people with whom viewers find it increasingly easy to sympathize. In either case, of course, the effect is strategic alienation: we're forced to recognize ourselves in the other, the other in ourselves.

I have already noted that one of the film's most insistent motifs is the way in which all of the characters' "perversions"—behaviors that involve the deployment of a fetish as a defense against the reality of castration or radical loss—clearly derive from or are at the very least enacted within specific family legacies. Francis is the most dramatic case of this phenomenon. A regular visitor to the club Exotica, apparently with eyes for no dancer but Christina, Francis is actually drawn to her in part because of their shared personal history, which is fragmentedly revealed through flashback and fully clarified only toward the film's end. As a high school student, Christina babysat for Francis's eight-year-old daughter, Lisa, before the child was kidnapped and murdered. In fact, in a scene we eventually witness in flashback, Christina and Eric are the two people who actually find Lisa's body in the course of a communal search. In these search scenes, numerous volunteers walk slowly in line across an open field. Though we later learn that they are looking for Lisa's body, the shots of the search initially appear as pastoral visions whose beauty has the effect of relieving the film's general air of depressive urban vulgarity. Only much later do we learn that the bucolic scene is the site of a discovery that brings Eric, Christina, and Francis together at the Exotica.

For Francis, the vision of Christina dancing in a uniform identical to the one in which his daughter was both photographed (in family photos shown in shots of the interior of Francis's house) and found dead is, on the one hand, a return to the vision of his daughter alive. On the other hand, the fact that Lisa's "return" is achieved in a strip club suggests how overdetermined is Francis's relation to Christina, and to Lisa. One significant aspect of Francis's loss of his child is that the police briefly considered him a suspect in that crime. Because a significant dimension of Francis's trauma is the loss of his sense of himself as a father who could protect his child from the dangers posed by others *and* by himself, Francis needs not just to see Christina, to have her "stand in" for his dead daughter. Even more desperately, he requires her to behave in an arousing way so that he can assure himself that he *does not* think of or respond to her sexuality. Part of Francis's obsession with Christina, that is, involves precisely the prohibition at the center of the dance club's operation: the dancers are to be watched, they can even be "purchased" for individual lap dances, but patrons may never touch the girls. In the midst of Christina's titillating act, therefore, he speaks to her only paternally, protectively, never as a "customer" would be expected to speak. In the following exchange, Francis speaks first and Christina responds:

> "What would happen if someone were to hurt you?"
> "How could anyone hurt me?"
> "If I'm not there to protect you."
> "You'll always be there to protect me."

In this conversation, Christina reassures Francis of his own omnipotence, her faith in him a confirmation of his status as "the law," precisely what his own daughter's tragic death has shown to be a delusion.

I should mention here several secondary but critical elements of Francis's trauma: the police investigation of Lisa's abduction revealed to Francis his wife's long-term affair with his brother Harold, and it also called in question the paternity of Francis's daughter, the object of his proud adoration.[17] It was this latter uncertainty the police felt gave Francis a motive for harming Lisa. And two months after Lisa's murder, Francis's wife was killed in an automobile accident that also partially paralyzed Harold. Thus, all the film's allusions—by photo, flashback, and home video shots—to Francis's happy pre-trauma homelife are revealed in the course of the film to have been delusions on his part, his sense of himself as part of a coherent network of stable relations entirely false. This, perhaps even more than the two tragic deaths, is the trauma he struggles to deny throughout the film.

Another of Francis's fetishistic covers for his losses is his niece, Tracey (Harold's daughter), whom he hires to "babysit" for him when he goes to the club Exotica. There is, of course, "no baby to sit" (as Tracey later points out commonsensically to Francis), but Francis works elaborately to provide cover and justification for Tracey's presence in his house when he leaves her there: he goes so far as to have his piano tuned so that Tracey, who lives with her paralyzed father above a seedy storefront in obviously less than well off circumstances, can have an instrument on which to play and practice. Since Lisa played the piano, to Francis's great pride, Tracey thus becomes further identified with the dead child. Clearly, Francis is fond of Tracey, but equally clearly, the girl is functioning as part of a tense fraternal dynamic. Like Christina, Tracey stands in for the dead daughter, but she also becomes a means by which Harold compensates his brother for his earlier betrayal.

Of course, none of these family strategies can be named or discussed; all are silently enacted, their success dependent on *not* being spoken. In fact, Tracey's innocent participation in the ritual, as long as it persists, suggests the efficacy of the child in sustaining adults' capacities for the magical thinking that is at work in fetishistic disavowal. According to Mannoni, "The child can, as someone who is both present and an outsider, play a non-negligible role by assuming . . . the burden of our beliefs after disavowal. He is not privy to the adults' secrets" (77). On the brink of adulthood, however, the teenaged Tracey begins to resist her role in the brotherly dynamic; her refusal to go along with it precedes and perhaps presages the collapse of Francis's other rituals.

Tracey's first defiance of her passive role in the exchange occurs ironically after and possibly in response to Francis's request that she talk to him (this occurs in the first scene of his driving her home). In this scene, Francis responds to Tracey's silence in the car by asking "I'm not really that boring am I?" and gesturing ironically at her headphones; he then reminds her of earlier occasions when they had talked on these same trips, and she had asked him questions. Tracey, typically adolescent, replies "You want me to ask you questions?" in a deliberate ironization of Francis's nostalgia for their earlier intimacy. But in a later car scene, Tracey obliges Francis with questions that both recall that intimacy and simultaneously challenge the stability of his ritual conduct with both her and Harold. In the following exchange, Tracey speaks first:

> "Do you consider my Dad a friend?"
> "Does he consider me a friend?"
> "I don't know."

"Why?"

"Because he always seems different when you're around."

"In what way?"

"Tense."

"Is that bad?"

[half-laughing] "Well, I don't really like to feel tense around my friends."

"Well, sure, I didn't like to feel tense around my friends when I was your age."

"You do now?"

"It's not a question of liking it or not; it's just something that happens. . . . As you get older you become aware that the people you meet and the person you are are carrying a certain amount of baggage, and that baggage creates tension."

"So what do you do about it?"

"Well, you can pretend it's not there, or you can choose not to have friends, or you can acknowledge that it's there and have friends anyway."

[reflective pause] "I don't think I like my Dad when he's around you."

"Hmm, well that's because your dad doesn't like himself when he's around me. But that's ok; that's part of what friends do to one another."

In this simultaneously moving and hilarious conversation, played absolutely straight, Francis tries his best to be the good father that we see throughout the film he most wants to be. But this impulse comes into conflict with his reliance on Tracey's innocence. He tries to answer Tracey's difficult questions without either giving her more information than she should have or sacrificing the naiveté that's necessary for her effective participation in his ritual.

Ultimately, however, Tracey proves able to break out of the dynamic in which she has until now been an unwitting participant. In a late scene in which Francis drives her home after having been beaten up by Eric, Tracey expresses concern over Francis's condition. He deflects her apprehension by asking "You worry about me, don't you?" as if to imply that she needn't. Tracey replies irritatedly, "You think [what we do] is normal?" When Francis feigns confusion, asking "What do we do?"

Tracey announces her frustration: "That's just it; we don't speak about it." Later, to her father, Tracey announces bluntly, "I'm not going to babysit for Uncle Francis anymore." When Harold evokes the old lie that she goes there to practice, she says "That's absurd" and mentions the money Francis pays her as evidence that "he pretends I'm still babysitting for him. . . . He wants to believe that Lisa's still there. I make it easier for him to convince himself." Tracey's directness here provokes Harold to speak, albeit elliptically, about his brother: "Francis always had strange ways to convince himself of many things. Things that never happened, things that might happen. People who did things for reasons but they didn't." Tracey, of course, can't understand her father's musings, but draws Harold back to the pertinent issue: "What has any of this got to do with me, Dad?" Finally forced to recognize his and Francis's exploitation of Tracey, Harold answers, finally, "Nothing at all."

By naming the absence that Francis's rituals are designed to cover over, Tracey manages to extricate herself from the disturbing drama, but it takes more than Tracey's resistance to demolish Francis's defenses. What more powerfully disrupts Francis's ritual conduct is his violent ouster from the club: Eric, no longer able to tolerate Francis's special relationship with Christina, follows him to the bathroom one night and convinces Francis to break the club's cardinal rule and touch Christina, thereby enabling the DJ to attack Francis and literally throw him out of the club into the rain-soaked street.

For the rest of the film, Francis works to reinstate himself in the club so as to resume his rituals with Christina, but these efforts paradoxically force him and others to speak explicitly about his life and his losses for the first time. In so speaking, Francis can't help undermining the rituals' power to disavow those losses. First, he blackmails Thomas, whom he's investigating for tax fraud, into visiting the club, wearing a wire, and interrogating Christina over what she thinks his touching her meant. This latter issue is the crucial one: Francis wants to know why Christina thinks he touched her. It is in Christina's talk with Thomas, which she first resists and then pursues enthusiastically, as if grateful for the chance to tell her own and Francis's story, that we learn of Francis's dead wife and child. We also witness Francis listening to Christina tell his story, forced because of his own plan to hear his history repeated by and to another.

During this talk, in which Christina refers to Francis as "a very particular case," we also learn of Francis's importance to Christina. When
she first explains to Thomas why Francis was banned from the club, she
says, "He touched me. And when you're dancing for the customer, they
can't touch"; this last line is uttered emphatically, but more importantly
in a tone that suggests a child's absolute commitment to and faith in a
rule. Christina goes on: "Francis and I have a very special type of relationship. And I've never minded. But then he chose to violate it. . . .
We've always had this understanding. I mean, I need him for certain
things and he needs me for certain things. I mean that's the way it's
been. . . . He violated that in his—his, in his role and what he was supposed to do for me . . . because I was doing things for him and he's
done things for me" (she cries). Christina's sense of betrayal emerges
here clearly: despite her inability or unwillingness to say exactly what
the two did for one another, her sadness at the loss of this reciprocity is
powerful, as is her desire to continue talking to Thomas.

When Francis discovers that it was Eric who had tricked him into
touching Christina and had thereby orchestrated his expulsion from the
club, he confronts Zoë and begs to be readmitted to Exotica. Zoë is
sympathetic, but she emphasizes the importance of the rule that Francis
violated. When she asks Francis why he touched Christina, his answer
inadvertently forces her to confront how her club has come to function in Francis's resistance to his loss. Francis says he touched Christina
because "I needed to make sure." Confused, Zoë asks, "If she had let
you?" And he replies, "I would have been disappointed. . . . It's not the
way she was raised." Here, Francis's confusion of Christina with Lisa
forces Zoë to speak the unspoken knowledge that all in the club possess: "We're all aware of what you've gone through. You've suffered a
lot." But Francis's answer obviously also frightens Zoë, because she refuses despite Francis's mounting distress to readmit him to the club,
thereby reasserting the limits of the club's function: it's for entertain-
ment only, not therapy, and the people who attend are there only to have
a good time.

The night that he is beaten and thrown out of the club, Francis asks
Tracey, "You know that feeling you get sometimes . . . that you didn't
ask to be brought into the world?" To her affirmative reply, he continues: "If you think you didn't ask to be brought into the world, who

did? All I'm saying is, nobody asked you if you wanted to be brought into the world. So the question is now that you're here, who's asking you to stay?" Francis's rituals have apparently functioned since Lisa's death to give him a reason "to stay," to continue living: he exists to guard Christina from the harm that may befall her. When that role is denied him—when he loses another little girl—Francis's outrage leads to his plan to murder Eric. But to do so also requires him to become more involved with Thomas: to convince Thomas to help him, and to give him the gun Thomas inherited from his father, Francis must tell the rest of his story, and here is where we learn of the police investigation that informed Francis of his wife's affair. Francis desires to redress the past losses he's suffered and the past crimes against him—by Lisa's murderer and by his wife and brother—by displacing his previously impotent anger onto Eric. And in curious ways, Francis both fails and succeeds in achieving his desire. In the film's penultimate scene, Eric and Francis approach one another, Francis's gun in hand, but matters don't play out as we might expect (particularly if this were an American film). In the dialogue that follows, Eric speaks first:

> "Don't be afraid. I know everything about you."
> "What do you know about me?"
> "I found her."
> "You found who?"
> "Your little girl."
> [cut to Eric and Christina in the field discovering Lisa's body]
> [Eric to Francis] "I found her."

Silently, Francis embraces Eric, as if Eric's role in finding Lisa's body had actually served in some way to restore her to her father, safe and alive.

Francis's powerful impulse first to preserve the possibility of the ritual at Exotica and then to avenge himself on Eric for destroying that possibility paradoxically forces Francis to move outside his limited relations and the closure of his world. But it is that enforced movement into new modes of relations with the familiar figures in his ritual that may actually enable him to find another strategy for dealing with his losses. In this sense, the "law" of limits—on what strangers could do to little girls, on what he could do to his own little girl—that Francis tried to call into being through his conduct with Christina was more effectively if punitively called into being by Eric's trickery. And the forced disruption of his ritual conduct may permit Francis to reattach himself to the symbolic order that so radically failed him with the collapse of his family and paternal identity. The most "optimistic" conclusion of all the stories, this one still promises nothing very concrete, except for Tracey's healthy removal of herself from the system of debts and payments between Harold and Francis.

Christina, the former babysitter, is also revealed through the film's final scene (a flashback to one of the narrative's earliest chronological moments) to be suffering from her own ambiguous traumatic family legacy. In that last scene, as Francis drives Christina home from a babysitting gig at his house, he waxes enthusiastic about Lisa's intelligence and musical talent, which a shy Christina notes admiringly and somewhat wistfully. When Francis tries to reassure her that her own parents no doubt talk about her with similarly affectionate interest, she stonily replies, "I don't think so." Recognizing Christina's unhappiness, Francis praises the girl in the only way he can think of at the moment, calling her "a very responsible young woman." Christina faintly wails, "Responsible to what?" suggesting the absence for her of a stable structure of meaning, of rules. Francis himself offers to listen to Christina anytime she wants to talk about her problems, identifying this scene as perhaps the "origin" of his later car-chat with Tracey. But Christina makes no revelation at this time, leaving viewers to speculate just what her family situation lacks or includes and how it has informed her later, current work as a dancer at Exotica. She may be attempting through those performances to gain, finally, the attention (such as she receives so complexly from Francis) from paternal figures that has previously been denied her. Or if, as Egoyan himself has suggested in an interview, Christina had an incestuous relationship with her father, she may in fact be using her provocative but ultimately frustrating act both to provoke and to repudiate the desire of older men as she perhaps felt herself to provoke and yet was *unable* to reject her father's desire for her.[18] In either case, Christina's dancing at the club seems to function as a repetition—she wears the uniform that Francis's daughter was wearing when she was killed, but presumably it is also a uniform she might herself have worn as a schoolgirl—by which she continues simultaneously to live out and to transform a previous trauma by which she has been marked. For

Christina, the club functions as both the site of her tempting of older men and a guaranteed limit to their power over her, as perhaps no one could limit her father's power. Again, we recall how adamant Christina was to Thomas about the club's rule: "When you're dancing for the customer, they *can't touch*."

Zoë, the current owner of the club, inherited it from her mother. Pregnant by Eric in a contractual arrangement rather than as the result of a relationship and desperate for a child, she may now be having a romantic relationship with Christina, Eric's former girlfriend and the object of his current obsession. And Zoë, not unexpectedly in this movie, seems obsessed with making her own life re-embody her mother's: in addition to running her mother's business, she wears her mother's clothes and wigs. When Christina expresses doubt about Zoë's choice to keep the club, Zoë explains: "When mom died, my immediate idea was to get rid of this place, just sell it"; but, she continues in explanation, "I used to be very shy as a child. I used to watch my mother for hours, just admiring her sense of freedom. So when the opportunity came up, I thought I would take on the challenge."

Zoë's nurturing relations with Christina, Eric, and even Francis when she has to expel him from the club, suggest that whatever else Zoë may be, she is motivated most powerfully by a desire to be a mother, though we don't necessarily have a sense that her own mothering of the other characters repeats her mother's treatment of her. Christina mocks Zoë's admiration of her mother, for example, by telling her how the previous owner of the club lied to the women in her employ: she built an observation hallway above the stage that would enable her, she said, to observe the women being observed by their clients. Zoë's mother claimed to be doing so to protect her employees, but in fact, she built the structure to serve the voyeuristic desires of a wealthy patron. We don't know if, in the earlier history of the club, Zoë's mother had ever been a performer, but she was clearly a powerful presence in the establishment, confidently mingling with customers and overseeing proceedings as Zoë continually expresses her wish to do. Despite Christina's evocation of the mother's deceptiveness, of her subservience to the whims of a rich client, for Zoë the club provides a context in which both roles—literal mother-to-be/motherly nurturer of clients and employees *and* confident orchestrator of sexual license—combine to grant her the only authority she desires to achieve. Significant in his absolute absence from either Zoë's memories or her present life is, of course, her father. His literal lack may suggest the failure of the paternal function for Zoë.

Christina is contemptuous of Zoë's explanation of her occupation: "So you feel better adopting her options instead of creating your own?" But this question might well be asked of all the characters in the film whose options seem profoundly determined by family legacies. It's certainly true for Thomas, the gay exotic pet shop owner/smuggler, who has also inherited his foundering business from his father. Whether Thomas inherited the very successful smuggling operation too is unclear, but the presence of his father's gun in Thomas's desk drawer suggests that he might have. The dank, dim store, full of leaking tanks whose murky waters obscure whatever the inhabitants might be, is absent any shoppers. Indeed, until his involvement with the ballet and then later with Francis, Thomas's only encounters with other people occur with the yuppie cab-sharer and, by means of an angry phone conversation, with the contractor/painter who has failed to complete a remodeling job on Thomas's apartment. This conversation is the only occasion on which he manifests much assertiveness at all. His encounters at the ballet suggest the attenuated nature of his sexuality and perhaps of his life: on his first visit to the performance, he sells the extra ballet ticket he received from the yuppie to a very attractive (and somewhat exotic looking) dark young man who's seeking admission to the theater. After the performance is over, Thomas insists on giving his money back to the young man on the grounds that the tickets were a gift to him, not something he paid for. In response, the young man invites Thomas for a drink, but Thomas declines, walking away with a slight and ambiguous smile on his lips. Thomas's second encounter at the ballet follows this exact same script, including the return of money at the end of the performance, despite the fact that this time he actually did purchase both tickets. On the third encounter, however, Thomas accepts the invitation of the attractive young man, and a later shot shows them both in Thomas's bedroom, near the incubator containing the smuggled eggs, on the verge of a romantic encounter. But, it turns out, his lover is the black customs officer we had first seen observing while Thomas smuggled the illegal eggs into the country. When the officer departs Thomas's apartment, he takes the illegal eggs with him, but later, when Thomas is still sleeping, he leaves a phone message identifying himself as both an agent of the law and a lover desirous of another rendezvous. Thus, Thomas's single sexual encounter, mediated and indeed distanced initially through the exchange of tickets and money and through the script he *almost* follows, ends up subjecting him to the complicated intimacy he appears to have been avoiding in his otherwise isolated existence. Thomas's insistent privacy is further undermined, of course, when Francis's investigation of his books makes him vulnerable to blackmail.

The other young man in the film, bitter, obsessed, jealous, and angry Eric, is revealed in flashbacks of his first encounter with Christina (searching the field with her) to have been a sweet if aimless sort of drifter, ambitious to make something of himself and yet worried about his future, fearfully confessing to Christina the way his days just go by. He further confides his fear that he will lose anything he values, a prophecy borne out in his loss of Christina and in his continued presence at the club, which presence preserves his relation to Christina only as something lost. Christina seems to have intuited as much in her earliest conversation with Eric: when he expressed his fear that everyone he cares about will "slip away" from him, Christina replies, "Maybe you want them to slip away."

In an early exchange between Christina and Zoë, when the latter had worried about Eric's remaining at the club, Christina had stated somewhat contemptuously, "Zoë, not all of us have the luxury of deciding what to do with our lives." But what the film consistently depicts is that the characters who make up this small community have, consciously or not, produced the particular scripts calculated both to maintain and manage their relation to the traumatic losses they have suffered. Their lives have not simply been given to them by some ruling authority. The absence of Zoë's father emphasizes the nonexistence of any "official" functioning father in the entire narrative, because the paternal function is precisely what has failed in this world: what "everybody knows" is that real fathers are dead, wounded, lost, deluded, or criminal. The only authorized figure of the law—Francis as tax auditor—turns his power over Thomas to the service of his own desperate coping strategies. Even the customs officer retrieves the smuggled eggs only accidentally and has no intention of subjecting Thomas to any further penalty for his crime.

Clearly, the club, through its staging and facilitation of perverse rituals, provides a much needed context for and even fraternity of similarly suffering people. Because the symbolic order has so clearly failed these characters, the rituals they engage in hold their lives together by staging the emergence of a comfortingly consistent rule. Each character is enabled at the club—or in Thomas's case, at the ballet—to enact the rites that call into being the only sustaining order and consistency in his or her life. These rituals are clearly not progressive and do not promise their performers any eventual transcendence of their need, but neither are they judged within the film as wrong, immoral, or diseased. Nonetheless, the rituals and their sustaining framework are limited, for they would have the potential to damage the girl Tracey if she had not been able to extricate herself from her role in Francis and Harold's relationship. In exposing those limits, the film suggests its own commitment to the preservation of the symbolic order. Insofar as the film introduces its own subject matter as a mystery—a logical trauma—that threatens to overwhelm the world of stable meaning, it necessarily motivates the interpretive work of viewers to *understand* the mystery, to resubmit the material to the symbolic order and thereby render it no longer mysterious, but merely sad—and safe.

Notes

1   Mannoni's essay is included in this volume; all parenthetical page citations following quotes from Mannoni's essay refer to its appearance in this volume. This quotation is from pg. 91.

2   "So in growing to adulthood, and thereby becoming positioned within sexual difference—masculine or feminine, with each of these governed by a prescriptive heterosexuality—perverse desire is not eliminated but transformed, via repression and sublimation, into other kinds of energy which civilization then draws upon—indeed depends upon" (Jonathan Dollimore, *Sexual Dissidence: Augustine to Wilde, Freud to Foucault* [Oxford: Oxford University Press, 1991], 105).

3   Jacques-Alain Miller, "On Perversion," in *Reading Seminars I and II: Lacan's Return to Freud,* eds. Richard Feldstein, Bruce Fink, and Maire Jaanus (Albany: SUNY Press, 1996), 311.

4   Ibid., 310.

5   Ibid., 311.

6   Sigmund Freud, "Fetishism," in *The Standard Edition of the Complete Psychological Works of Sigmund Freud,* trans. James Strachey (London: The Hogarth Press, 1961), 21: 154.

7   Bruce Fink, *A Clinical Introduction to Lacanian Psychoanalysis: Theory and Technique* (Cambridge, Mass.: Harvard University Press, 1997), 180.

8   Ibid., 176.

9   Miller, "On Perversion," 316.

10 Ibid., 316–17.

11 The internal quotation is from Freud's "Fetishism" (153). Mannoni also notes of the fetish that "it represents the last thing seen before the shock of the discovery of the female body. The memory of this discovery is blotted out by an act of forgetting that Freud quite simply likens to traumatic amnesia. What thus comes into being is, however, only a screen memory; it is not yet a fetish. But a belief in the phallus that is preserved in magical form, on the one hand, and, on the other, a screen memory associated with the anatomical discovery and tied to it in various ways, can very easily exist side by side—this is extremely common—in subjects who are not fetishists" (90).

12 For the song's lyrics, see one of the many websites devoted to Leonard Cohen's works.

13 According to Slavoj Žižek, the structure of disavowal also operates in what he calls, following Peter Sloterdijk, "cynical reasoning": "This cynicism is therefore a kind of perverted 'negation of the negation' of the official ideology" (Slavoj Žižek, *The Sublime Object of Ideology* [London: Verso, 1989], 30). The stance of cynical reasoning obviates the need for any sort of analytic discourse, since it's predicated on the assumption that we all "know" the same things, are above the banalities of explanatory discourse. This is precisely what makes the stance ideological in Žižek's terms.

14 In fact, however, the music is Schubert's *Impromptu,* op. 90, no. 4, rendered strange by Indian instruments. It occurs at other moments during the film, played by Francis's niece Tracey, and over the final credits. The traditional piano performance is by Egoyan's sister, Eve Egoyan, a professional musician.

15 Egoyan's interest in voyeurism is manifest in most of his films. See in particular *Next of Kin* (1984), *Family Viewing* (1987), *Speaking Parts* (1989), and *The Adjuster* (1991).

16 Egoyan wrote the film in part in response to his experience of a tax audit: "No one can think of an audit without some sort of terror, because of what power that they have to reveal and discover things that you might not have even known you'd done wrong. When I was audited, at first I thought, I have nothing to hide, and I made my books open to this person. But the moment that you get that first question . . . , this person looks at you very blankly, and he nods. And you think, is he onto something? Are they onto something that I don't even know about myself? It was really irresistible, to have this man [Francis] going to the club, so we were auditing, taking stock of his private life, and of course during the day he's doing that to someone else" (Fuchs interview).

17 The wife, we learn from family photographs, happens to be black; this fact for most U.S. viewers qualifies as another example of "exoticism," though Egoyan himself claims that the biracial marriage is simply not the same issue to Canadians that it is to other North Americans (Fuchs interview).

18 Fuchs interview with Egoyan. Egoyan discusses his interest in incest more specifically in an interview with Richard Porton regarding a subsequent film, *The Sweet Hereafter* (1997).

Slavoj Žižek

The Ambiguity of the Masochist Social Link

In *Gasparone,* a silly German musical from 1937, the young Marika Roekk, when reproached by her father for treating unkindly her rich and powerful fiancé, promptly answers: "I love him, so I have the right to treat him in any way I want!" There is a truth in this statement: far from obliging me to be respectful and considerate (all signals of cold distance), love in a way allows me to dispense with these considerations. Does this mean that love gives me a kind of carte blanche, justifying every brutality? No, and therein resides the miracle of love: love sets its own standards, so that, within a love relationship, it is immediately clear when we are dealing with love and when we are not (the same as with politically incorrect terms, which can also be used as proof that I am a real friend of the concerned person). As we already learned from Christianity, true love and violence are never simply external to each other— sometimes, violence is the only proof of love. David Fincher's *Fight Club* (1999), an extraordinary achievement for Hollywood, directly tackles this knot of love and violence.

The Perverse Organ without a Body

Jack, the film's insomniac hero and narrator (superbly played by Edward Norton), follows his doctor's advice and, in order to discover what true suffering is, starts visiting the support group of victims of testicular cancer. However, he soon discovers how such practice of the love for one's neighbors relies on a false subjective position (of voyeurist compassion), and soon gets involved in a much more radical exercise. On a flight, he meets Tyler (Brad Pitt), a charismatic young man who explains to him the fruitlessness of his life filled with failure and empty consumer culture, and offers him a solution: Why don't they fight, beating each other to pulp? Gradually, a whole movement develops out of this idea: secret after-hours boxing matches are held in the basements of bars all around the country. The movement quickly gets politicized, organizing terrorist attacks against big corporations. In the middle of the film, there is an almost unbearably painful scene, worthy of the most weird David Lynch moments, which serves as a kind of clue for the film's final surprising twist: in order to blackmail his boss into paying him for not working, the narrator throws himself around the man's office, beating himself bloody before building security arrives; in front of his embarrassed boss, the narrator thus enacts on himself the boss's aggressivity toward him. The only similar case of self-beating is found in *Me, Myself & Irene*, in which Officer Charlie Baileygates (Jim Carrey) beats himself up—here, of course, in a comic (although painfully exaggerated) way, as one part of a split personality pounding the other part.[1] In both films, the self-beating begins with the hero's hand acquiring a life of its own, escaping the hero's control—in short, turning into a partial object, or, to put it with Deleuze, into *an organ without a body* (the obverse of the body without an organ). This provides the key to the figure of the double with whom, in both films, the hero is fighting: the double, the hero's Ideal Ego, a spectral/invisible hallucinatory entity, is not simply external to the hero—its efficiency is inscribed within the hero's body itself as the autonomization of one of its organs (the hand). The hand acting on its own is the drive ignoring the dialectic of the subject's desire: drive is fundamentally the insistence of an undead "organ without a body," standing, like Lacan's *lamella,* for that which the subject had to lose in order to subjectivize itself in the symbolic space of the sexual difference.

What, exactly, is the status of this "organ without a body"? At the beginning of Monteverdi's *Orfeo,* the goddess of music introduces herself with the words "Io sono la musica." Is this not something which soon afterward, when "psychological" subjects had invaded the stage, became unthinkable, or, rather, irrepresentable? One had to wait until the 1930s for such strange creatures to reappear on the stage—in Bertolt

Brecht's "learning plays," an actor enters the stage and addresses the public: "I am a capitalist. I'll now approach a worker and try to deceive him with my talk of the equity of capitalism." The charm of this procedure resides in the psychologically "impossible" combination in one and the same actor of two distinct roles, as if a person from the play's diegetic reality can also, from time to time, step outside himself and utter "objective" comments about his acts and attitudes. This second role is the descendant of Prologue, a unique figure that often appears in Shakespeare but that later disappears, with the advent of psychological-realist theater: an actor who, at the beginning, between the scenes, or at the end, addresses the public directly with explanatory comments, didactic or ironic points about the play, and so on. Prologue thus effectively functions as the Freudian *Vorstellungsrepräsentanz* (representative of representing): an element which, on stage, within its diegetic reality of representation, holds the place of the mechanism of representing as such, thereby introducing the moment of distance, interpretation, ironic comment—and for that reason, it had to disappear with the victory of psychological realism. Things are here even more complex than in a naive version of Brecht: the uncanny effect of Prologue does not hinge on the fact that he "disturbs the stage illusion" but, on the contrary, on the fact that he does not disturb it—notwithstanding his comments and their effect of extraneity, we, the spectators, are still able to participate in the stage illusion.

And this is how one should also locate Lacan's "C'est moi, la vérité, qui parle" from his *La Chose freudienne:* as the same shocking emergence of a word where one would not expect it. In his extraordinary philosophical novel *Les Bijoux indiscrets* (1748), Denis Diderot claims that a woman speaks with two voices.[2] The first one, that of her soul (mind and heart), is constitutively lying, deceiving, covering up her promiscuity; it is only the second voice, that of her *bijou* (the jewel, which, of course, is the vagina itself), that by definition always speaks the truth— a boring, repetitive, automatic, mechanical truth, but truth nonetheless, the truth about her unconstrained voluptuousness. This notion of the "talking vagina" is not meant as a metaphor, but quite literally: Diderot provides the anatomic description of the vagina as *instrument à corde et à vent* capable of emitting sounds. (He even reports on a medical experiment: after excising the entire vagina from a corpse, doctors tried to "make it talk" by blowing through it and using it as a string.) This, then, would be one of the meanings of Lacan's *la femme n'existe pas:* there are no talking vaginas telling the truth directly, there is only the elusive lying hysterical subject.

However, does this mean that the concept of the talking vagina is a useless one, just a sexual-ideological fantasy? A closer reading of Diderot is necessary here: his thesis is not simply that woman has two souls, one—superficial, deceiving—expressing itself through her mouth, and the other through her vagina. What speaks through woman's mouth is her soul, which tries desperately to dominate her bodily organs—and, as Diderot makes it clear, what speaks through her vagina is not the body as such, but precisely vagina as organ, as a subjectless partial object. The speaking vagina thus has to be inserted in the same series as the autonomized hand in *Fight Club* and *Me, Myself & Irene.* It is in this sense that, in the case of the talking vagina, it is not the woman, the feminine subject, who compulsively tells the truth about herself—it is rather the truth itself that speaks when the vagina starts to talk. "It's me, the truth, that speaks here"—me and not I. What speaks through the vagina is drive, this subjectless *moi.*

The ultimate perverse vision would have been that the entire human body, including the head, is nothing but a combination of such partial organs, where the head itself is reduced to just another partial organ of *jouissance,* as in those unique utopian moments of hard-core pornography when the very unity of the bodily self-experience is magically dissolved, so that the spectator perceives the bodies of the actors not as unified totalities, but as a kind of vaguely coordinated agglomerate of partial objects—here a mouth, there a breast, over there the anus, close to it the vaginal opening. The effect of close-up shots and of the strangely twisted and contorted bodies of the actors is to deprive these bodies of their unity, somewhat like the body of a circus clown, which the clown himself perceives as a composite of partial organs that he fails to coordinate completely, so that some parts of his body seem to lead their own particular lives (suffice it to recall the standard stage number in which the clown raises his hand, but the upper part of the hand doesn't obey his will and continues to dangle loosely). This change of the body into a desubjectivicized multitude of partial objects is accomplished when, for example, a woman is in bed with two men and does fellatio on one of them, not in the standard way, actively sucking his penis, but so that she lies flat on the bed and leans her head over its edge downward into the air—when the man is penetrating her, her mouth is above her eyes, her face is turned upside down, and the effect is one of an uncanny change of the human face, the seat of subjectivity, into a kind of impersonal sucking machine being pumped by the man's penis. The other man is meanwhile working on her vagina, which is also elevated above her head and thus asserted as an autonomous center of jouissance not subordinated to the head. The woman's body is thus transformed into a multitude of "organs without a body," machines of jouissance, while the men working on it are also desubjectivized, instrumentalized, reduced to workers serving these different partial objects. Within such a scene, even when a vagina talks, it is just a "talking head" in the same way that any other organ simply exerts its function of jouissance. This perverse vision of body as a multitude of sites of partial drives, however, is condemned to failure: it disavows castration.[3]

How to Dissolve a Masochist Symptom?

What, then, does the self-beating in *Fight Club* stand for? In a first approach, it is clear that its fundamental stake is to reach out and reestablish the connection with the real Other, that is, to suspend the fundamental abstraction and coldness of the capitalist subjectivity best exemplified by the figure of the lone monadic individual who, alone in front of the PC screen, communicates with the entire world. In contrast to the humanitarian compassion that enables us to retain our distance toward the other, the very violence of the fight signals the abolition of this distance. Although this strategy is risky and ambiguous (it can easily regress into a proto-fascist macho logic of violent male bonding), this risk has to be assumed—there is no other direct way out of the closure of the capitalist subjectivity. The first lesson of *Fight Club* is thus that one cannot pass directly from capitalist to revolutionary subjectivity: the abstraction, the foreclosure of the others, the blindness for the others' suffering and pain, has first to be broken in a risk-taking gesture of directly reaching toward the suffering other—a gesture that, since it shatters the very kernel of our identity, cannot but appear as extremely violent. However, there is another dimension at work in *self*-beating: the subject's scatological (excremental) identification, which equals adopting the position of the proletarian who has nothing to lose. The pure subject emerges only through this experience of radical self-degradation, when I let/provoke the other to beat the crap out of me, emptying me of all substantial content, of all symbolic support that could confer on me a minimum of dignity. Consequently, when Jack beats himself in front of his boss, his message to the boss is: "I know you want to beat me; but, you see, your desire to beat me is also my desire, so, if you were to beat me, you would be fulfilling the role of the servant of my perverse masochist desire. But you are too much of a coward to act out your desire, so I will do it for you—here you have it, what you really wanted. Why are you so embarrassed? Are you not ready to accept it?" Crucial here is the gap between fantasy and reality. The boss, of course, would have never actually beaten up Jack: he was merely fantasizing about doing it, and the painful effect of Jack's self-beating hinges on the very fact that he stages the content of the secret fantasy his boss would never be able to actualize.

Paradoxically, such a staging is the first act of liberation: by means of it, the servant's masochistic libidinal attachment to his master is brought to the daylight, and the servant thus acquires a minimal distance toward it. Already at a purely formal level, the fact of beating up oneself renders clear the simple fact that *the master is superfluous:* "Who needs you for terrorizing me? I can do it myself!" It is thus only through first beating up (hitting) *oneself* that one becomes free: the true goal of this beating is to beat out that which in me attaches me to the master. When, toward the end, Jack shoots at himself (surviving the shot, effectively killing only "Tyler in himself," his double), he thereby also liberates himself from the dual mirror-relationship of beating: in this culmination of self-aggression, its logic cancels itself; Jack will no longer have to beat himself—now he will be able to beat the true enemy (the system). And, incidentally, the same strategy is occasionally used in political demonstrations: when a crowd is stopped by police ready to beat them, the way to bring about a shocking reversal of the situation is for the individuals in the crowd to start beating each other. In his essay on Sacher-Masoch,[4] Gilles Deleuze elaborated in detail this aspect: far from bringing any satisfaction to the sadistic witness, the masochist's self-torture frustrates the sadist, depriving him of his power over the masochist. Sadism involves a relationship of domination, while masochism is the necessary first step toward liberation. When we are subjected to a power mechanism, this subjection is always and by definition sustained by some libidinal investment: the subjection itself generates a surplus enjoyment of its own. This subjection is embodied in a network of "material" bodily practices, and, for this reason, we cannot get rid of our subjection through a merely intellectual reflection—our liberation has to be staged in some kind of bodily performance, and, furthermore, this performance *has* to be of an apparently "masochistic" nature, it *has* to stage the painful process of hitting back at oneself.

And did Sylvia Plath not adopt the same strategy in her famous "Daddy"? "What she does in the poem is, with a weird detachment, to turn the violence against herself so as to show that she can equal her oppressors with her self-inflicted oppression. And this is the strategy of the concentration camps. When suffering is there whatever you do, by inflicting it upon yourself you achieve your identity, you set yourself free."[5] This also resolves the problem of Plath's reference to the Holocaust, that is, the reproach of some of her critics that her implicit equation of her oppression by her father to what the Nazis did to the Jews is an inadmissible exaggeration: what matters is not the (obviously incomparable) magnitude of the crime, but the fact that Plath felt compelled to adopt the concentration camp strategy of turning violence against herself as the only means of psychic liberation. For this reason, it is also far too simplistic to dismiss her thoroughly ambiguous hysterical attitude toward her father (horror at his oppressive presence and, simultaneously, her obvious libidinal fascination by him—"Every woman adores a Fascist, the boot in the face"). This hysterical knot[6] of the libidinal investment of one's own victimization can never be undone. That is to say, one cannot oppose the "redemptive" awareness of being oppressed to the "pathological" enjoyment the hysterical subject gains from this very oppression, interpreting their conjunction as the result of the liberation from patriarchal domination as an unfinished project (to paraphrase Habermas), that is, as the index of split between the "good" feminist awareness of subjection and the persisting patriarchal libidinal economy, which chains the hysteric up to patriarchy, making her subordination into a *servitude volontaire*. If this were the case, then the solution would be simple: one should enact what, apropos of Proudhon, Marx characterized as the exemplary small bourgeois procedure, that of distinguishing in every phenomenon a "good" and a "bad" aspect, and then affirming the good and getting rid of the bad—in our case, struggling to keep the "good" aspect (awareness of oppression) and discard the "bad" one (finding pleasure in oppression).

The reason this "untying of the knot" doesn't work is that *the only true awareness of our subjection is the awareness of the obscene excessive pleasure (surplus enjoyment) we get from it.* This is why the first gesture of liberation is not to get rid of this excessive pleasure, but to assume it actively—exactly what the hero of *Fight Club* does. If, following Fanon, we define political violence not as opposed to work, but, precisely, as the ultimate political version of the "work of the negative," of the Hegelian process of *Bildung,* of the educational self-formation, then violence should primarily be conceived as self-violence, as a violent reformation of the very substance of subject's being—therein resides the lesson of *Fight Club.*

In his autobiography, Bertrand Russell reports how he was trying to help T. S. Eliot and his wife Vivien in their marital troubles, "until I discovered that their troubles were what they enjoyed"[7]—in short, until he discovered that they enjoyed their symptom. How, then, are we to draw a clear line of separation between this redeeming violence and the brutal acting out that just confirms one's entrapment? In an outstanding reading of Walter Benjamin's "Theses on the Philosophy of History," Eric Santner elaborates Walter Benjamin's notion that a present revolutionary intervention repeats/redeems the past failed attempts.[8] The "symptoms"—past traces that are retroactively redeemed through the "miracle" of the revolutionary intervention—are "not so much forgotten deeds, but rather forgotten *failures* to act, failures to *suspend* the force of social bond inhibiting acts of solidarity with society's 'others' ":

> Symptoms register not only past failed revolutionary attempts but, more modestly, past *failures to respond* to calls for action or even for empathy on behalf of those whose suffering in some sense belongs to the form of life of which one is a part. They hold the place of something that is *there,* that *insists* in our life, though it has never achieved full ontological consistency. Symptoms are thus in some sense the virtual archives of *voids*—or, perhaps, better, defenses against voids—that persist in historical experience of "normal" so-

cial life, like the participations in the obscene rituals of the reigning ideology.

Was not the infamous *Kristallnacht* in 1938—this half-organized half-spontaneous outburst of violent attacks on Jewish homes, synagogues, businesses, and people themselves—a Bakhtinian "carnival" if ever there was one? One should read this *Kristallnacht* precisely as a "symptom": the furious rage of such an outburst of violence makes it a symptom— the defense formation covering up the void of the failure to intervene effectively in the social crisis. In other words, the very rage of the anti-Semitic pogroms is a proof *a contrario* of the possibility of the authentic proletarian revolution: its excessive energy can only be read as the reaction to the ("unconscious") awareness of the missed revolutionary opportunity. And is not the ultimate cause of the *Nostalgie* (nostalgia for the Communist past) among many intellectuals (and even "common people") of the defunct German Democratic Republic also the longing, not so much for the Communist past, for what effectively went on under Communism, but rather, for what might have happened there, for the missed opportunity of another Germany? Consequently, are the post-Communist outbursts of neo-Nazi violence also not a negative proof of the presence of these emancipatory chances, a symptomatic outburst of rage displaying the awareness of the missed opportunities? One should not be afraid to draw a parallel with the individual psychic life: in the same way the awareness of a missed "private" opportunity (say, the opportunity of engaging in a fulfilling love relationship) often leaves its traces in the guise of "irrational" anxieties, headaches, and fits of rage, the void of the missed revolutionary chance can explode in the "irrational" fits of destructive rage.

The Redeeming Violence

So, back to *Fight Club*. Is then the very idea of the "fight club," the evening encounters of men who play the game of beating up each other, not the very model of such a false transgression/excitation, of the impotent *passage à l'acte* that bears witness to the failure to intervene effectively into the social body? Does *Fight Club* not stage an exemplary case of the *inherent transgression:* far from effectively undermining the capitalist system, does it not enact the obscene underside of the "normal" capitalist subject? This aspect was developed in detail by Diken and Laustsen, in their outstanding "Enjoy Your Fight!," the most representative analysis of *Fight Club*:

> The normalised and law abiding subject is haunted by a spectral double, by a subject that materializes the will to transgress the law in perverse enjoyment. . . . Thus *Fight Club* is hardly an "anti-institutional" response to contemporary capitalism, just as creativity, perversion or transgression are not necessarily emancipatory today. . . . Rather than a political act, *Fight Club* thus seems to be a trancelike subjective experience, a kind of pseudo-Bakhtinian carnivalesque activity in which the rhythm of everyday life is only temporarily suspended. . . . The problem with *Fight Club* is that it falls into the trap of presenting its problematique, violence, from a cynical distance. *Fight Club* is of course extremely reflexive and ironic. It can even be said that it is an irony on fascism.[9]

The ultimate ground of this irony is that, in accordance with the late-capitalist global commodification, *Fight Club* offers as an "experiential commodity" the very attempt to explode the universe of commodities: instead of concrete political practice, we get an aestheticist explosion of violence. Furthermore, following Deleuze, Diken and Laustsen discern in *Fight Club* two dangers that invalidate its subversive thrust. First, there is the tendency to go to the extreme of the spectacle of ecstatic (self) destruction, so that revolutionary politics is obliterated in a de-politicized aestheticist orgy of annihilation. Second, the revolutionary explosion "deterritorializes, massifies, but only in order to stop deterritorialization, to invent new territorializations": "In spite of a deterritorializing start, *Fight Club* ends up transforming into a fascist organization with a new name: Project Mayhem. Violence is now turned outwards, which culminates in a plan for 'organized' terror to undermine the foundations of the consumerist society." These two dangers are complementary, since "the regression to the undifferentiated or complete disorganization is as dangerous as transcendence and organization."

Is the solution really the "just measure" in between the two extremes, neither the new organization nor the regression to the undifferentiated violence? What one should problematize here is, rather, the very opposition between de- and re-territorialization, that is to say, Deleuze's idea of the irreducible tension between the "good" schizophrenic-molecular collectivity and the "bad" paranoiac-molar one: molar/rigid versus molecular/supple; rhizomatic *flows*, with their molecular segmentarity (based on mutations, deterritorialization, connections, and accelerations), versus *classes* or *solids*, with their rigid segmentarity (binary organization, resonance, overcoding).[10] This opposition—a variation of Sartre's old thesis, from his *Critique of Dialectical Reason*, about the reversal of the *praxis* of the authentic group dialectics into the "praticoinert" logic of the alienated institution (Deleuze himself often directly refers to Sartre)—is a false ("abstract") universalization, insofar as it offers no space to articulate the key distinction between the two different logics of the very connection between micro- and macro-, local and global. The "paranoiac" State that "reterritorializes" the schizophrenic explosion of the molecular multitude is not the only imaginable frame of the global collective social organization; the Leninist revolutionary party gives body to (or, rather, it announces) a totally different logic of collectivity. (What lies beneath this opposition is, of course, Deleuze's profoundly anti-Leninist distrust of any form of global firm organization.)

As it was clear already to Deleuze, one cannot provide in advance an unambiguous criterion allowing us to delimit the "false" violent outburst from the "miracle" of the authentic revolutionary breakthrough. The ambiguity is here irreducible, since the "miracle" can only occur through the repetition of previous failures. And this is also the reason why violence is a necessary ingredient of a revolutionary political act. That is to say, what is the criterion of a political act proper? Success as such clearly doesn't count, even if we define it in the dialectical way of Merleau-Ponty, as the wager that the future will retroactively redeem our present horrible acts (this is how, in his *Humanism and Terror*, Merleau-Ponty provided one of the more intelligent justifications of the Stalinist terror: retroactively, it will become justified if its final outcome will be true freedom);[11] neither does the reference to some abstract-universal ethical norms. The only criterion is the absolutely inherent one: that of the enacted utopia. In a proper revolutionary breakthrough, the utopian future is neither simply fully realized, present, nor simply evoked as a distant promise that justifies present violence. Rather, it is as if, in a unique suspension of temporality, in the short circuit between the present and the future, we are—as if by grace—for a brief time allowed to act as if the utopian future is (not yet fully here, but) already at hand, just there to be grabbed. Revolution is not experienced as a present hardship we have to endure for the happiness and freedom of future generations, but as the present hardship over which this future happiness and freedom already cast their shadow — in it, we already are free while fighting for freedom, we already are happy while fighting for happiness, no matter how difficult the circumstances. Revolution is not a Merleau-Pontyan wager, an act suspended in the *futur antérieur,* to be legitimized or delegitimized by the long-term outcome of the present acts; it is, as it were, its own ontological proof, an immediate index of its own truth.

Let us recall the staged performance of "Storming the Winter Palace" in Petrograd, on the third anniversary of the October Revolution, on November 7, 1920. Tens of thousands of workers, soldiers, students, and artists worked round the clock, living on kasha (tasteless wheat porridge), tea, and frozen apples, and preparing the performance at the very place where the event "really took place" three years earlier; their work was coordinated by Army officers, as well as by avant-garde artists, musicians, and directors, from Malevich to Meyerhold. Although this was acting and not "reality," the soldiers and sailors were playing themselves, for many of them not only actually participated in the event of 1917, but were also simultaneously involved in the real battles of the civil war that were raging in the near vicinity of Petrograd, a city under siege and suffering from severe shortages of food. A contemporary commented on the performance: "The future historian will record how, throughout one of the bloodiest and most brutal revolutions, all of Russia was acting";[12] and the formalist theoretician Viktor Shklovski noted that "some kind of elemental process is taking place where the living fabric of life is being transformed into the theatrical."[13] We all remember the infamous self-celebratory First of May parades that were one of the supreme signs of recognition of the Stalinist regimes — if one needs a proof of how Leninism functioned in an entirely different way, are such performances not the supreme proof that the October Revolution was definitely *not* a simple coup d'état by a small group of Bolsheviks, but an event that unleashed a tremendous emancipatory potential?

The archetypal Eisensteinian cinematic scene rendering the exuberant orgy of revolutionary destructive violence (what Eisenstein himself called "a veritable bacchanalia of destruction") belongs to the same series: when, in *October*, the victorious revolutionaries penetrate the wine cellars of the Winter Palace, they indulge there in the ecstatic orgy of smashing thousands of the expensive wine bottles; in *Bezhin Meadow*, after the village Pioneers discover the body of the young Pavlik, brutally murdered by his own father, they force their way into the local church and desecrate it, robbing it of its relics, squabbling over an icon, sacrilegiously trying on vestments, heretically laughing at the statuary. In this suspension of the goal-oriented instrumental activity, we effectively get a kind of Bataillean "unrestrained expenditure"—the pious desire to deprive the revolution of this excess is simply the desire to have a revolution without revolution. It is against this background that one should approach the delicate issue of revolutionary violence which is an authentic act of liberation, not just a blind passage à l'acte.[14]

Notes

1   There is, however, a scene in Don Siegel's *Dirty Harry* that somehow augurs the self-beating in *Fight Club*: the serial killer, in order to denounce Dirty Harry (Inspector Callahan, played by Clint Eastwood) for police brutality, hires a thug to beat his face into a pulp—even when his face is already soaked in blood, he continues to instruct him: "Hit me harder!"

2   Denis Diderot, *Les Bijoux indiscrets*, in *Oeuvres complètes*, vol. 3 (Paris: Hermann, 1978). I rely here on Miran Bozovic, "Diderot and l'âme-machine," *Filozofski vestnik* (Ljubljana) 3 (2001).

3   There is, of course, a long literary and art tradition of talking vagina—from the 1975 French cult film *Le sexe qui parle* (*Pussy Talk;* Frederic Lansac and Francis Leroi) to Eve Ensler's recent, notorious monodrama *The Vagina Monologues*. However, what happens here is precisely the wrong step: the vagina is subjectivized, transformed into the site of woman's true subjectivity. In Ensler, sometimes ironic, sometimes desperate . . . it is the woman who speaks through her vagina, not vagina-truth itself that speaks.

4   See Gilles Deleuze, *Masochism and Coldness* (New York: Zone Books, 1993).

5   Quoted in Claire Brennan, *The Poetry of Sylvia Plath* (Cambridge: Icon Books, 2000), 22.

6   I borrowed this term from Elisabeth Bronfen's study of hysteria, *The Knotted Subject* (New York: Columbia University Press, 2000).

7   Bertrand Russell, *The Autobiography of Bertrand Russell* (London: Routledge, 2000), 295.

8   Eric Santner, "Miracles Happen: Benjamin, Rosenzweig, and the Limits of the Enlightenment" (unpublished paper, 2001).

9   Bulent Diken and Carsten Bagge Laustsen, "Enjoy Your Fight!—*Fight Club* as a Symptom of the Network Society" (unpublished manuscript).

10 For the most systematic exposition of these two levels, see Gilles Deleuze and Felix Guattari, *A Thousand Plateaus* (Minneapolis: University of Minnesota Press, 1987).

11 Maurice Merleau-Ponty, *Humanism and Terror: The Communist Problem* (Oxford: Polity Press, 2000).

12 Quoted from Susan Buck-Morss, *Dreamworld and Catastrophe: The Passing of Mass Utopia in East and West* (Cambridge, Mass.: MIT Press, 2000), 144.

13 Quoted from Buck-Morss, *Dreamworld*, 144.

14 With regard to this point, the crucial figure of the Soviet cinema is not Eisenstein, but Alexander Medvedkin, appropriately named by Chris Marker "the last Bolshevik" (see Marker's outstanding documentary *The Last Bolshevik* from 1993). While wholeheartedly supportive of the official politics, including forced collectivization, Medvedkin made films that staged this support in a way that retained the initial ludic utopian-subversive revolutionary impulse. For example, in his *Happiness* from 1935, in order to combat religion, he shows a priest who imagines seeing the breasts of a nun through her habit—an unheard-of scene for the Soviet film of the 1930s. Medvedkin thus enjoys the unique privilege of an enthusiastically orthodox Communist filmmaker whose films were *all* prohibited or at least heavily censored.

Confessions

of a

Medieval

James Penney | **Sodomite**

Meet Gilles de Rais

"Sodomite," pederast, infanticidal criminal, and enthusiast of the black arts, Gilles de Rais is the most infamous monster of French cultural history. A nobleman and warrior of the early fifteenth century, Gilles distinguished himself in battle, most notably alongside Joan of Arc during the Hundred Years War, earning the prestigious title of Marshal of France at the precocious age of twenty-six. Orphaned at eleven, Gilles became one of the richest and most powerful men in all medieval Europe upon the death of his grandfather and guardian, Jean de Craon. The transcripts of the trial of Gilles de Rais, preserved through the centuries in a Nantes archive, convey the testimonies of dozens of witnesses who claim that the members of Gilles's entourage kidnapped, over a period of about eight years, more than a hundred adolescent and preadolescent children, almost exclusively boys, whom Gilles then submitted to disturbing rituals of erotic torture, then summarily murdered by strangulation, decapitation, or dismemberment.

Not surprisingly, during the centuries after his execution at the stake for the crimes of heresy, sodomy, and invocation, Gilles de Rais became the stuff of folkloric legend, frightening countless generations of Breton schoolchildren through his figuration in the Bluebeard tale, which nonetheless holds few resemblances to the facts the trial documents relay.[1] After Voltaire, in his *Essai sur les mœurs*, expressed doubt about Gilles's guilt, early twentieth-century historians, most notably Salomon

Reinach,[2] reawakened interest in the case when they began to question the authenticity of the documents and the legality of the trial.[3] Most recently, Pierre Klossowski's 1965 translation from the Latin of the trial's proceedings, accompanied by Georges Bataille's analysis of the cultural and historical importance of Gilles de Rais, has brought the case to the attention of the contemporary literary public, and has raised important questions about the conceptual stakes involved in our engagement with Gilles's perversion.[4] Clearly, Gilles de Rais has been the source of endless fascination for more than five hundred years; but one senses that the tradition of critical literature on Gilles has yet fully to come to terms with the mysterious contradictions and seemingly incredible goings-on of the trial phenomenon.

The record of the trial's proceedings documents the scandalous confession of a man of unsurpassed feudal privilege and unshakeable faith who, accused of the most unthinkable crimes, managed nonetheless to obtain, despite his eventual execution, a symbolic pardon by the Inquisition in the form of reincorporation into the religious community. The preservation of Gilles's remains in the church of the Carmelite monastery of Nantes further demonstrates the church's strangely conciliatory attitude with respect to Gilles. Adding to the strangeness of the trial is the reaction of the public who witnessed Gilles's confession. While describing the atrocious crimes before the parents and relations of his victims, Gilles managed to elicit the empathy of his audience, which followed him in a procession to the gallows and offered prayers to God for his redemption. What follows is an attempt to clarify the nature of the dynamic informing both the church's and the public's strange complicity in the spectacle of Gilles's trial, and to spell out in detail how a psychoanalytic approach to the case helps to fill in the blanks the exclusively sociohistorical account of Georges Bataille and others tends to leave open. In short, we will suggest that Gilles's confession demonstrates the logic of what Lacan defined as the perverse psychic structure; in addition, we will put forth that the Inquisition took advantage of this perversion, as well as the trial audience's transferential fascination with its spectacle, to consolidate its political dominion over the believers of Nantes.

At issue will be the theoretical status of the relation between the transcripts of Gilles's confession and the sociohistorical context in which

the trial was inscribed. Our main premise will be that in spite of its tremendous historical perspicacity, Bataille's description of the tragic dimension of the Gilles phenomenon fails to account for the trial audience's willingness to forgive the criminal, and works against Bataille's
own efforts to describe Gilles's position with respect to his own conditions of historical possibility. Bataille's inability to recognize the significance of the audience's relation to Gilles's confession symptomatically
repeats the logic of fascination that accounts for the audience's sympathy in the first place. For this reason, Bataille's historicist[5] consideration
of Gilles's confession must be supplemented by an account of the dimension of desire—both Gilles's own and that of his audience—if we
are properly to understand the trial phenomenon. Bataille's reduction of
Gilles's subjectivity to his circumscription in and by the discourses of
late medieval France results not only in a contradictory psychologiza-
tion of Gilles that portrays the criminal at once as an evil manipulator
and a suggestible simpleton, but also in a disturbing depoliticization of
the church's agency in the manipulation of the trial proceedings for its
own material gain.

The Spectacle of Perversion

It is now commonly acknowledged that the medieval church required its
heretics in order to construct its ideology of faith and to impose its political dominion. The Inquisition served as a political instrument through
which faith became an imperative of submission to the earthly representatives of divine authority rather than to the command of the divine will
itself.[6] One of the most striking elements of the trial of Gilles de Rais is
surely the judicial apparatus's theatricalization of the criminal and his
perversion, or perhaps more accurately the complicity of this apparatus with Gilles's own desire to create a spectacle of himself. The trial
took place in the great room of the Tour Neuve castle in Nantes before
a large and attentive audience. The transcripts of the trial vividly convey the thoroughly public character of the proceedings, highlighting the
scandalous juxtaposition of Gilles's graphic evocations of the infanticides with the formal procedures of the church's judicial machinery.

In the text of Gilles's citation, Jean de Malestroit, bishop of Nantes,
decries the enormity of Gilles's crimes—their "unheard-of perversity"—

declaring that they could not be described in such ceremonial circumstances owing to their utterly scandalous nature. When he announced
that the full extent of Gilles's transgressive acts would be "disclosed in
Latin at the appropriate time and place,"[7] the bishop attempted to situate these acts on the other side of the iterable, sheltered from the im-
pressionable ears of the vulgate-speaking audience. Jean de Malestroit's
letter of citation announcing the trial of Gilles de Rais to the people of
Nantes participated in this manner in a quest for the sensational; the
ecclesiastical authorities tantalizingly proclaimed a coming spectacle at
the same time that they nominally denounced its outré contents. Here
one finds an emblematic example of a splitting in the church's position of enunciation that characterizes the entirety of its dealings with
Gilles. While overtly denouncing the criminality of Gilles's activities,
the church covertly participated in the transformation of the trial into
a sensational event designed to consolidate the institution's ideological
power over the community of believers. From the beginning of the trial
phenomenon, so it appears, the church was fully cognizant of the opportunity the Gilles case provided to consolidate its oppressive political
authority.

The representatives of divine justice, however, were not the only
parties responsible for the trial's titillating publicity. With the aristocratic haughtiness of a grand personage accustomed to the accordance
of his most capricious whim, Gilles also sought after the diffusion of the
news of his crimes in an apparent effort to increase the eventuality of his
religious rehabilitation and divine pardon. The fundamental paradox of
Gilles's attitude with regard to his trial immediately presents itself: in
spite of the seriousness of the accusations mounted against him, Gilles
unfailingly considered throughout the trial proceedings the dramatiza-
tion of his own brutality as favorable to his prospects for clemency on
the part of the church authorities and his status under the gaze of God.
Subsequent to the public reading of his bill of indictment, for example,
Gilles gave his assent to the publication in French of the full depositions
of the witnesses in order that these testimonies reach the widest possible
audience. Additionally, having made his initial "out of court" confession
under threat of torture, Gilles confirmed the validity of his testimony
when he reappeared during official court procedure, adding in the process further self-incriminating details. As the documents indicate, Gilles

desired to repeat his out of court confession in the public confines of the
trial "to remedy its faults in the event that he had omitted anything, and
to make more thorough declarations of the points developed summarily
in the . . . articles [of the indictment]" (189; 241–42). Menaced with excommunication and torture, Gilles decided not only to participate fully
in his own incrimination, but also to do so in the most theatrical fashion
possible.

Only moments prior to the most explicit description of his crimes,
during which he acknowledged having cut open the bodies of his young
victims in order to delight in "the view of their internal organs" (189;
244–45), Gilles repeated his request that his confession be published in
French "for any and all of the people present [at the trial] . . . in order . . .
to attain more easily the forgiveness of his sins and God's grace in absolv-
ing them" (190; 242–43). According to Georges Bataille's interpretation
of the trial, a cynical desire to horrify his public while allowing himself to wallow theatrically in his own monumental evil set the stage for
Gilles's precise and clinical exhibitionism. After the judges of the Inquisition threatened Gilles with excommunication, Gilles began his grisly
evocation of the crimes in order to reveal, according to Bataille, their
"horrible grandeur, that grandeur that would leave [the audience] trembling" (60; 74; translation modified). At the moment when the Inquisition issued its threat, Gilles realized, in this view, that he had nothing
to lose. Having lost the dignity of his privileged position in the feudal
social structure, Gilles had left only the terrible spectacle of his crimes,
and he certainly was not going to forego the opportunity to flaunt them
in the most grisly manner possible.

Given the evidence provided by the trial documents, however, the
motivation for Gilles's unfettered confession appears more straightforwardly to lie in his fear of the consequences of being jettisoned from the
community of God and so deprived of a chance for salvation. The Inquisition's threat of excommunication is the unambiguous turning point
that changed Gilles's attitude with respect to the legal authority of the
church over his indictment. Oddly, however, Gilles did not consider the
description of his crimes as grounds for the potential reinstitution of
the excommunication. Indeed, Gilles thought that his chances at absolution increased in proportion to the morbid completeness of his confession. This is what is so astounding about Gilles's self-perception with

respect to his crimes; it is also what should turn our attention to that aspect of his confession that points to the specificity of his relation to the sociosymbolic Other. At no point did Gilles waver from the inclusion of himself in the set of believers blessed by God's favor. Though the luxury of his enormous feudal privilege no doubt played a significant role in the adamancy with which Gilles espoused this position, the fact remains that not once during his confession did Gilles consider himself, as well as the crimes he committed, as either in some manner alien to the human fabric, or as beyond the reach of God's forgiveness. This strange complicity between his compulsion to narrate the crimes and his conviction in the clemency of God begins to demonstrate what we will later qualify as the perverse structure that characterizes the confession. Additionally, it also points to the ethical ambivalence of Gilles's discourse: on the one hand, Gilles underlines that the enormity of his perversion is simply an intensified version of a perversity of universal human reach but, on the other hand, he also gives evidence of the ethical short circuit that distinguishes his brand of criminality from the hysterically transferential response of the trial audience to his confession.

Before advancing to a more technical exploration of Gilles's perversion and the trial audience's response to it, let us first consider in greater detail the main characteristics of the confession itself. It is crucial to note, for example, the manner in which Gilles's insistence on emphasizing the potential human universality of the dark forces that motivated him link up with the trial audience's counterintuitive empathy with the criminal. While the apparatus of the Inquisition attempted to display Gilles in all his horrific glory as a means of gaining public sanction for its acts of capital punishment, Gilles reveled in his own spectacularization, all the while premising his confession on the hypothesis that anyone, in the proper circumstances, could be led to commit crimes as unthinkable as his own. Whatever evil force compelled him to perform the horrific infanticidal acts lies dormant, he implied, in each of his confession's auditors. Witness the transcription of Jean Petit, notary public, who recorded as follows this crucial aspect of Gilles's testimony:

> The said Gilles de Rais, the accused, voluntarily and publicly, before everyone, confessed that, because of his passion and sensual delight, he took and had others take so many children that he could not determine with certitude the number whom he'd killed and

caused to be killed, with whom he committed the vice and sin of sodomy; and he said and confessed that he had ejaculated spermatic seed in the most culpable fashion on the bellies of the said children, as much after their deaths as during it; on which children sometimes he and sometimes some of his accomplices inflicted various types and manners of torment; sometimes he severed the head from the body with dirks, daggers, and knives, sometimes they struck them violently on the head with a cudgel or other blunt instruments, sometimes they suspended them with cords from a peg or small hooks in his room and strangled them; and when they were languishing, he committed the sodomitic vice on them.[8] (190; 243)

Clinically and nonchalantly reported, this shocking parade of details concerning the crimes of Gilles de Rais could only have horrified, one would certainly think, the trial's audience. It is difficult to imagine five centuries after the fact the effect of the evocation of the murders on the parents who, during the latter years of Gilles's crimes, had handed over their children to his accomplices when the rumors of his strange practices had already spread throughout Brittany and the Vendée. Oddly, however, there is no indication in the records of the trial that Gilles's confession provoked an outcry among the audience members. In fact, the opposite is the case. Michel Bataille's fictionalized account of the trial plausibly depicts the audience's reaction to Gilles's confession and accords with the evidence of the transcripts. "The crowd did not reply, uttered no insult, did not scale the barriers to do harm to Gilles, did not lynch him," he writes. "But rather, in light of the enormity of facts that could be appreciated through no known criterion, the crowd fell to its knees and began, as he asked, to pray for him" (my translation).[9]

The reader of the trial's documentation is confronted with this nearly incredible scenario: At the moment of Gilles's in-court confession, the members of the communities to which the victims belonged calmly, empathetically listened to the narration of the crimes, as if in the presence of a patently evil but wise prophet. The audience serenely received Gilles's moral exhortations to pay close attention to the rearing of future generations of children to prevent them from succumbing to the temptations to which he himself succumbed. While laying blame for the crimes on his bad upbringing, Gilles "entreated the parents among the auditors to impart good principles to their children and provide them with the habit of virtue during their youth and childhood." [10] How is it possible to explain this theatrical transformation of Gilles from a detestable, homicidal monster to a sublime conduit of moral pedagogy more credible than the authorities of the Inquisition themselves? And how do we come to terms with the transference of the audience with regard to Gilles— the means, in other words, by which he is attributed with moral knowledge in the very presence of the ecclesiastical authorities whose judicial powers were at that moment in full display? To the extent that the Gilles de Rais phenomenon schematizes the dependence of religious hegemony on a surreptitious transgression of dogma, what was the nature and importance of the transferential identification of the trial's audience with Gilles? Did this transference, more specifically, constitute a subversion of the ideology of Christian faith, and hence of the church's political power, or was it rather an act of complicity on behalf of the general public in the church's cynical participation in the perversion of its most sacred beliefs? And finally, is it possible to conclude, from the evidence provided by the trial of Gilles de Rais, that there is a certain complicity between perversion and hysterical neurosis that lends itself to the formation of a group dynamic especially conducive to political manipulation? How, more specifically, did the church authorities take advantage of this complicity? Before grappling with these questions, however, let us first bring further detail to our view of Bataille's interpretation of the trial as a means of establishing a context for the present intervention.

The Tragedy of History According to Georges Bataille

Georges Bataille's introduction to *The Trial of Gilles de Rais* presents the criminal as a grotesque monster who personifies the tragedy of a social class decadently abusing its privilege and discovering itself outmoded by the remarkable forces of a nascent bourgeois humanism. Bataille's interpretation situates the importance of the trial entirely within the particular historical circumstances of the transitional period of early fifteenth-century France. In its quest to consider the case amid the multiple and conflicting historical forces of this moment, Bataille's text fails to ask a number of important questions. In spite of its careful and suggestive analysis of the historical context of the trial, Bataille's introduction may too easily be summarized by the following historicist thesis, which, though certainly not incorrect, remains nonetheless unsatisfying:

The Gilles de Rais phenomenon symptomatizes the sensual decadence and warmongering violence of an outdated social class issuing a futile protest against a democratizing bourgeoisification that would increase in importance with the emergence of an urban commercial middle class during the transition to the French Renaissance.

Without denying, of course, the relevance of the trial's placement in its historical context, as well as the lucidity and richness of Georges Bataille's evocation of it, it is nevertheless necessary to state that it may not properly be understood outside of the reaction to the scandal of perversion unveiled by the transferential relation between Gilles and his public, as well as the properly perverse machinations of moral consciousness through which Gilles attempts to justify his actions to God—his sociosymbolic Other. Implicit in our approach will be the assumption that the trial, considered as a historical event, is not reducible to the material traces that have survived it. It is possible, in other words, to read these traces as a means of describing with adequate plausibility phenomena that these traces may not articulate in positive terms, and that inform contemporary cultural dynamics in a way similar to their illumination of the context in which they occurred.[11] Where Bataille explains Gilles's crimes as a determinate effect of his sociohistorical location, we will instead attempt to recover Gilles's subjective *sovereignty*[12] by drawing conclusions from the manner in which his speech orients him with respect to the available representations of his actions, and positions him with respect to the Other's desire, that is to say with the lack of completion characterizing the sociosymbolic order. Our approach, in other words, will insist on reading Gilles's testimony psychoanalytically with the view of describing the nature of the desire inscribed therein. It is only in this manner that we may ascribe *responsibility* to Gilles for his crimes, to attribute their causation to a force other than that of a traumatic historical transition that succeeds in fully instrumentalizing the subjects who experienced it. By restoring to Gilles's confession the dimension of desire, we wish to open a gap in the seamless continuum of Bataille's historicist analysis, a gap in which Gilles positions himself with respect to his own confession, and onto which the audience projects a consoling narcissistic fantasy of its irreproachableness.

Georges Bataille's analysis of the trial of Gilles de Rais pivots around a particular understanding of tragedy: "The principle of tragedy is crime," he explains, "and this criminal, more than any other, perhaps, was a character of tragedy."[13] It is thus necessary to examine in some detail how the concept of tragedy informs Bataille's interpretation of Gilles's confession. Bataille's understanding of the tragic is exclusively social and historical in nature; it is devoid of any relation to the category of the subject psychoanalytically defined as subject of the unconscious. Bataille's formulation of the subject of tragedy, in other words, presupposes a subject without desire. For Bataille, Gilles is a "character": the feudal lord seamlessly embodies the qualities of the discourse through which his social class historically expressed itself. The figure of Gilles de Rais acquires his tragic cast neither through the particularity of his subjective structure, nor through the specificity of his mode of reacting to the circumstances of his fate, but rather through the tidiness with which he personifies the futile aristocratic resistance to the sociohistorical forces of late medieval France.

Bataille takes great pains, for example, to situate Gilles de Rais in the uppermost echelons of late feudal culture. Issuing forth from the great houses of Laval-Montmorency, Craon, and Rais, Gilles's ancestors belonged to the "noblest, richest, and most influential houses of the feudal society of the time" (20; 25). Each of Gilles's peers was a great lord, owner of vast feudal properties and opulent castles. Living in easy luxury, the society to which Gilles belonged entertained itself through the gallant quest for glory. Supplementing the tedious nonchalance of its material comfort with the manufactured dangers of chivalric antagonism, the participants in this quest sought after the strengthening of alliances, the distinction of feats of bravura in battle, and the flaunting of means and privilege through the conspicuous expenditures of mysteries and *fêtes*. Bataille thus describes a late medieval social setting characterized by manifest inter-clan violence and enormous lordly egos — a carefree but cruel field of ambitions realized at any expense. As Denis Hollier has pointed out, the Middle Ages represented for Bataille, who was trained as a medievalist, the historical apex of Christianity's cultural influence. The medieval period was the moment of "greatest taboo" and consequently "also the place of the most astounding crimes."[14] Through his reckless bravery on the battlefield, his aggressive provocation of feudal rivals, and his profligate spending on the accoutrements of devotion and carnivalesque spectacle, Gilles exhibits, according to Bataille's understanding, his neat exemplariness, his perfect personification of the ethos of noble privilege at the late medieval moment. Gilles's historical circumscription thereby *causes* him to perform the crimes. There is no logical solution of continuity between the circumstances surrounding Gilles's life and his "being"; he is fully articulated by, perfectly expressed through, the discourses through which we have access to him. In short, Bataille fails to attribute to Gilles the chance *to fail* to subjectivize himself, to become a subject of desire, to resist the perverse, sacrificial logic through which he paradoxically tries to exculpate himself through crime.

More specifically, the notion of tragedy comes into play, according to Bataille, when we take into account the lateness of this feudal mode of being, in other words the fact that, throughout fifteenth-century France, the feudal elite found itself overcome by historical forces that even the resources of its enormous privilege failed to subdue. Bataille refers, for example, to the increasingly administered approach to war: "heavy cavalry" is replaced by "infantry and archers, arrows and pikes."[15] War is no longer a chaotically playful field open to personal distinction through feats of bravery, but a carefully managed and strategized activity in which the warrior becomes a soldier: an anonymous instrument of another's will who sacrifices his desire for glory to duty, cause, or nation. At the moment of Gilles's military distinction, the act of war had already begun to lose its ludic function as it became tethered to a project for collective assertion and national identity formation. Socialized to participate in violent conflict as a means of demonstrating his aristocratic essence, Gilles and those of his privileged ilk were suddenly stripped of their means of distinction, bereft of a medium through which to channel the force of their warmongering energies and the violent aggressiveness of their fragile narcissism. According to Bataille, Gilles was "riveted to war by an affinity that marked a taste for cruel pleasures." And now that war no longer existed in the way it once did, Gilles, as Bataille pathetically puts it, "had no place in the world" (41; 51). The tragic nature of the case of Gilles de Rais devolves from the impact of these sociohistorical developments on one particular "type," on an individual trained to perform a historical function that had been superseded by history itself. Late feudalism introduced into elite culture a structural conflict between the calculation, moderation, planning, and sacrifice of the emerging bourgeoisie with the daring, playfulness, spontaneity, and profligacy integral to the aristocratic style of life. With the appearance of humanism on the Western European cultural scene, life itself became a value, and one was no longer required, as were the feudal nobles, to go to heroic lengths to prove oneself worthy of it.

In this way, Bataille's sociohistorical methodology allows him to qualify tragedy as an essentially aristocratic mode. "Without the nobility," he asserts, "without the refusal to calculate and to reflect, . . . there would be no tragedy" (53; 42). Tragedy thus becomes the sole domain of the noble class; it articulates in historical actuality the nobility's impotent protest against the hegemonization of reflection. Bataille does not appear too concerned by the extreme desubjectivation of Gilles his definition of tragedy implies, by his dismissal, in other words, of the relevance of what we might learn if we were to consider Gilles in his subjective particularity, as the expression of a structure of psychic life. We read, for instance, that Gilles "differs from all those whose crime is personal." The murders have no psychical significance; their meaning may be reduced without distortion to "the convulsive tremblings of [the] world" that the victims' "slit throats" expose. "The crimes of Gilles de Rais," Bataille summarizes, "are those of the world in which he committed them" (43; 54). Gilles emerges as a kind of template on which were set in motion great historical conflicts that were not only utterly beyond his control, but that transformed him into an instrument for their own abstract ends. Perfectly sutured to his representation of the class to which he belonged, Gilles is deprived, at least at this level of Bataille's analysis,[16] of even the most modest capacity for agency, of any ability to reflect upon or mediate the concrete historical circumstances through which his experience was necessarily articulated. Or, to put it in a way best suited to the perverse meaning of the case, Bataille deprives Gilles of the chance *to fail* to mediate his historical circumstances by issuing a protest against them or by assuming the direction of his fate—by establishing a position of enunciation, in other words, with respect to his very discursive circumscription.

As one might well imagine, the trial transcripts suggest that Bataille's carefully constructed social diagnosis of Gilles's criminality leaves a number of things, as it were, to be desired. Indeed, there is ample evidence in Bataille's own interpretation of the trial that his notion of tragedy fails to elucidate every detail of the case. All the evidence suggests, for example, that Gilles's first acts of morbid criminality coincide with the death of Jean de Craon, his grandfather, guardian, and initiator into the violent world of the feudal warrior. As Bataille himself underlines, the most obvious instigating factor in the onset of Gilles's criminal behavior is an event of primarily "personal," psychodynamic significance, one related to the demise of the concrete person most likely to have represented for Gilles the agency of symbolic castration. When he makes reference to Craon's death and to his turbulent childhood during his testimony, for example, Gilles himself invites us to read his crimes psychoanalytically: as a response to a trauma indeed inscribed within a specific sociohistorical context, but additionally linked to a properly psychical meaning that betrays a particular structural orientation with respect to the Other's desire. Indeed, Gilles's self-diagnosis is so perfectly modern and spontaneous it acquires, from our perspective, a truly comic dimension not wholly dissimilar to the zealously confessional and puerile ethos of North American daytime talk-show television; in no uncertain terms Gilles blames his criminality on his screwed-up childhood—on the lack of direction, discipline, and authority characterizing his overly privileged early years.[17] In the absence of any more objective insight into his psychical predicament, Gilles "psychologizes" his pathological behavior in a way that requires no historicization.

Revealing the subterranean complicity of an allegedly anti-humanist historicism with a tendency toward a resolutely humanist psychologism, Bataille presents a truly contradictory portrait of the criminal in which Gilles emerges simultaneously as a "type" and an aberration, a historical example and an idiosyncratic perversity. Bataille fully participates, in other words, in Gilles's own psychological confessional method. Bataille's Gilles manifests dark tendencies innate to the human fabric while embodying a properly monstrous negation of what Bataille mysteriously refers to as "human values." This confusion is at work, for instance, in the critic's consideration of Gilles's agency. Working against the grain of his description of Gilles as an infantile simpleton without a will of his own, Bataille occasionally imbues his subject with a redoubtable and malicious cunning, with an inhuman ability to seduce both his public and the church authorities. "The character of Rais . . . is a force that seduces and dominates," he writes. Moreover, comparing the feudal warrior class to which Gilles belonged to the Germanic Barbarian tribes, Bataille attributes Gilles's nobility with "a violence respecting nothing, before which nothing fails to cede" (37; 47; translation modified). It is at textual moments such as this that Bataille symptomatically psychologizes Gilles: he endows the criminal with the capacity to apprehend his desire transparently, to represent a conscious intention to himself and to bring it straightforwardly to fruition. In such passages Bataille also betrays his own transferential seduction by Gilles; it is as if he had suddenly taken a seat among the trial's audience members and succumbed to the logic of their fascination. In such instances Gilles is imagined as a virile, sexually threatening, and "hardened" (12; 15) Other capable of instrumentalizing his subjects after his own evil will while at the same time remaining a naive simpleton, a "*niais*" (34). Bataille's self-contradictory critical moves bear witness in this way to the paradox of the transference: the subject's unconscious attribution of impotence to the Other is precisely what fuels the fantasy of omnipotence. Paradoxically, in other words, the two aspects of the fantasy work in tandem. Indeed, the splitting of the subject's fantasmatic image of the Other is the surest sign that the transferential dynamic is in full effect. Breaking the smooth surface of the passive, tabula rasa version of Gilles he needs to illustrate his historicist thesis, Bataille's fantasy version of the diabolical, omnipotent Gilles emerges from time to time with disastrous results for the coherence of his argument. Gilles is simultaneously an exemplary incarnation of his social milieu and an utterly singular contradiction of human nature, both an infantile simpleton adrift in necromantic fantasy and a masterful, self-conscious manipulator of circumstance.

It is most interesting to note, in addition, that the properly homophobic aspects of Bataille's consideration of the trial are not unrelated to its contradictorily symptomatic portrait of the criminal. By way of contextualizing Bataille's strange comments about what we would now call Gilles's homosexuality, let us briefly open a historicizing parenthesis on the topic of sexuality and late medieval culture. First, as has been amply demonstrated in the past decades, our current understanding of sexuality as a term descriptive of a subject's identity does not predate the nineteenth-century invention of sexuality discourse. As Jonathan Goldberg notes with reference to the term's usage during the English Renaissance (and one fails to see how it would not also apply to fifteenth-century France), sodomy confusedly describes illicit sexual acts—virtually anything outside of procreative sex within marriage—

that are not associated with a presumed essence or identity of the subject. Theoretically, in other words, each subject is equally capable of falling victim to the temptation of sodomy, and the execution of such an
act will not necessarily tell us anything about who this subject "is." It is
also worthwhile noting that, as Goldberg argues, the crime of sodomy
emerged into visibility only on occasions when it was coupled with another act of criminality that threatened the authority of the church.[18]
Clearly, Goldberg's observation applies directly to the Gilles case. As
for what we would now call the "homosexual" aspect of the case—that
Gilles was almost exclusively interested in adolescent boys and probably had sexual relations with a number of his male cohorts, including
his Florentine invoker François Prelati—there is evidence that we should
not overestimate the extent to which this aspect would have been perceived at the time as scandalous. According to Philippe Reliquet, male
homosexual activity among late feudal nobles in France was relatively
common.[19] Young lords of Gilles's level of privilege habitually sponsored
the company of *mignons*, adolescent male pages who often performed
services of a sexual nature for their masters. Indeed, Gilles's cronies re-
cruited the young boys who would become Gilles's victims to serve as
the great lord's pages.

   It is crucial to remark that Bataille directly relates Gilles's monstrous aberrance to his erotic preference for young male victims. Gilles's
"homosexuality," according to Bataille, is a function of the "archaic"
quality of his "personality," of the fact that the criminal failed to obey
an imperative of civilization during his lawless, undisciplined, and over-
privileged childhood. Gilles personifies, very precisely, the bloodthirsty
and violent "archaic human nature" present in late medieval culture.[20]
The homoerotic networks linking Gilles and his numerous lackeys serve
to highlight this depraved, perverse archaism characteristic of both
Gilles and the entire feudal aristocracy. To illustrate his contention, Bataille interprets Gilles's melodramatic goodbye to his cherished alche-
mist—and, in all likelihood, his lover—François Prelati not as evidence
that Gilles, despite his brutality, was also capable of that most "human"
of emotions, namely love, but rather as proof of Gilles's infantilism and
naiveté, of the location of his intellect beneath the threshold of universal rationality (19–20; 24–25). For Bataille, the homosexual practices of
Gilles and his male class peers were not simply another instance of their

debauchery, but rather the very *mode* of their devolution into brutality, lawlessness, and excess. Homosexuality thus "facilitated," as Bataille puts it, the descent of the young feudal warrior into chaotic archaism (31; 38). Phobically, Bataille makes Gilles's homosexuality an essential feature of his perversion, a condition of possibility for the crimes. Homosexuality becomes synonymous with transgression, to the point that it is impossible to imagine crime—and hence the tragic—within Bataille's framework in the absence of its homosexual element. Clearly, this is another danger of Bataille's historicist understanding of tragedy. Since the tragic mode for Bataille features concrete and particular historical content, Bataille is able to make homosexuality itself an attribute of the historical dislocation of the feudal social structure in late medieval culture. This gesture not only implies a highly problematic historicist understanding of homosexuality that collapses homosexual desire into its concrete historical manifestations,[21] but also relates homosexuality in an essential, necessary way to the themes of decadence, lateness, profligacy, and excess with which Bataille describes the feudal aristocracy in mid-fifteenth-century France.[22]

Thus, it is precisely Bataille's symptomatic othering of Gilles—the facility, in other words, with which his suggestive gestures toward the notion of a universally shared human monstrosity or radical evil[23] devolve into accounts of Gilles's idiosyncratically diabolical foreignness to the human—that prevents him, along with the vast majority of the trial documents' readers, from grasping in its disturbing nuance the significance of the audience's transference with respect to Gilles. Bataille will refer, for example, to the "insensitivity" and "indifference" that "situate [Gilles] beyond the feelings of ordinary humanity" (16; 20; translation modified). Here it becomes necessary to inquire after the type of object Gilles constituted for his confession's auditors. Bataille, for his part, attributes Gilles's apparent seduction of the crowd to a strange power of persuasion traceable, but not perfectly reducible, to the impressiveness of his feudal authority. Of what metaphysical attribute does this charismatic supplement consist? Bataille explains the "compassion" of the audience for Gilles de Rais by claiming that its members were able, during the trial, "to realize through [their] tears that this great lord who was to die, being the most notorious of criminals, was like everyone in the crowd" (58; 73; translation modified).

Though Bataille needs to argue for Gilles's particular monstrosity in order to avoid a confrontation with the trial's most unsettling universal ramifications, he asserts nonetheless that the audience's relation to the criminal was mediated by an empathic identification — a positioning of the ego at the locus of the other — that counteracts the spontaneous, visceral disgust one would intuitively attribute to the response of the auditors of Gilles's confession. At the same time that the crowd views him as an object of horror, Gilles is "offered for the terrified sympathy, for the compassion of those who see him cry" (61; 77). The substance of the audience's identification, according to Bataille, is Gilles's particular brand of extreme criminality: that which separates him, in other words, from what is allowed to be associated with the human. Bataille appears to imply that this idea of a shared monstrosity is a function of the crowd's fully and consciously cognized representation of Gilles. When an audience member looks at the accused, he sees a deviance, a perversion, he recognizes in himself. The fascination of Gilles is a function, in this view, of a shared transgression, a communion in guilt. Watching Gilles break down before the evidence of the evil inside him, the spectator can weep vicariously at the evil he senses in himself. Bataille's argument here features an intuitive, commonsensical persuasiveness. Although we do not disagree that the libidinal dynamic motivating the public's sympathy is related to such a fraternity in transgression, it is nonetheless unlikely, however, that this transgression constituted the public's point of identification. Among the presuppositions behind Bataille's argument is the notion that a group consolidates its identification solely around a representation of its shared guilt. Let us now return to psychoanalysis to discover in what manner it renders more complex and *intellectually* persuasive the trial audience's transference with respect to Gilles and his grisly confession, and to explore in further detail the manner in which this confession exemplifies the logic of the perverse structure.

The Transference and the Group

The manifest and aware identification Bataille attributes to the trial's public is not only highly improbable, given in particular the extreme suffering the crimes surely brought upon the audience members, but also implicitly predicated on an improperly theorized notion of transference. Transference, by its very nature, is put in motion by forces of resistance and disavowal that distract the subject from a traumatic confrontation with unconscious material through a relation to a fascinating, consoling object imbued with knowledge of its desire. The dynamic of identification constitutive of the transferential relation is therefore fundamentally narcissistic: the knowledge I suppose in the subject to whom I address myself is the knowledge that will allow me to see myself in the way I wish to be seen. In Lacanian terms, then, the audience attributes to Gilles the knowledge pertaining to how one might "remain" innocent in the light of traumatic intuitions of guilt. By qualifying the audience's relation to Gilles as transferential, we wish to point out the means it offers to avert an encounter with unconscious conflict, in this case with the recognition of unconscious guilt associated with the subject's experience of *jouissance*, of the death drive. The logic of transgressive communion Bataille sees at work in the case is indeed the cement that binds the trial audience to Gilles's confession; *contra* Bataille, however, this guilty communion need be unconscious, and it is therefore with Gilles's conviction in his innocence, rather, that the audience identifies, properly speaking. Thus, we can describe the audience's relation to Gilles as a collective transference—one that exemplifies the dynamic of the Freudian "group"—because it defers a traumatic encounter with unconscious guilt.[24] As assiduous readers of Freud, we all know that our most deep-seated intuitions of culpability, traceable to the murder of the primal father in unconscious fantasy, are not reducible to any concrete wrongdoing for which we could existentially assume responsibility. Nonetheless, given both the length of time between the emergence of unconfirmed knowledge of the crimes and the first actions undertaken against Gilles—not to mention the apparent facility with which most of the children were handed over to Gilles's cronies—it could indeed be argued that numerous audience members undoubtedly, in their "empirical" lives, had much to feel guilty about.

On this alternative reading, then, Gilles acquires this attribute of transferential fascination for the crowd not through his admissions of guilt, but rather through his protestations of innocence. Or, more precisely put, the audience's fascination takes hold as a result of the manner in which its narcissistic identification with Gilles's sense of his own innocence creates a kind of alibi for the shadily shared transgression to which Bataille refers. What is so moving about Gilles, in other words, is not the manner in which he presents an externalization of the public's guilty regret at having in some manner contributed, however unwittingly, to the children's grisly end. Instead, Gilles's strange charisma should be explained with reference to the means he provides to his audience to exorcise these intuitions, to eradicate them through the unfurling of a beautiful image of divinely sanctioned purity. Gilles's furnishing to the audience of a means of escape from a messy interrogation of its own complicity in the demise of the children explains the apparent lack of any dissenting voices at the trial. Gilles is able to confess in such morbid detail precisely because he premises his testimony on an unshakeable conviction in a properly metaphysical innocence, an innocence that remains pristinely independent of anything of the order of empirical reality, and that paradoxically increases, in consequence, in direct proportion to the "objective" guilt Gilles accrues through the confessional narration of his crimes.

With reference to linguistic theory, we might state that the radical self-incrimination of Gilles's *énoncé*, or statement, is enabled by the unswerving faith in innocence that frames his *énonciation,* or enunciation. Absolute innocence is the enunciative perspective from which Gilles confesses his guilt. Gilles's moral authority therefore accrues from the willingness with which the crowd attributes him with knowledge of its own innocence. Here we witness, in psychoanalytic terms, the properly narcissistic structure of the ego ideal. The persuasiveness with which Gilles exonerates himself encourages the public to take the criminal as the point of its symbolic identification: the perspective from which it appears worthy—good—to itself. This narcissistic structure also allows the crowd to shield itself from the traumatic kernel of truth in Gilles's confession, namely, that he is not, in fact, an inhuman, monstrous incarnation of radical evil, but rather a manifestation, extreme to be sure, of evil in its universal "banality," of perverse, sado-masochistic tendencies operative on some level in any "normal" subject's libidinal economy. Contrary to Bataille's interpretation, then, the audience binds itself to the spectacle of Gilles's perversion not in order explicitly to commune with the scandal of his crimes, but rather to construct an absolute barrier disqualifying any effort to establish a continuum between Gilles's radical brand of bestiality and "everyday" human wickedness.

If it is in fact the case, as he appears so passionately to believe, that Gilles can be forgiven for even these truly despicable crimes, then surely the light of grace will shine at least as brightly on the "everyday" sinners of which the crowd was constituted. In his classic essay *Group Psychology and the Analysis of the Ego*, Freud details the relationship between the type of empathic identification forming the basis of the transference of the trial audience and the vicissitudes of the subject's moral life: its relation, in other words, to the superegoic vectors of conscience, of internalized self-surveillance and judgment. In the context of his analysis of the logic of group formation Freud first defines identification as "the earliest expression of an emotional tie with another person,"[25] then contrasts the identificatory phenomenon with a libidinal object cathexis, suggesting that we identify with the other as an alternative to taking this other as a sexual object. Here it becomes apparent how the audience's identification served to desexualize its spectatorial position with respect to Gilles, and to repress in the process any libidinal investment it may have had in Gilles's dangerous and transgressive sexuality. For this reason it is possible to qualify the crowd's reaction to Gilles's confession as defensive. In order to avoid the interrogation of its own fascination with Gilles's criminality, the audience transforms the accused's rhetoric of innocence into the perspective from which it can view itself as beyond moral reproach.

More crucially, however, Freud also shows in this same essay how identification subtends a kind of egoic sympatico in which the subject, in this case the collective subject constituted by the trial's auditors, "moulds" its ego "after the fashion of the one that has been taken as model" (106). Through this process Gilles's public manages to reconstruct itself on the model of the criminal's noumenal innocence, in so doing constituting itself as a "group" in the Freudian sense of the term by consolidating itself, so to speak, from the point of view of Gilles's guiltless enunciation, all the while deriving the dividend in jouissance in the sharing of Gilles's guilty transgressions. It is also tremendously significant to the case of Gilles de Rais that Freud relates the selection by a group of an ego ideal through the identificatory act to what he calls "self-observation, the moral conscience," and "the censorship of dreams." Its identification with Gilles permitted a part of the audience's collective ego to "cut itself off from the rest of the ego," thereby allowing the simultaneous coexistence of the reassuring, conscious narcissistic structure and the subterranean, disavowed transgressive one. But instead of structuring the critical self-relating agency that characterizes the classical "bourgeois" superego, however, this dual-faceted structure, according to Freud, extends "the original narcissism in which the childish ego enjoyed self-sufficiency" (110). From a historical perspective, one could even go so far as to say that the decline of the rigid feudal social structure is a factor in this process. Insofar as the phenomenon of the emerging capitalist mode of production displaces the subject's critical agency from the "external" figure of the feudal superior (lord, guild master, etc.) to an "internal," critical voice of "bourgeois" moderation and frugality, it might be said that a general cultural anxiety related to the subjectivation or individuation of the moral voice in part contributed to the audience's inability to fashion a more autonomous, "responsible" relation to Gilles's confession. In this view, at the historical moment of the trial, the feudal masses, subject to increasing urbanization and greater independence with respect to the landed lords, were confronted with the anxious hysteria to which their very (relative) freedom gave rise. Subject to the new, abstract, and unpredictable laws of commercial exchange that for us have long since become overfamiliar, the subjects of Nantes came to recognize that the trial of Gilles de Rais presented the prospect of creating a kind of cult premised on both a covert nostalgia for the old, however oppressive, social certainties, and the dissimulation of a traumatic yet irresistible enjoyment.

The Sacrificial Logic of Perversion

It will be necessary to examine in greater detail the transcripts of the trial in order to understand how Gilles de Rais was able to consider himself worthy of divine grace while divulging the most inconceivable transgressions. Such an examination will enable us, moreover, to come to terms with the properly perverse quality of Gilles's confession. The speech at the ultimate moment of the trial is especially demonstrative of the logic of Gilles's subjective structure. This discourse clearly conveys the illicit complicity between Gilles's theatricalization of his innocence and the guilty transgression not only of the crimes themselves but also of the church hierarchy's cynical manipulation of the spectacle. Additionally, the coda of the confession underscores how, during the entirety of the proceedings, Gilles never once vacillated from his absolute faith in both his exemplary piousness with respect to the religious law and the imminent pardon of God. Even while relaying the most shocking details of his crimes, Gilles continuously viewed himself as within the reach of the redemptive powers of divine clemency. Indeed, as the following passage from the transcript ably shows, Gilles's faith in God's forgiveness increased in direct proportion to the grisliness of the confession's details. So great was his sense of God's love and favor that Gilles proved himself abundantly capable of bestowing moral counsel on his accomplices as they prepared for their own encounters with the final judgment. Notary Jean de Touscheronde recorded Gilles's final words as follows:

> The said Gilles de Rais confessed and exhorted his aforesaid servants [Henriet and Poitou] on the subject of the salvation of their souls, urging them to be strong and virtuous in the face of diabolical temptations, and to have profound regret and contrition for their misdeeds, but also to have confidence in the grace of God and to believe that there was no sin a man might commit so great that God in His goodness and kindness would not forgive, so long as the sinner felt profound regret and great contrition of heart, and asked Him for mercy with a great deal of perseverance. And God was closer to forgiving and receiving the sinner in His grace than the sinner was to asking His forgiveness. And they should thank God for having shown them such a sign of love, He who required them to die in the fullness of their strength and memory, and did not permit them to be punished suddenly for their wrongs, and who gave them such an ardent love of Him and such great contrition for their misdeeds that they no longer had anything in this world to fear from death, which was nothing but a short death, without which one could not see God in all His glory. And they ought very much to desire to be out of this world, where there was nothing but misery, so as to enter into eternal glory. And thus, as soon as their souls left their bodies, those who had committed evil together would thereby meet each other again in glory, with God, in paradise.[26]

And to this declaration of faith in the imminent salvation of those united in a community of evil, the notary added the following continuation, which underscores the dimension of Gilles's perversion that solicited the transferential identification characterizing the public's response:

> After having exhorted them thus, Gilles got down on his knees, folding his hands together, begging God's mercy, praying to Him to be willing to punish them not according to their misdeeds, but, being merciful, to let them profit by the grace in which he put his trust, telling the people that as a Christian, he was their brother, and urging them and those among them whose children he had killed, for the love of Our Lord's suffering to be willing to pray to God for him and to forgive him freely, in the same way that they themselves intended God to forgive and have mercy on themselves. Recommending himself to holy Monsignor Jacques, whom he had always held in singular affection, and also to holy Monsignor Michel, begging them in his hour of great need to be willing to help him, aid him, and pray to God for him, despite the fact that he had not obeyed them as he should have. He further requested that the instant his soul left his body, it might please holy Monsignor Michel to receive it and present it unto God, whom he begged to take it into His grace, without punishing it according to its offenses. And the said Gilles then made beautiful speeches and prayers to God, recommending his soul to Him. (279; 337)

The climactic moment of the Gilles de Rais trial brings to its point of greatest intensity the complicity between, on the one hand, Gilles's perverse desire to sacralize himself while theatricalizing to the utmost his criminality and, on the other, the efforts of the institutional apparatus of the church to consolidate its political power under the guise of an ideology of faith. As far as Gilles is concerned, his final discourse betrays the properly perverse short circuit through which his crimes are performed as a means of establishing his innocence before the eyes of God. It is precisely by becoming guiltier before the divinity, by performing the most taboo actions according to church doctrine, that Gilles secures his innocence, and therefore his salvation. Gilles performs his crimes, in other words, in order to secure the guilt from which he will then be able to beseech God for forgiveness. In ethical terms, Gilles performs evil as a means of safeguarding the good—in this case his favor with respect to God's grace; he distinguishes himself through evil in order to benefit all the more from the goodness of the divine. Confident in the knowledge that God's desire is to bestow forgiveness on his straying flock, Gilles proceeds to the not altogether illogical conclusion that the subject with the greatest sins, and therefore the most spectacular acts of contrition, will best conform to the divine will to grant the grace of salvation. Far from perverting the theological position on grace in late medieval Christianity, Gilles's confession uncovers the authentically perverse kernel of forms of Christian casuistry that safeguard a realm of illicit taboo by granting divine pardon to the believer in advance.

There is a tendency in the available interpretations of the trial of Gilles de Rais—that of Georges Bataille being the supreme example—to overstate the oddity of the paradox of Gilles's faith: the facility, in other words, with which his increasingly obsessive solicitation of his invokers' forbidden powers of black magic segues into an equally obsessive promise of moral cleansing coupled with vociferous protestations of innocence. According to Bataille's thesis, Gilles's unceasing oscillation between transgression and faith, devilishness and saintliness, offers further evidence of his radical distance from normative rationality. Indeed, this very coincidence of high religious piety and murderous criminality constitutes for Bataille Gilles's foreignness to the human. But is it not the case that Gilles's mania for both the black arts and divine redemption manifests the same, properly perverse, subjective structure of abdication and sacrifice? Are they not both desperate efforts to escape the enigma of the Other's desire? If we take Gilles at his word when he adamantly denies his monstrosity and stresses the resemblance of the temptations that plagued him to those of his auditors, then how are we to interpret the phenomenon of the strange complicity of guilt and innocence in this description of his subjective state? In his reformulation of the problematic in psychoanalytic theory, Lacan shifted the emphasis of the interrogation of perversion from the concrete details of the subject's sexual comportment to a description of the pervert's position with respect to the Other's desire. In Lacan's view, the pervert circumvents the uncertainty the neurotic experiences about what kind of object it is for the Other's desire by presenting itself as the object-instrument of the Other's enjoyment.[27] "The pervert," as Bruce Fink sums up, "plays the role of . . . the object that fills the void in the mOther" (175).[28] From this perspective, the apparently contradictory logic of Gilles's innocence in guilt gains new significance as a kind of short circuit of the moral framework of Christianity. By indulging in such unambiguously transgressive actions, Gilles acquires for himself the certainty of his guilt in the eyes of God; Gilles knows what he is from the perspective of God's desire because he has transgressed His law. Yet by framing his entire confession around the premise that the sole condition for divine forgiveness is a genuine gesture of clemency, Gilles ensures for himself that he will be *especially* forgiven for his particularly scandalous crimes. Through his criminality Gilles's becomes the instrument of the jouissance of divine clemency. Rather than being perturbed, in neurotic fashion, by the uncertainty of the conformity of his actions with God's indeterminate desire, Gilles interprets the divine faculty to bestow forgiveness as a kind of obscene jouissance and then positions himself through the execution of the crimes as its guarantee. In more theological terms, Gilles's perversion consists in his taking to its extreme limit the already perverse logic of Jesuitical casuistry that subtended the possibility of earning grace through acts of contrition and self-justification.[29] In a theological framework that allows for certainty with respect to the content of the final judgment, the subject acquires divine forgiveness and favor by means of the very transgression of the terms of the covenant. One receives proof of God's love by meriting his forgiveness; in consequence, the surest, most direct way of executing the will of God becomes crime.

The attraction of the kind of absolute religious faith Gilles constructs for himself is that it permits the complicity of an illusory ideal of innocence with a subterranean world of transgression that paradoxically enables this innocence. One detects in the trajectory of Gilles's testimony a moral self-justification reminiscent of the fetishistic logic Freud elucidated in his 1927 essay "Fetishism" (SE XXI, 152–57). Gilles, on a level not too deeply hidden, knows he is guilty. Otherwise it is impossible to account for Gilles's deep-seated need for the moral purgation for which his plan for a holy pilgrimage to Jerusalem, for example, provides evidence. Yet Gilles repeatedly posits during his confession that he is "always already," as some now like to say, pardoned for his sins; that the unceasing act of contrition he performs at the trial serves to preserve him in a pure, beatific state of divine favor. The believer of Gilles's ilk—the moral[30] fetishist—says to himself: I know I am guilty of reprehensible injustices, but still, such actions do not tarnish my fundamental, inalienable innocence.[31] In fact, such crimes serve as proof to the Other of the subject's worthiness with respect to God's grace; the crimes secure, in this way, the very power of forgiveness through which they are expiated. While the neurotic subject indulges in crime as a result of an irrational, pathological motivation beyond its conscious control, and then chastises itself as a means of both intensifying the enjoyment of transgression and reconstituting the contours of its symbolic universe, the pervert commits the crime in order retroactively to present himself as the object-cause of redemption. The pervert, in short, must commit the sin with reference to which he will subsequently rationalize his innocence. Rather than experience the split inherent in subjectivity to which the neurotic's suffering bears witness, the pervert transfers this splitting onto the object of his act in order to present himself as the object that fills the gap, that heals the wound in the Other. The lifeless, bloody bodies of the young victims function precisely in Gilles's subjective economy as the evidence of this wound that Gilles then "heals" by offering himself as the very image of divine purity and innocence.

Gilles's testimony demonstrates in this fashion the effects of his over-zealous protestations on his psychic life: the more he announces his innocence, the more he feels the need for absolution, for some assurance that he remains within the community of God. The very criminality ensuring that God must step in to bestow forgiveness requires the unceasing gestures of contrition meant to secure it. It is for this reason— one that furnishes the required supplement to the historicist-culturalist rationalization that the valorization of membership in the church was an inherent discursive feature of Gilles's particular sociohistorical context—that the prospect of excommunication was so intolerable to Gilles. Excommunication confronted Gilles with the full, traumatic prospect of his radical guilt; it would provide irrefutable, objective proof that Gilles, in light of his perverse criminality, is not an *object* of innocence, but rather a *subject* of guilt.

Gilles's eventual execution at the stake for his crimes clearly evinces the danger he posed to the church's moral and political authority. But the apparent facility with which Gilles was reincorporated into the church after his brief excommunication and later laid to rest on the property of a Nantes church also bears witness, more significantly, to the church's complicity in the identificatory structure that allowed the audience to forgive Gilles or, more precisely perhaps, to posit a transferential convergence between the criminal's paradoxical "innocent guilt" and its own. It is here where we may discern a disturbing sympathy between Gilles's perversion and the trial audience's hysterical identification with him. The moral authority with which the audience endowed Gilles enabled an identification whose underlying trauma was nevertheless kept at bay by the apparently self-evident fact that its guilt could not possibly be as extreme as that of the murderer before it. By attending the spectacle of Gilles's trial, the audience vicariously experienced the cleansing expiation of Gilles's confession from the safe distance of the gulf between its ordinary crimes and failures and the unthinkable transgressions of the great feudal lord. The trial of Gilles de Rais acquired a calming, seductive, reassuring effect precisely by virtue of its shocking morbidity. By participating in the strange pardon of Gilles de Rais, the audience forgave itself for its own complicity in the most atrocious social crimes, for its disavowed participation in the cruelty and violence of late medieval French culture. It is also clear that the church authorities became aware of this complicity at the earliest stages of the trial, and it is undoubtedly for this reason that Gilles's scandalous confession was allowed to proceed in such an unbridled way. The trial audience's fascination with Gilles discouraged any critical effort to uncover the church's manipulation of it. Witnessing the symbiotic interaction of Gilles's perversion with the public's hysterical identification, the church stepped in to secure the spoils derived from its manipulation of the spectacle of Gilles's self-destruction, confident that the creation of a cult around Gilles would prevent any critical scrutiny of its actions.

Indeed, there is ample evidence in support of the claim that the political elites of Brittany and the Vendée, as well as the authorities of the Inquisition, wanted Gilles dead at least in part for self-interested economic reasons, and that the church benefited enormously from the manner in which the public's desire to be seduced by Gilles occluded the more disturbing political motivations for the trial. More specifically, during the last five or six years of his life, Gilles's outrageous expenditures had brought him near ruin, and it was with increasing desperation that he turned for assistance to the counsel of alchemists and the liquidation of his property. It appears eminently plausible to think that the ecclesiastical and political authorities—in particular Jean V de Montfort, duke of

Brittany, and Jean de Malestroit, archbishop of Nantes, both of whom, not coincidentally, acquired a significant portion of Gilles's property during the years leading up to the trial—delayed for so long the organization of their investigation because several years had to pass from the time of the emergence of the initial evidence of the crimes before these authorities could no longer profit from Gilles's moral and financial self-destruction.[32] Given the intensely polemical nature of much of the criticism concerning the trial's political aspects, it is necessary to point out what should be obvious, namely that the identification of the political and ecclesiastical elites' interest in delaying Gilles's arrest and ordering his execution need not lead us to the conclusion that there was a massive "conspiracy" against Gilles, that his trial was a hoax. As Jacques Heers has succinctly put it, "Villainous judges are perfectly capable of recognizing true crimes."[33]

Viewed against the backdrop of this dark political intrigue, Gilles's articulation of his radical evil, so naively and unselfconsciously enunciated, acquires an unanticipated dimension of heroism when juxtaposed with the manipulations of the church authorities and the astounding complicity of the trial audience. In fact, the ultimate paradox of the case of Gilles de Rais might be that the confession of his perversion— the uncensored transparency of his self-delusion and morbid criminality, as well as the lucidity with which he makes available to us the perverse short-circuiting of subjectivity that characterizes his psychic structure—provides us with the tools required to bring to light the cynically neurotic perversity of the church's and the public's investments in his crimes.

Notes

1   Thomas Wilson provides a useful overview of the relation between the facts of the trial and the development of the Bluebeard motif in Breton folklore. Leonard Wolf elaborates on the differences between the events of Gilles's life and their distorted representation in the Bluebeard tradition (Leonard Wolf, *Bluebeard: The Life and Crimes of Gilles de Rais* [New York: Clarkson N. Potter, 1980]).

2   Reinach's article "Gilles de Rais" is the best known and most influential attempt to rehabilitate Gilles de Rais through the argument that the trial was the instrument of a political conspiracy that entirely fabricated Gilles's crimes (Salomon Reinach, "Gilles de Rais," *Cultes, mythes et religions* 4.8 [1912]: 267–99). None of the recent

interpretations of the trial, however, subscribes to this thesis; for example, Georges Bataille, in *The Trial of Gilles de Rais*, argues vehemently against it (Georges Bataille, *The Trial of Gilles de Rais,* trans. Richard Robinson [Los Angeles: Amok, 1991]). Clearly, Reinach's article must be placed in the context of a post-Dreyfus affair revisionist effort to comb French legal history for instances of abuses of power against political undesirables. Though Reinach demonstrates analytic acumen in his discussion of the political motivation for the trial, and in fact we draw significantly on his work in our own concluding discussion, we agree with most commentators that the strength of the evidence against Gilles should not allow us to go as far as to question the authenticity of the witnesses' depositions. Ludovico Hernandez's text is another example of the effort to "rehabilitate" Gilles de Rais (Ludovico Hernandez, *Le procès inquisitoriale de Gilles de Rais* [Paris: Curieux, 1921]).

3   The late-nineteenth-century reawakening of interest in the trial of Gilles de Rais was largely due to the publication of Eugène Bossard's historical biography (Eugène Bossard, abbé, *Gilles de Rais, maréchal de France dit Barbe-Bleue* [Paris: Champion, 1886]). Most of the subsequent studies that argue in favor of the influence of Gilles's biographical life on his criminality make reference to Bossard's pioneering text.

4   Pierre Klossowski supplied Bataille with the French translation of the trial for *The Trial of Gilles de Rais* (1991).

5   Joan Copjec has provided the most concise definition of historicism: "The reduction of society to its indwelling network of relations of power and knowledge" (Joan Copjec, *Read My Desire: Lacan against the Historicists* [Cambridge, Mass.: MIT Press, 1994], 6). An example of Bataille's historicism is offered in this statement: "[Gilles] represents exactly the feudal society of a period when the bourgeois ideal of management and the exploitation of goods wins out over the concern with traditional virtues, linked to the notion of feudal honor" (*The Trial*, 22 [English translation], 27–28 [French original]; translation modified by author for greater clarity). In such arguments Gilles "disappears" under the discourses surrounding him; he is deprived of an unconscious, deprived of desire. All subsequent page references to *The Trial of Gilles de Rais* are to the English translation and the French original respectively.

6   Henry Charles Lea provides contextual information on the history of the Inquisition in medieval France (Henry Charles Lea, *A History of The Inquisition of the Middle Ages* [New York: Harper, 1888], 2: 113–61). James B. Given examines the question of the political power exercised by the Inquisition in thirteenth-century Languedoc in a way that usefully illuminates the case of Gilles de Rais (James B. Given, *Inquisition and Medieval Society: Power, Discipline, and Resistance in Languedoc* [Ithaca, N.Y.: Cornell University Press, 1997]).

7   G. Bataille, *The Trial*, 150; 191.

8   It is not clear from the evidence of the trial documents of what consisted this oft-evoked "sodomitic vice." Étienne Corrillaut, known familiarly as Poitou in the Gilles entourage, provided the most detailed account of what occurred during the rituals of abuse. According to him, Gilles "first took his penis or virile member into one or the other of his hands, rubbed it, made it erect, or stretched it, then put it between the

thighs or legs of the said boys and girls, bypassing the natural vessel of the said girls, rubbing his said penis or virile member on the bellies of the said boys and girls with great pleasure, passion, and lascivious concupiscence, until sperm was ejaculated on their bellies" (219; 275). It is entirely possible, indeed probable, that anal penetration never featured among Gilles's practices with his young victims. Corrillaut's account also underlines the tremendously broad late medieval understanding of sodomy, extending, as it did, to any sexual activity that may not directly lead to conception.

9   Michel Bataille, *Gilles de Rais* (Paris: Mercure de France, 1972), 20.

10 G. Bataille, *The Trial*, 189; 242; translation modified.

11 Although it is impossible to detail this point here, the Gilles case cries out for comparison with mass media treatments of serial killers, in particular those whose cases involve child or adolescent victims and same-sex eroticism. As the Gilles phenomenon exemplifies, the spectacularization of cases of perversion has as much to say about the anxieties and social antagonisms of the culture in which the crimes are committed as they do with the subjectivities of the perpetrators. The case of Jeffrey Dahmer, for example, provided an alibi for the venting of ugly homophobic prejudices, and the media coverage of instances of child molestation routinely expresses intense social discomfort at the reality of child and adolescent sexualities. For a lucid analysis of the figure of the serial killer in popular culture, see Mark Seltzer (*Serial Killers: Death and Life in America's Wound Culture* [New York: Routledge, 1998]).

12 It is crucial to distinguish this idea of subjective sovereignty from any erroneous voluntarist, psychologistic interpretations. The subject is sovereign in the precise sense that it remains unexpressed through its utterances; the subject, in other words, is necessarily indeterminate. This notion has a patently paradoxical application to the Gilles case. The infanticides are the means by which Gilles attempts to express the inexpressible, to occlude his desire, to defer the necessary splitting constitutive of subjectivity. In order to assert that Gilles fails to subjectivize himself, to become a sovereign subject, the subject must first be defined *as sovereign* in the manner here described.

13 G. Bataille, *The Trial,* 10; 12; translation modified.

14 Denis Hollier, *Against Architecture: The Writings of Georges Bataille* (Cambridge, Mass.: MIT Press, 1989), 36–37.

15 G. Bataille, *The Trial,* 40; 50.

16 As we shall go on to explore, Bataille's historicist account of Gilles's relation to discursive context has the somewhat paradoxical effect of psychologizing the criminal in a deeply contradictory way. This is also an opportune moment to distinguish our use of the terms subject, subjective, and subjectivity from their psychologistic usage. By reclaiming Gilles's subjectivity we defend the gap, the chasm—the contradiction, even—between Gilles's discourse and the desire it articulates. The psychoanalytic subject is defined precisely by an unconscious desire. The subject of psychology, by contrast, is an intentional, coherent "self" transparent to desire.

17 Gilles claimed that he was led to a life of crime "on account of the bad upbringing [*mauvais gouvernement*] he had received in his childhood" (189; 242; translation

modified). There is indeed some evidence of the traumas the young Gilles suffered, enough to persuade us to take seriously the effects of these experiences on his future criminality. When Gilles was eleven years old, his father, Guy de Rais, was gored by a wild boar on a hunting expedition and died four years later. It was at this point that Gilles's maternal grandfather, Jean de Craon, assumed Gilles's guardianship after successfully appealing Guy's deathbed attempt to accord responsibility for the boy to a distant cousin. Evidently, Gilles's father had little confidence in his father-in-law's merits as a parental figure, and Gilles's own testimony reveals that Craon allowed his ward to indulge his most savage tendencies. Further, only months after the death of his father, Gilles's mother appears to have abandoned her two boys, owing either to sudden death or to remarriage (Michel Herubel, *Gilles de Rais et le déclin du Moyen-Age* [Paris: Librairie académique Perrin, 1962], 49–73). The other standard-issue view concerning the influence of lived trauma on Gilles's criminality presents the execution of Joan of Arc as the source of an extreme disillusionment that causes Gilles, in essence, to lose faith in humanity. For a suggestive, though highly speculative, account of this angle, see M. Bataille, *Gilles de Rais*, 92–105. Michel Tournier turns this insight into a novella entitled *Gilles et Jeanne,* and Mireille Rosello uses this fictional material to interpret Gilles's execution through the lens of René Girard's theory of the scapegoat. Our own analysis of Gilles, in contrast to these (not *absolutely* value-less, in our view) psychobiographical approaches, will focus exclusively on the logic of the rationalization of his criminality he offers in his confession.

18   Jonathan Goldberg, *Sodometries: Renaissance Texts, Modern Sexualities* (Stanford, Calif.: Stanford University Press, 1992), 9, 19.

19   Philippe Reliquet, *Le Moyen-Age. Gilles de Rais: maréchal, monstre et martyr* (Paris: Editions Pierre Belfond, 1982), 244–45.

20   G. Bataille, *The Trial*, 12; 15.

21   We can revisit Copjec's definition of historicism via the theme of homosexual desire. A historicist conception of homosexuality is one that subsumes same-sex desire under the discourses through which it is represented. This way of thinking about homosexuality features the absurd corollary that one cannot conceive of homosexual desire in the absence of a "discourse" about it.

22   Another clear indication of Bataille's deeply symptomatic relation to the idea of homosexuality occurs in a bizarre passage of his interpretation in which the French critic imagines the decadent orgies Gilles allegedly organized as a prelude to the staging of his bloody scenes of torture. Gilles apparently had a particular fondness for the voices of young choirboys and, in reference to two of Gilles's musical recruits, André Buchet and Jean Rossignol, Bataille unaccountably avers that they "undoubtedly had the voices of homosexual angels" (43). Elsewhere, with reference to the increasingly self-destructive nature of Gilles's comportment leading up to his arrest, Bataille refers to Gilles's self-enclosure in "the solitude of crime, homosexuality, and the tomb" (52). Clearly, homosexuality appears to bring out in Bataille a peculiar taste for the oxymoronic. And finally, evoking too-familiar images of plague and contagion, Bataille makes reference to the Florentine origin of Gilles's favorite necro-

mancer when he claims that François Prelati "came from a city where homosexuality was widespread" (67).

23 For a provocative introduction to the controversy surrounding this Kantian philosophical motif, see Joan Copjec's edited volume, *Radical Evil* (London: Verso, 1996).

24 Here we use the term transference in its strictly psychoanalytic sense. In Lacanian clinical psychoanalysis, the phenomenon of transference occurs when the analysand unconsciously attributes to the analyst knowledge about his or her desire. A more conventionally Freudian understanding would consider the transference a projection onto the analyst of affects—often, but not always, aggressive ones—that originate in psychical conflicts with parental figures. Both understandings share the acknowledgment of a displacement of unconscious material derived from a "past event," necessarily distorted or constructed by the subject's fantasy, onto the dynamics of an inter-subjective encounter (one which Lacan would later describe as dialectical) occurring in the present. In *Studies on Hysteria,* Freud first described the transference as a "false connection" or "*mésalliance*" that dissociates the content of a wish from "the surrounding circumstances that would have assigned [the wish] to a past time" (SE II, 303). Later, Freud would underline how the transference emerges "precisely at the moment when particularly important repressed contents are in danger of being revealed" (J. Laplanche and J.-B. Pontalis, *The Language of Psycho-Analysis,* trans. D. Nicholson-Smith [New York: Norton, 1973], 458). In an early paper on the Dora case, Lacan underlines how the transference halts the emergence of unconscious material when he describes it as "a moment of stagnation in the analytic dialectic" ("Intervention sur le transfert," in *Écrits* [Paris: Seuil, 1966], 225).

25 Sigmund Freud, "Group Psychology and the Analysis of the Ego," SE XVIII, 105.

26 G. Bataille, *The Trial,* 278; 336–37.

27 Joël Dor and Serge André describe Lacan's understanding of perversion as psychic structure. See also Bruce Fink's *A Clinical Introduction to Lacanian Psychoanalysis* for a detailed interpretation in English of Lacan's contribution to the clinical understanding of perversion (this volume, 38–67).

28 Bruce Fink, *A Clinical Introduction,* reprinted in this volume, 49.

29 This is precisely the moral tradition against which Pascal would launch his famous polemic in the *Lettres provinciales,* ed. Louis Cognet (Paris: Garnier, 1965).

30 A comment on our use of the term *moral:* We are not arguing in favor of moralism or a moralistic perspective on Gilles de Rais, which we would define as a structure of judgment or action that takes as its point of self-legitimation ambient, commonly acknowledged criteria that inhere in any particular historical discourse. The word moral as we are using it here refers instead to the manner in which a subject rationalizes its thoughts and actions to itself in the context of a dialogue not between the subject and "society," but rather between the subject and his or her Other, defined psychoanalytically as the sociosymbolic network from the perspective of which every subject views itself as worthy and unworthy, innocent and guilty. The moral realm, in other words, indexes the very nexus of the psychic and the social at which the subject "pays the price" for its narcissism. The psychical agency that allows us to view our-

selves approvingly, in other words, is the selfsame agency through which we reproach ourselves for our inadequacies. The movement from morality to ethics may be defined as coinciding with the subject's ability to liberate itself from such egoic dependencies and to *self-legislate:* to rationalize its act *ex nihilo,* with reference to nothing other than the sacred legality of desire. Obviously, it is precisely this movement that Gilles and his auditors failed to effect.

31 One may suggestively juxtapose the tremendous comfort and pleasure with which Gilles seems to adopt the role of the moral pedagogue with the serenity of the fetishist who, according to Freud, shows himself "quite satisfied" with his fetish. It is also possible to compare the paradox of Gilles's idea of his empirical guilt and metaphysical innocence with the fetishist's ability to entertain two contradictory propositions concerning his psychical experience of castration: "The woman has still got a penis," says the fetishist at the same time that he admits "[his] father has castrated the woman." See Freud, "Fetishism," SE XXI, 152, 157.

32 This is just the tip of the iceberg, as the saying goes, of the evidence in favor of the political stakes involved in the trial of Gilles de Rais. Indeed, only when the ecclesiastical and political authorities had fully taken advantage of Gilles's declining situation did they begin to amass the evidence required for an arrest. As Salomon Reinach has argued, Gilles's profligacy was not entirely out of control, for he made a condition for the sale of his most strategically located castles that his right to reacquisition be recognized for a full six years after the transaction. As a result of this clause, the buyers clearly developed a vested interest in the obliteration of Gilles, since only his death or long-term incapacitation could have safeguarded their ownership of Gilles's property, and since Gilles had no sons to whom he could bequeath his fortune. Further, Reinach suggests that Jean de Malestroit, allied to the English during the Hundred Years War, had a personal vendetta against Gilles, having been arrested in the battle of Saint-Jean de Beuvron by the constable de Richemont under whom Gilles served (Reinach, "Gilles de Rais," 269–70). As Michel Bataille succinctly puts it, "Gilles was not beaten by judges, but by political and financial rivals" (*Gilles de Rais,* 175). Jean Benedetti provides additional details about the duke of Brittany's political and material interest in Gilles's downfall (*Gilles de Rais* [New York: Stein and Day, 1972], 156–90).

33 Jacques Heers, *Gilles de Rais. Vérités et légendes* (Paris: Perrin, 1994), 12.

"As If Set Free into Another Land": Homosexuality, Rebellion, and Community in William Styron's *The Confessions of Nat Turner*

Michael P. Bibler

Published at precisely the moment when the arguments about race had reached crisis proportions in the United States, William Styron's 1967 novel *The Confessions of Nat Turner* became one of those rare sticks of literary dynamite that threatened to blow the already fragile nation into irreparable fragments.[1] In retrospect, it was almost inevitable that the bulk of the novel's readers would immediately divide into polarized camps presenting only two ways to read the text: either we must carefully praise this white southerner for daring to write from the perspective of a black hero, or we must condemn him forthwith.[2] Yet, surprisingly, as the academic battles over race, history, and literary representation spread into the streets, the textual ingredient that made the novel so explosive—the part that inflamed and rallied readers the most—involved an altogether different category of identity than race: homosexuality. Without any historical evidence to support him, Styron ignored the real Nat Turner's marriage to a woman and instead represented his controversial protagonist as having only one sexual encounter in his entire life, this time with a male slave named Willis. Many in the black community interpreted this change as a serious affront and attacked Styron for it. Indeed, in perhaps the most organized response to the novel—*William Styron's Nat Turner: Ten Black Writers Respond* (1968)—each of the contributors treats Styron's admittedly unusual decision to include this homosexual scene as the one thing that, above all else, should galvanize the black community into an angry and cohesive whole. Charles V. Hamilton's words are especially revealing: "Styron's literary mind can wander [sic] about homosexuality and the like, and his vast readership can have their stereotypes strengthened by an image of a black preacher who is irrational and weak . . . and uncertain. But black people should reject this; and white people should not delude themselves."[3] Equating homosexuality with irrationality and weakness, Hamilton describes the scene with Willis as a reinforcement of racist stereotypes that will predictably expose white readers' gullible passivity while it prods black readers into activism. Reading communities give way in Hamilton's mind to larger communities built on a shared racial identity, but those communities apparently don't take form until the point in the novel when the readers must decide how they feel about Nat's homosexuality. For Hamilton, the construction of a community built on race depends first and foremost on the regulation of sexual desire, for the black community will come together, he implies, mostly through the act of rejecting homosexuality.

If we can generalize from Hamilton's assumptions and say that the construction of community depends on the exclusion, or at least control, of same-sex desires and homosexual identities, such a claim is possible only if we define homosexuality not as an alternate form of affection or desire, but as a force much like infection that threatens to undermine all forms of social relation through deficiency, inferiority, weakness, and degeneracy. If community depends on the rejection of homosexuality, then homosexuality itself must be intrinsically negative and disruptive of culture—never constitutive. In *Ten Black Writers*, Alvin F. Poussaint says as much when he argues that Nat's homosexual encounter "implies that Nat Turner was not a man at all. It suggests that he was unconsciously really feminine."[4] As a psychologist, Poussaint was trained at a time when the American Psychological Association still classified homosexuality as a disorder.[5] Therefore, we need to recognize that Styron's portrayal of Nat Turner in an explicitly homosexual situation was a horrible slap in the face to the black community, in effect identifying one of their heroes as a sick and dirty queer. But it is also important to acknowledge both the implicit homophobia of responses like Poussaint's that automatically read Styron's Nat as effeminate and weak, and the way that this homophobia determines the ten black writers' readings of the rest of the novel. Poussaint, for example, is especially clear in claiming that this one homosexual encounter invalidates the rest of the entire narrative: "Thus, throughout the book he is revealed as an emasculated and 'abnormal' character. There is even the suggestion here that the rebellion was participated in reluctantly by the 'sensitive' Nat Turner who really only wished to sleep with Miss Margaret to salvage his manhood. The depiction of the young rebel as a would-be deviant carries the implication that the whole revolt against slavery and racism was somehow illegitimate and 'abnormal.' "[6]

For Poussaint, Nat's isolated affair must mean that he is "emasculated" and therefore taking part in the rebellion only to alleviate the pain of his personal degeneracy. Poussaint implies that homosexuality and rebellion against an unjust society are mutually exclusive because homosexuals are "abnormal" and want only to tear society down to their level. Thus, every aspect of Nat's rebellion is false because it naturally lacks any concomitant ambition to build a better way of life after slavery—as though a gay slave could not resent his condition as much as a straight one.

As Poussaint's condemnation shows, the ten black writers' homophobic assumptions about the supposed effeminacy of gay men limit their assessment of just what role this homosexual interruption plays within the novel. And more recent critics have done no better to explain why Styron might have decided to include such a controversial scene in an already controversial book. But what if we allow ourselves to read Nat's only sexual encounter as central to the novel in a more positive sense? What if we approach the text as a gay novel that happens to include a slave revolt, and not vice versa? To begin with, reorienting our critical perspective, as it were, to the novel's homosexual dynamics shows us that there is no evidence to support the idea that the affair emasculates Nat or makes him effeminate and weak. Instead, the description of Nat's homosexual encounter identifies it as a watershed moment that moves Nat into adulthood and points him in the direction of his career both as a preacher and as a rebel conspiring for freedom on the behalf of all black people. In addition, this homosexual force leads Nat to a full-scale revolt against slavery by giving him a radical new understanding of the power of black community. Instead of repeating the patterns of domination and submission that typically define both sexual and social relations within the slave institution, Nat's homosexual encounter gives him a new experience of mutuality and sameness—what Leo Bersani calls "homo-ness." Bersani argues that same-sex desire possesses a unique structure that privileges sameness instead of difference. Unlike heterosexuality, which is a desire for an Other who is different from the self, homosexuality is "a desire in others of what we already are," a desire "to repeat, to expand, to intensify the same."[7] That is, whether or not gays or lesbians actually long for partners who are as identical to themselves as possible, the dominant discourses surrounding homosexual desire situate sexual sameness as the defining characteristic, and any expression of that desire must be read accordingly. Consequently, any analysis of homosexuality in a social or literary context would potentially benefit most from a focus on this dynamic because sameness indicates a totally different *alternative* to heterosexual relations, and not a failure, corruption, or deviation from them.

Moreover, this association of homosexuality with sameness proposes a distinct form of interpersonal sexual relations that also makes homosexuality a powerful source for rethinking the hierarchical networks of mainstream *social* relations. In Bersani's definition, homo-ness evokes a profoundly alternative form of relationality in which individuals would relate to each other identically, each person socially the same like "points along a transversal network of being in which otherness is tolerated as the nonthreatening margin of, or supplement to, a seductive sameness."[8] Homo-ness intimates a system of human relations that is explicitly anti-hierarchical and provides for the absolute equality of every citizen on the premise that they are all, ultimately, the same. This definition needs to be complicated in relation to Styron's novel, of course, but reading Nat's encounter with Willis as an expression of homo-ness helps make sense of the nature and purpose of Nat's bloody revolt, for the experience not only provides him with a necessary sexual release, but also shows him an image of the freedom and the community that blacks could enjoy outside of slavery. Instead of making the revolt illegitimate, this instance of homo-ness acts as the driving force behind it because it simultaneously provides Nat with the sense of a new model of social relations grounded in sameness and equality. In this way, homosexuality truly *can be* constitutive of community—not through the reification of differences by way of its exclusion, as the ten black writers would have it, but through the presentation of a radical new form of homo-relationality that could heal the rifts *between* communities. Of course, this model is utopian, and Styron's construction of Nat's rebellion ultimately fails to account for and resolve the web of complications involved in building a new form of social equality based on the highly subjective concept of sameness. Yet even in Nat's, and by extension, Styron's, failures, the text nevertheless offers a profound example of the ways that same-sex desire and homosexual relations can possess this remarkable structural potential for resisting the dominant networks of social power in favor of a much more equitable alternative.

Homo-ness, Freedom, and Baptism

Occupying a place in the text that is almost precisely central, Nat's homosexual encounter with Willis marks a momentous transition in Nat's life. Reflecting on the encounter later, Nat claims that it felt like a "promontory" on the way toward both the salvation of "the distant hills of the Lord" and the "astonishing abyss" and "howling winds" of warfare, murder, and revolt.[9] Although the scene is hardly the only cause for Nat's movement toward rebellion, Styron positions this brief homosexual encounter within Nat's confession as the seminal moment, as it were, that begins Nat's treacherous path to the uprising he organizes years later. In what begins as a very idyllic scene, Nat and Willis are fishing one Sunday when Willis pricks his finger and curses, "fuckin' Jesus!" Ever religious, Nat takes offense and "so swiftly that I hardly knew what I was doing I rapped him sharply across the lips, drawing a tiny runnel of blood" (204). Nat's blow hurts Willis emotionally, of course, and Nat, realizing what he has done, suddenly feels "a pang of guilt and pain at my anger, a rush of pity . . . mingled with a hungry tenderness that stirred me in a way I had never known." He reaches up to wipe away the blood on Willis's lip, and the two end up making love: "I reached up . . . pulling him near with the feel of his shoulders slippery beneath my hand, and then we somehow fell on each other, very close, soft and comfortable in a sprawl like babies; beneath my exploring fingers his hot skin throbbed and pulsed like the throat of a pigeon, and I heard him sigh in a faraway voice, and then for a long moment as if set free into another land we did with our hands together what, before, I had done alone. Never had I known that human flesh could be so sweet" (204). The initial violence of Nat's response corresponds to the code of interpersonal behavior established within the slave institution. Although his own master is fairly tolerant, violence nevertheless remains the primary method of control and punishment within slavery at large, and Nat reiterates the lesson almost perfectly. But his act of striking Willis also fosters a painful identification with him on the basis of their shared status at the bottom of the social hierarchy. Himself a slave, Nat cannot assert any real power over Willis by physically correcting his behavior. The blow's symbolic emptiness thus pairs with Willis's hurt feelings to remind Nat of his own disenfranchisement and pain. As a result, the scene quickly turns into a description of some other kind of relationship based in this identification—not quite the surrender of either man so much as the simple sharing of pleasure between them.

Within the hierarchies of the slave plantation, Willis and Nat's equal status as black male slaves creates a situation in which their identities appear to cancel each other out. Although there are real differences between the men, the cultural nexus of slavery renders those differences irrelevant because they share the same fundamental relationship to the networks of power. Without a significant racial, gender, class, or even age difference to unbalance the power relation between them personally, and without a narrative voice to infer one, the two men thus share a moment of homo-ness in which their homosexual union renders their identities not only the same, but also virtually interchangeable. In much the same way that the institutions of slavery prompt an initial violent response from Nat, they also foster the realization and the pleasure of a profound mutuality and sameness that appear to contradict the logic of violence. This experience of homo-ness paradoxically blurs, and even seems to eliminate, the very categories of identity that define the two men because their localized sameness actually neutralizes the axes of difference that support definition. Moreover, this evacuation of identities derives a large part of its power not so much from the simple recognition of similarity as from the temporary release from the self through sexual orgasm. Within the act of their mutual masturbation, their identities do not remain distinct, but merge into one, so that the sexual act they perform on each other becomes an extension and repetition of the sexual acts they have previously performed on themselves. Nat's contact with Willis represents an extension of both men's selves in the psychological as well as the physical sense, because they each place the other in the position of the self—"we did with our hands together what, before, I had done alone." In this way, it is impossible to read the scene as a sign of Nat's emasculation, as early critics wanted to, because Nat's pleasure derives specifically from the replication—and not the assertion or surrender—of his own masculinity with another male body.

Although the plantation society's constructions of identity initially enable Nat's experience of homo-ness, the temporary release both from those categories and from the self liberates him, transporting him not only to a new level of pleasure and satisfaction, but also to a state that makes him forget his status as a slave. Describing homo-ness as a kind of emancipation where he feels "as if set free into another land," Nat comes to recognize a new system of relations that aren't governed by the laws of domination, force, violence, inequality, and ownership that govern the "land" of Virginia in which he actually lives. Thus, the temporary shift into freedom indicates the socially revolutionary potential of homosexuality. Contrary to the opinions of Styron's critics, homo-ness is not a sickness or a failure to live up to the dominant constructions of mainstream identities. And contrary to those who would argue that gays and lesbians or any other minorities can simply be absorbed into mainstream society—giving homosexuals or African Americans "a place at the table," as it were—homo-ness does not simply rearrange the terms of dominant culture or soften their powers to classify, control, and subjugate individuals through a hierarchy of differences. Instead, homo-ness invokes the possibility of taking the power away from those identities and terms entirely by creating a new system of relations grounded in sameness and equality. It is a radical disruption of culture that does more than simply expose or test the limits of social relations because it offers a contrary vision of what may lie beyond those limits. Although it is largely the product of the plantation's symbolic order, Nat's brief affair also offers him a glimpse of what may be possible *outside* of that symbolic order. More importantly, the erotic component of homo-ness makes that brief glimpse fully experiential, for the dissolution of self necessarily incorporates the simultaneous dissolution of those terms that define and control him within the plantation. Thus, Styron clearly situates this transcendent sexual moment as Nat's most empowering inspiration for both the idea and the real possibility of slave revolt.

The extent to which homo-ness pushes Nat toward insurrection becomes most evident in the particular manner in which he tries to build
and justify his revolution. But if we are to accept the power of Nat's
experience of homo-ness with Willis, Styron's novel shows that we
shouldn't rush into assuming that homosexuality offers this model for
social transformation consistently, as though same-sex relations would
always mean the same thing between men or between women every
time. Just as, for Nat, the specific hierarchies of race, class, and gender enable his experience of sameness with another black male slave,
they will also enable or restrict the experience and significance of sexual
sameness depending on the identities of those involved. Indeed, Styron's
novel makes it perfectly clear that not every expression of same-sex
desire is also an example of homo-ness. In contrast to Nat's sexual encounter with Willis, and just a few pages after it, the novel provides an
image of same-sex relations that incorporates the significantly different
pattern of domination and submission. In the scene, Nat begins his account of his life with his new master, the Reverend Eppes, by describing
the way that Eppes blatantly tries to "ravish" him (239). Riding on the
buggy away from Turner's plantation, Eppes strikes up a religious discourse with Nat to disguise his more sinister proposition that Nat should
submit to Eppes sexually. Eppes claims that King Solomon made it clear
in the Bible that women are "whores" who always cause the downfalls of
men; then he infers that since the Scripture also identifies men as "good"
and "beautiful," sexual contact between men must be acceptable and
safe in comparison (236–37). Then, after a pause, Eppes stops the buggy,
puts a hand on Nat's thigh, and tries more directly to seduce Nat by
getting him to verify the myth of black men's larger penises: "I hear tell
your average nigger boy's got a member on him inch or so longer'n ordinary. That right, boy?" (238). In this simple question, Eppes reasserts
the social difference between himself and Nat by invoking several other
axes of difference—race ("nigger"), physiology (a penis "longer'n ordinary"), age ("boy"), and mental capability (also the infantilizing "boy").
Proving that he is neither an emasculated deviant nor a hopeless sub-
missive, Nat resists this advance, and the frustrated Eppes ends the encounter with a remark that further puts Nat "in his place" as a slave:
"You goin' to mind me, boy?" (238). Eppes focuses his sexual desire for
Nat on the idea of Nat's difference, eroticizing his racial difference to the
point of obsessing about the size of his penis while also getting a thrill

from the idea of being able to dominate someone with a supposedly superior potency. And when he can't dominate Nat sexually, he reasserts his own superiority by calling attention to Nat's legal powerlessness as a slave. Consequently, this scene lacks any evidence of the eroticization of sexual sameness that Nat experiences with Willis. Eppes wants to use sexuality to reinforce slavery's hierarchy of differences and also gets sexual pleasure from the exploitation of those differences.

In addition to showing us that homo-ness is a unique, and perhaps uncommon, phenomenon, because not all same-sex relations are characterized by the willful subordination of interpersonal differences in the name of sexual sameness, the novel also reminds us that homo-ness when it does occur is not always automatically political in nature. Even when homo-ness does represent the main component of same-sex relations, homosexuality is not *necessarily* opposed in an active sense to the dominant arrangements of hierarchical differences. In the scene of Nat's encounter with Willis, their mutual orgasm gives Nat a brief glimpse of a world defined by total emancipation, but it also ironically creates a narrative interruption that threatens to alter or halt the course of Nat's progression toward insurrection. Although Nat has not yet figured out exactly what his calling is at this moment, he feels that God has chosen him for some reason. Yet his encounter with Willis presents him with the opportunity to digress from that chosen path and hide from his destiny. Moments after the two men climax together on the bank of the stream, Willis "murmurs" contentedly to Nat: "Man, I sho liked dat. Want to do it agin?" (204). Willis wants to repeat the pleasure of their contact and presents Nat with what is actually a very important decision for him to make. If he reenters Willis's embrace, he risks forming a private relationship that will potentially limit his ability to fulfill any larger purpose ordained for him as a chosen disciple of God. As a gay couple, Nat and Willis would occupy a safe and satisfying bubble of private liberation on the Turner plantation, but leave intact the structure of the slave institution. Homo-ness may possess antisocial or outlaw tendencies because of its paradoxical intolerance for the hierarchical relations that enable it, but the sexually transcendental scene also testifies to the dangers of forming an emotive relationship in place of a political community. Linking Nat and Willis through their recognition of an erotic, shared sameness, the repetition of the act would present Nat with the chance to "settle down," as it were, and find a kind of contentment

within his position as a slave. Though the men would be outlaws in a
sense, homosexuality would give them the chance to build a new community by acting both as their point of commonality and as their buffer
against the oppression of the slave institution. However, if Nat were to
accept that alternative, this scene would seriously interrupt his narrative
by pointing him away from religion and rebellion and leading him instead toward complacency and private satisfaction. The experience certainly doesn't show Nat *how* he should rebel. But while it does give Nat
the glimpse of freedom that will eventually lead him to adopt a deeply
outlaw position as an insurrectionist, it also interrupts the narrative by
threatening to close it down entirely.

Nevertheless, Nat does not allow his experience of temporary sexual
emancipation to give him an easy out from the daily miseries of slavery.
In fact, the truly radical potential of his experience of homo-ness lies in
the larger sense of community that it inspires in him. This sense of community is most evident in the scene immediately following his sexual
encounter when he leads Willis into the river and baptizes them both.
Needless to say, this movement from homosexual liaison to righteous
baptism has been the subject of much heated controversy, and most critics have dealt with it by disregarding the baptism as a testament to Nat's
confusion, guilt, and sin.[10] But these readings are too easy when explaining Nat's turn to God at this moment because there are other dynamics
at work in the language of the scene that suggest an expansion, rather
than a repudiation, of the homo-ness he has just experienced sexually.
Although he does ask that the " 'Lord . . . witness these two sinners who
have sinned and have been unclean in Thy sight and stand in need to
be baptized' " (205), the method and the description of his baptism are
quite sexual, as well, repeating his physical encounter with Willis in a
sublimated, spiritual way. In this manner, Nat does not use baptism to
erase or nullify the sexual act he just committed, but to change that act
into something larger and more suitable to his sense of a divine purpose.
As the two men enter the water, Nat waits eagerly for a revelation from
God, and the language of his description becomes increasingly erotic, as
though building not toward a revelation but to an orgasm:

> In the warmth of the spring air I suddenly felt the presence of the
> Lord very close, compassionate, all-redeeming, all-understanding.
> . . . He seemed about to reveal Himself, as fresh and invisible as

a breath of wind upon the cheek. It was almost as if God hovered in the shimmering waves of heat above the trees, His tongue and His almighty voice trembling at the edge of speech, ready to make known His actual presence to me as I stood penitent and prayerful with Willis ankle-deep in the muddy waters. Through and beyond the distant roaring of the mill I thought I heard a murmuration and another roaring far up in the heavens, as if from the throats of archangels. Was the Lord going to speak to me? I waited faint with longing, clutching Willis tightly by the arm, but no words came from above — only the sudden presence of God poised to shower Himself down like summer rain. . . . For an instant indeed I thought He spoke but it was only the rushing of the wind high in the treetops. My heart pounded wildly. (205–6)

The language of this passage repeats much of the same anxious phrasing and diction that describe his encounter with Willis, transposing the "throb" and "pulse" of Willis's throat to the "shimmering," "trembling," and "rushing" of the Lord's "tongue" and the archangels' "throats." The rhythm in the passage builds intensely as Nat waits for the ejaculatory moment in which God will "reveal himself" and "shower Himself down like summer rain." And, as Nat becomes "faint with longing," he "clutches" Willis "by the arm" and infects him with his own ecstatic spirit, until Willis himself seems about to climax again: " 'Amen!' Willis said. Beneath my fingers I could feel him begin to stir and shudder and another 'Amen!' came from him in a gasp. 'Das right, Lawd!' " (206).

By including Willis in this scene, Nat makes the act of baptism a powerfully communal event whose purpose fulfills more than a selfish need to eliminate his own personal guilt or sin. The sexualized description proves that Nat is not turning away from his homosexual encounter, but rather capitalizing on his newfound recognition of homorelationality to bring Christianity more powerfully into his life. Nat chooses a verse for baptism that stresses the fundamental equality of every baptized person: " '*For by one Spirit are we all baptized into one body,*' I said, '*whether we be Jews or Gentiles, whether we be bond or free, and have been made all to drink into one Spirit*' " (206). This quotation invokes a kind of spiritual homo-ness that is intrinsic to Christian belief and that exposes the thematic connection between his baptism and his homosexual encounter. With the power to unite all people into "one body" and "one Spirit," baptism can build a new community that re-defines identity through a fundamental Christian sameness instead of through individual differences in ethnicity, race, gender, or class. In this way, the act of baptism allows Nat to enlarge his newfound awareness of the possibility for homo-relationality. By moving from homosexuality to baptism, Nat takes the private recognition of homo-ness and sub-limates it into a religious agenda with a more public purpose. At the moment of his own self-baptism, Nat pledges to God, "Let me hence-forth be dedicated to Thy service. Let me be a preacher of Thy holy word" (206–7). Thus committing himself to God, Nat vows to repeat his sexual experience of homo-ness in a specifically religious way, for God's orgasmic revelation never comes in this scene. With "a thrill of joy," Nat believes that God is just "testing" him, "sav[ing] his voice for another time" when orgasm and the fulfillment of religious purpose will again coincide in the creation of a new world. Consequently, he decides to adopt an activist position that is profoundly inspired by the homo-sexual act and vows to build a radically new system of social relations by spreading the idea of a Christian egalitarianism. And, by baptizing Willis with him, Nat already begins creating this new kind of homo-community.

Homo-Community and the Limits of Homo-ness

Nat's baptism with Willis indicates that homo-ness has the power at least to open the possibility for creating a new sense of community even as it simultaneously disrupts the existing cultural hierarchies that enable it. But while Nat's experience of the power of homo-ness is absolutely vital to the revolution he plots later in the novel, the way he proceeds from the baptism becomes highly problematic in part because he actu-ally tries to remain true to that experience. Consequently, the limits of the insurrection that Nat imagines also reveal many of the limitations of homo-ness itself. The first problem Nat encounters is that the constitu-tive power of homo-ness doesn't actually give him a clear plan of action. Homo-ness empowers a new sense of an egalitarian society opposed to the existing structure of the slave plantation, but does not offer a prac-tical model for organizing or stabilizing that new political community. To compensate for this gap, Nat tries to build on his experience and fulfill his commitment to reinvent society according to "the Lord's will" by drawing on other models of egalitarian community already theorized within culture. Yet these models are themselves limited in their potential, and when Nat tries to reconcile them with the transformational impetus of homo-ness, he moves beyond revolt into much more problematic ideological ground. He becomes increasingly fascistic in his ideology by disallowing any form of difference beyond a common racial identity, and thus plots to eliminate whites through genocidal warfare. And when he finally decides that *some* whites might deserve to live after his revolt, he again accepts them into his community with a subtly revised notion of their *ideological* sameness as opponents to slavery. Moreover, at every stage of his plan, he insists that all women of both races be excluded from any real participation in his community. Thus it seems again that Styron's depiction of Nat's rebellion is as doomed to fail as the rebellion itself—though not, perhaps, because of Styron's implicit racism or sexism, as others have argued. For although Styron offers a profound image of the idea of homo-ness that supports Nat's insurrection, he does not acknowledge the way that homo-ness implicitly depends on difference for its own eruption into culture, or the way that it depends on an extremely relative notion of sameness to the self. Nevertheless, even if Nat and Styron both fail, the novel still works as a remarkable example in which we can better understand the emancipatory possibilities of homo-ness by also learning to recognize the limits of its power.

In the weeks immediately following the baptism, Nat imagines creating a new community that is quite typical of every other vision of evangelical Christianity. But this attempt fails because while he privileges a notion of sameness, he also ignores the disruptive capability within homo-ness to change the oppressive networks of slave society. At this point in his thinking, Nat decides to build a community of two people not by entering into a full-fledged homosexual relationship with Willis, but by trying to educate him and prepare him for freedom:

> As for Willis—well, I realized now that loving him so much, loving him as a brother, I should do everything within my power to assure his own progress in the way of the Lord. I must first try to teach him to read and write . . . that accomplished, maybe it was not beyond the bounds of possibility that Marse Samuel might be persuaded that Willis, too, was fit for freedom and could be set loose in the

outer world—Richmond perhaps!—with a grand job and a house
and family. It would be hard to describe how much it pleased me to
think of Willis free like myself in the city, the two of us dedicated to
spreading God's word among the black people and to honest work
in the employ of the white. (207)

This new concept of community is small, and Nat wants to form with
Willis a more closely knit relationship that develops both men's senses of
their shared sameness. Nat wants to educate Willis so that Willis will be
equally literate, intelligent, and spiritual—a second Nat "like myself,"
ready for freedom and ready to branch out to make even more Nats by
"spreading God's word among the black people." Then, with this new
evangelical army of educated blacks, Nat and Willis will gradually create a new society in which all black people are the same because of their
education and spiritual training. More importantly, Nat's vision also implies that he believes black people will finally be free in this new society
because their new identity as intelligent and capable beings will prove
to whites, as he hopes it would prove to "Marse Samuel," that slavery
actually is unjust and illogical.

    However, Nat's plan here is obviously flawed because it depends en-
tirely on white benevolence. It tries to situate a larger version of homo-
relationality—one that is evangelical instead of privately sexual—within
a slave society whose hierarchies of social differences and domination
have been left intact. He attempts to reconcile a Christian demand for
unity and sameness with a liberal model of political community in which
the umbrella of citizenship still allows for social differences. This flaw
in his thinking immediately becomes apparent in the events following
the baptism. When Turner sells Willis to help pay off some debts, Nat
painfully realizes that education, faith, and trust will never win freedom
for any black. Freedom will never work as long as whites remain in the
dominant position and can decide at whim whether or not a black person is actually qualified to live as a complete human being. Even freedom after manumission is not a true freedom because whites will still
set the terms that define black identity, and blacks will still remain sub-
ordinate to them—"free in the city" but still having to work "in the honest employ of the white." Christian evangelism by itself would fail to
change anything, even if Nat were able to convert as many people as
possible, for instead of being set free into "another land," his converts

would simply become free in slave Virginia. Thus, for Nat to replace the slave institution with a new society governed by a system of homo-relations that affirms the fundamental sameness of every person, he will have to recognize that a dramatic change can only come about through dramatic methods.

Suffering his master's betrayal, which is then followed by a string of other betrayals and setbacks, Nat quickly abandons his evangelical plan for a benign Christian society. But he does not give up his attempt to reconcile his religious purpose with his political quest to end slavery. He becomes increasingly committed to his faith and resentful of the whites around him until he finally experiences a religious vision that inspires him to all-out bloody revolt. In the vision, a black angel vanquishes a white angel in the sky and then tells Nat, *"These shall make war with the Lamb and the Lamb shall overcome them. . . . This is the fast that I have chosen, to loose the bonds of wickedness, to undo the heavy burdens, to let the oppressed go free, and that ye break every yoke"* (292). This vision leads Nat to decide that the only way to liberate himself and his fellow blacks completely is actually to destroy those who "make war with the Lamb." Instead of trusting the good intentions of white slaveholders, Nat must strive to "break every yoke" and assert freedom through direct action. Yet, in forming this plan for warfare, he ultimately decides that the best way to correct the oppression of a rigidly hierarchical society is to destroy those whose power keeps that hierarchy intact. This vision builds on the inspiration of Nat's experience of homo-ness in which the categories of identity are wiped clean, and his desire to destroy the social and economic institutions of slavery illogically leads him to plot the murder of every white person in the vicinity. Whereas he learns that Christianity by itself lacks the power to transform his slave society and win the freedom of enslaved Africans as equal citizens, he evidently returns to the liberating experience of homo-ness by deciding simply to *kill* difference in the name of a greater social sameness. To reach the freedom of "another land," he must utterly destroy the very signs of difference that define and maintain the oppressive social structure of the "old" land.

Yet even though Nat decides to create his new society of sameness and equality by destroying the whites who perpetuate injustices through the institutions of racism and slavery, his vision of this bloody insurrection should not be misconstrued as the ravings of a sexual deviant who wants only the destruction of culture for his own self-gratification. If Nat wanted nothing more than personal revenge on the whites he blames for his real dehumanization and pain as a slave, then there would be no sign that he has any sense of the community he would build after his revolt. And yet, this is not the case. At a key moment when Nat watches two slaves whose masters have forced them to fight each other in public until they are bloody and exhausted, he becomes outraged and lectures the other slaves in the audience with the only sermon he makes in the entire novel. Preaching about the Jews' deliverance from their bondage in Egypt, he tells his "brothers" to learn to take pride in their blackness:

> Them Jews become *men*. But oh, my brothers, black folk ain't never goin' to be led from bondage without they has *pride*! Black folk ain't goin' to be free, they ain't goin' to have no spoonbread and sweet cider less'n they studies to love they own *selves*. Only then will the first be the last, and the last first. Black folk ain't never goin' to be no great nation until they studies to love they own black skin an' the beauty of that skin an' the beauty of them black hands that toils so hard and black feet that trods so weary on God's earth. (311)

In this passage and throughout the rest of the sermon, Nat appeals to his fellow slaves through a rhetoric of kinship in which all men are connected laterally as brothers. Nat replaces slavery's hierarchical arrangement of paternalistic relations—master/father, slave/child, mammy, uncle, and so on—with the more egalitarian political model of a fraternal brotherhood. More importantly, he invokes this notion of brotherhood to encourage them to take pride in themselves—to find their own sense of identity as proud, beautiful human beings, and not as bodies meant just for work and toil. Then, with a new pride in their own blackness and a new sense of social equality, this new community of "brothers" would, in Nat's imagination, ultimately spread to the far corners of the globe. Clearly imagining a rebellion larger than his personal desire to punish the white community, Nat decides that it should take place on the Fourth of July and describes his awareness of the effect this date would have on slaves all over the country:

> It seemed clear to me that when our eruption was successful . . . and when word of our triumph spread throughout Virginia and the upper southern seaboard, becoming a signal for Negroes every-

where to join us in rebellion, the fact that it had all arisen on the Fourth of July would be an inspiration not alone to the more knowledgeable slaves of the region but to men in bondage in even more remote parts of the South who might take flame from my great cause and eventually rally to my side or promulgate their own wild outbreaks. (353–54)

By staging his rebellion on the national holiday, Nat hopes to expand the practice of life and liberty that the Declaration of Independence promised in word. He still espouses violence, but he also hopes that his actions will convey an *ideological* imperative that emphasizes freedom and equality—and not the punishment of whites—as the basis for a new, cohesive community of blacks that spans the different regions of the country.

Although he is first inspired by the experience of sameness in his encounter with Willis, Nat's initial vision of an egalitarian Christian community fails to offer a solution to the real political problems associated with egalitarian citizenship because it leaves the institutions of culture unchanged. Inspired by a second vision that also dictates the radical transformation of society—only this time through violence instead of erotic attachment—Nat ultimately revises his version of Christianity to reconcile that tension between the religious and the political. Nat decides that the best way to destroy that rigid hierarchy of social differences is to destroy the *fact* of difference by killing whites. The sheer destructiveness of his plan for insurrection thus indicates the extension of his desire to be "set free into another land" because he intends not only to win the emancipation of enslaved Africans, but also to destroy completely every vestige of the hierarchical society built by white slaveholders. Legal equality, framed in the liberal discourses of fraternity and the American Revolution, will be easy because the economic, cultural, and ideological institutions that support difference will be gone, as will the phenomenon of racial difference itself. Everyone in his new land will satisfy his requirements for both a Christian sameness and a legal equality after slavery because the only people left will already be defined as the same as each other. Of course, these appropriations and revisions of the other forms of egalitarianism do not spring directly from Nat's experience of homo-ness, as if they were always the natural product of *any* experience of homo-ness. But this strange, new vision of community certainly testifies to the power and influence of that experience, for in his quest for a religious community of legal and social equals, he changes the existing modes of egalitarianism to approximate as closely as possible his initial feelings of liberation and equality through sameness.

At this stage in Nat's imagination of a post-rebellion community, however, his goal for revolution is fraught with the same core paradoxes that define homo-ness itself. His first problem is that he privileges the idea of sameness to such a degree that he actually wants to destroy differences outright. Secondly, in the same way that the feeling of homo-ness can occur only within the hierarchical arrangement of identities it seems to transcend, this particular plan to create sameness through the elimination of difference ironically depends on the very categories and definitions that Nat wants to eliminate. If killing whites leaves a new community of people who are the same as each other, they can only be identified as the same if the terms of the old culture are transposed into the new culture. The dissolution of racial oppression ironically relies on the preservation of the racial categories Nat wants to overthrow, as his sermon about blacks loving "they own black skin" shows. Nat is thus refusing to acknowledge the limitations intrinsic to homo-ness because he transforms homo-relationality into overt fascism. In this way, Styron's text is still extremely conservative in its politics because he very nearly transforms this heroic slave rebel into genocidal, megalomaniacal black Hitler. Moreover, what Nat—and possibly Styron—doesn't realize is that the fascist vision of an all-black society also shifts the axis of difference to the more expansive notion of a shared blackness. Whereas his first plan proposed to create a black race of Nats who are equally educated, equally religious, and equally free, his second plan redraws the line of sameness more broadly. Nat tries to remain true to his experience of homo-ness, but in doing so, he ironically redefines the ways by which any form of social sameness could now be realized.

And, as he resituates his idea of equality on the grounds of a broader racial sameness, he implicitly does so in a way that seems to privilege only black *men*. Throughout the novel, Nat's violent fantasies of raping women and his obsession with the young, white Margaret Whitehead indicate a deep-seated, and now almost legendary, misogyny. Assisted by this misogyny, Nat combines his experience of homo-ness with the single-gendered egalitarian model of fraternity to exclude women. Nat makes no mention of what role black women might play in his new society beyond that of the future "wife" he imagines will help relieve his sexual tension. In the afterglow of his most violent rape fantasy in the novel, he prays, "Lord, after this mission is done I will have to get me a wife" (347). Clearly sexist, such a prayer defines women as something like their own form of property whose purpose is to assist, calm, and satisfy him when he needs it. Where white women are concerned, his attitude is even worse. For while he ultimately decides that some white men need not be killed, as we will see, he continues to fight against his own better judgment and demand that all white *women* be killed.[11] This fascist exclusion of women is obviously the product of his own misgivings about sexual difference, but it may also signal another limitation of homo-ness itself. Because homo-ness evokes a model of social sameness that specifically privileges *sexual* sameness, this characteristic helps explain Nat's quick adoption of fraternity as a conceptual model. And while we should be careful not to confuse homo-ness as the natural source of antifeminist or misogynist sentiment—the old myth that gay men must hate women—its insistence on the subordination of differences to a greater sense of sameness may leave homo-ness wide open for misappropriation by those who would actively *suppress* differences on the basis of one sex's (or one race's or one class's) supposed superiority over the other.

However, even as Nat authors this genocidal and violently patriarchal plan, he also recognizes the irrationality of its extremism, albeit only slightly, and revises his vision of community once again. As the time of the insurrection draws nearer, Nat continues to redraw the line of sameness to suit his own politics. And while he does broaden the scope of his insurrectionist community to move away from overt fascism, this new basis for a community of sameness remains highly problematic in its own way. Soon after Nat makes his sermon, an interesting opportunity arises that enables Nat once again to revise his visions of Christianity and community into a form that nominally corresponds even more closely to the liberated "other land" he glimpsed with Willis. About a month after Nat makes his sermon, but immediately following it in the narrative, a white man named Ethelred T. Brantley approaches him and asks to be baptized. Brantley is a convicted "sotomite" who has been cast out from all the white churches in the area, and he sees Nat as his last hope for salvation (315). Nat finally agrees after some persuasion and thus performs the only other baptism besides his own and Willis's that he includes in his confession. This second baptism is extremely significant in that Brantley's oppositional relation to slave society prompts Nat to rethink his genocidal vision and decide to spare the white man from the slaughter. And, as Nat sees it, the core characteristic that sets Brantley at odds with the power structures of society is his sexual identity as a "sotomite." In making this decision, however, Nat seems to misread Brantley's character deliberately in order to foster an identification with him in a way that satisfies Nat's original experience of homo-ness. In the novel, Brantley's sexuality resituates homosexuality as crucial to Nat's vision of rebellion and at least reminds us of the power of homoness both to disrupt the web of social relations and to offer an alternative to them. But it also shows us the truly slippery and peculiar logic that can accompany any attempt to make that original vision of homo-ness into a social reality on a large scale.

The encounter with Brantley at first repulses Nat in part because Brantley has a grotesque appearance, which Nat describes almost homophobically: "a round womanish man of about fifty, with soft plump white cheeks upon which tiny sores and pustules congregated like berries amid a downy fringe of red hair" (313). In high novelistic fashion, this description of physical repulsiveness functions also to stress the apparent moral deformity of Brantley's sexual character, for as Nat paraphrases from Brantley's own admission, Brantley has imposed himself sexually on young boys: "He had been sent to jail once in Carolina. Now he was afraid again. Because—He had taken a woman—No! He hesitated, his eyes anxious behind flickering eyelids, a pink flush rising beneath the pustuled skin. That was wrong. No, he—He had done something *bad,* yesterday, with a boy. The son of a local magistrate. He had paid the boy a dime. The boy had told. He thought the boy had told. He wasn't sure. He was afraid" (314). Because Brantley has molested a young boy, the dynamic of the sexual encounter resembles the plantation's more common pattern of domination and submission suggested in Eppes's attempt to dominate Nat—not the homo-ness of Nat's encounter with Willis. The exchange of money even seems to replicate temporarily the economic contract of chattel slavery. Nevertheless, Styron seems to suggest that Brantley's particular form of predation still counts as taboo because it falls outside the acceptable forms of white male privilege in slave society. Even though he takes advantage of the child, Brantley's penchant for boys places him at odds with the hierarchical structure of Virginia society because he still tries to instigate a form of sexual relations that even the paternalistic culture of slavery cannot accommodate. This deviation from the normative mode of sexual relations consequently sets him apart from the normative mode of *social* relations and makes it possible for Nat both to identify with Brantley as an outlaw and to recognize that Brantley might not pose a threat to Nat's vision of a new community.

When Brantley breaks down and tells how the white churches have banished him for being a sodomite, Nat is "suddenly swept away by pity and disgust," and recognizes Brantley's wretched state as a white outcast. He agrees to baptize the man and then speculates about his reasons for agreeing: "It may be only that Brantley at that moment seemed as wretched and forsaken as the lowest Negro; white though he might be, he was as deserving of the Lord's grace as were others deserving of His wrath, and to fail Brantley would be to fail my own obligation as minister of His word. Besides, it gave me pleasure to know that by showing Brantley the way to salvation I had fulfilled a duty that a white preacher had shirked" (315). As "wretched and forsaken as the lowest Negro," Brantley is already an outlaw who is denied access to the white networks of power and security. No doubt fascinated by the idea that whites can exclude other whites from their own community, Nat consequently decides to baptize him out of an identification with the desperation of Brantley's status. Although Nat admits that he gets some satisfaction in doing the job as a "minister of His word" better than a "white preacher," and although he is moved in part by a "pity" that confirms his own spiritual superiority, he also bases his decision on more altruistic grounds that fall in line with his identification. Nat is clear that only some people deserve "grace" while others deserve "wrath," indicating that it is by no means his policy to help people indiscriminately. Nat is particular in choosing whom he will help, and he baptizes Brantley primarily because he sees Brantley as truly abject and deserving of salvation. And even though his white skin technically makes him superior to Nat, his appeal to Nat for help and guidance shows that Brantley actually disregards the dominant hierarchies as part of an unjust, oppressive, and un-Christian social apparatus. If Brantley subscribed to the notion of white supremacy, he would never approach Nat with this kind of request, and he would deserve wrath instead of grace. Therefore, when Nat agrees to baptize him, he is not making a gesture of pity so much as acknowledging the significance of Brantley's position in society.

Nat's identification with Brantley is further evident in the manner in which he baptizes the white man. Again emphasizing the communal nature of baptism, Nat tells Brantley, "We will be baptized together in the Spirit" (315). Brantley is the only other person besides Willis that Nat tells about baptizing in the novel, and both baptisms are significant in that Nat builds a community of sameness with each man "together in the Spirit." Nat may not like Brantley personally, but he is still willing to accept him into his symbolic religious community. Moreover, at the actual scene of the baptism, Nat's sense of a shared community with Brantley grows even beyond his identification with Brantley's outlaw status and his avowal of their sameness in the eyes of God. When the two men wade into the water of the pond, a "mob of forty or fifty poor white people" begins pelting the two men with "stones and sticks from fallen trees" (319). Their hateful reaction underscores the opposition between the dominant community—which Nat codes as morally and spiritually lost through the people's use of "fallen" materials—and the less judgmental community that he is working to create. Then, immersing himself in the millpond, Nat again experiences a transcendent moment that reminds him not only of his devotion to building a spiritual community, but also of his attempt to build a literal community through his violent insurrection: "I immersed myself with a prayer, then rose. Beyond the white faces blooming dimly on the far bank, heat lightning whooshed up in faint green sheets. Dusk had come down like the shadow of a great wing. I felt a sharp premonition of my own death. 'Brantley,' I said as we struggled back through the water toward my followers on the bank, 'Brantley, I advise you to leave the county soon, because the white people are going to be destroyed' " (319). By telling Brantley to leave before the insurrection, Nat clearly decides that killing him would be wrong or unnecessary. Brantley is already an outcast from the white community and personally has no stake in preserving the hierarchies that have shut him out as a sodomite. After the rebellion, when Nat has completely destroyed the idea of racial difference by destroying the fact of racial difference, this white man will thus pose no threat to the new social order because he will have no desire to return to the horrors of the old. Brantley's desire for baptism may be driven by his fear of damnation, but he still becomes part of Nat's spiritual community by default. As a sexual outlaw and now as a baptized Christian with an honest resentment for the sexualized and racialized hierarchies of the slave society, Brantley is thus an honorary member, as it were, in Nat's post-rebellion community of freedom, sameness, and equality.

Within the logic of the novel, the fact that Brantley's sexual identity as a sodomite helps provoke Nat's decision to spare him testifies to the importance of same-sex desire and homo-ness as a constitutive, rather than a negative, force in the formation of social relations and community. While his model for a larger political community of free blacks invokes the single-sex metaphor of brotherhood, his decision to spare Brantley again collapses explicit homosexuality and social isolation onto each other. As a result, Nat's decision to include Brantley in his new community now *appears* to be a move into a real system of homo-relationality that accepts difference as a mere supplement to sameness. This inclusion indicates a gesture toward the final dissolution of those hierarchical identities that enable the concept of sameness in the first place. Brantley's sexual identity, as Nat conveniently misconstrues it, destabilizes the categories of race, class, and gender, making him simultaneously masculine and "womanish," both white and worse than "the lowest Negro." By accepting him as the same in Christian terms and deciding to spare his life in his political rebellion, Nat thus embraces this destabilization of identities in an attempt to prove that he is not simply trying to invert the social order by giving blacks ascendancy over whites. His new society still emphasizes Christian sameness, but only for those Christians who also occupy a political opposition to the old order regardless of their material identities. In this way, Styron would apparently have us believe that by baptizing him, Nat clearly accepts Brantley's identity as a sodomite and creates a radically new version of Christian relations that is totally unlike either version he has imagined earlier. Nat personally dislikes Brantley, and Brantley himself shows no interest in Nat's political ambitions because he "hear[s] nothing" of Nat's warning to leave (320). Yet Nat still welcomes him into this new community, proving that there is now space for personal and political differences within this strange new world of sameness and equality. Although the flawed logic here obviously rests in the way that Nat personally forms his opinion about Brantley, Styron's inclusion of this second baptism seems to suggest that Nat's new vision of violent Christianity and bloody insurrection marks a final attempt to destroy the institutions and *definitions* of difference, as well as the people who support them, so that the realities of interpersonal differences between those who remain will no longer need to be suppressed.

But the flaw in Nat's thinking—and here, I think, in Styron's as well—cannot be ignored because Nat also allows the term "sodomy"—which we now more generally associate with homosexual acts performed by consenting adults—to absorb and obscure Brantley's much more problematic identity as a pedophile. He de-emphasizes the predatory form of Brantley's apparent sexual preference and recasts it as something much more amenable to his own political goals. This slippage conveniently allows Nat once more to redraw the axis of sameness and welcome only those who also live at odds with the hierarchies and ideologies he is struggling to overthrow.[12] He now redefines sameness on political grounds instead of racial ones by also misconstruing Brantley's habits of sexual domination as something more akin to his own experience of homo-ness. Nat seems to privilege a false notion of Brantley's sexual identity in order to reclassify himself and the white man as the *same kinds* of outlaws—men who are at odds with society not just because they've done something taboo sexually, but because their sexual histories have prompted them in one degree or another to modify and challenge the social limitations placed upon them. With this subtle error, Styron apparently wants us to read the scene as the full-circle return of homo-ness in a way that allows Nat to tolerate differences within a community built on a communal sameness. Superficially, Nat's embrace of Brantley seems almost like a realization of the utopian form of homo-relationality that homo-ness inspires—the place where social equality is grounded in the notion of a fundamental sameness and where differences can exist without mattering. But to reach this new system of homo-relational community, Nat must constantly redraw the lines of sameness to satisfy his personal criteria of who should be admitted and who should not. Again, the error here seems to stem in large part from Nat's personal idiosyncrasies. But the inconsistency of Nat's criteria for sameness may also result from the extreme subjectivity of that demand in homo-ness for sameness to the self. As he expands his notion of community, he becomes less and less able to define that community according to his original feeling of sameness that his and Willis's shared status as black male slaves enabled. Consequently, for every person Nat meets who is not like him, but whom he also wants to save as a member of his community, he must distort both his own and the other person's identities to create *some* kind of sameness that would justify a positive relationship between them. The disruptive and communal powers of homo-ness are localized and specific; and while they clearly offer a profound vision of what lies outside the hierarchies of difference, they do not offer any specific means for transforming culture or for stabilizing the categories of sameness on which any new culture would be built.

Nevertheless, if Styron's novel fails to examine these limits of homo-ness, we should not let that cloud us to the ways that same-sex desire and homosexual relations can still inspire a radical revision of the mainstream hierarchies of patriarchy, racism, and the oppressive class structure, even in our own society. In its shifting definitions of sameness, its total exclusion of women, and its near-total exclusion of whites, the rebellion of Styron's Nat Turner fails in its attempt to create a new system of open homo-relationality inspired by his initial experience of homo-ness with Willis. But insofar as Styron's novel portrays his rebellion as a failure for Nat both politically and personally, the text still attests to the positive capabilities of homosexual relations in the construction of community, for it suggests that homo-ness is the force that not only gives Nat his greatest push toward open rebellion as the way to end slavery, but that also informs his every attempt to imagine a society after slavery. Although homo-ness depends on the construction of differences to open a space for sameness, it also enables the temporary dissolution of differences through the orgasmic replication and extension of the self in an other. This dissolution thus offers a transformational and transcendent glimpse of a nexus of relations that actually defies the hierarchical arrangement of difference that fostered homo-ness in the first place. Attempting to realize this feeling of liberation in a more permanent and more social form, Nat appropriates other forms of egalitarianism and tries to modify them according to that original sexual inspiration. Yet even though these attempts ultimately fail, Styron's representations still open new ways for viewing homosexuality as a potentially constitutive force for community. If we treat Styron's novel as a meditation on the powers and limitations of homo-ness, we might allow it to prompt us to reconsider homo-ness and homosexuality as possible sites for challenging and correcting the hierarchical networks of racism, sexism, and even heterosexism that continue to dominate and fracture our society today. At the same time, we must be mindful of the variables and limitations associated with homo-ness, for privileging homosexuality and sameness as utopian absolutes may lead us not into "another land" marked by freedom and equality, but to the "astonishing abyss" of murder, revolt, and pseudo-fascism pioneered so controversially by Styron's Nat.

Notes

I would like to thank those who have assisted me in one form or another with the preparation of this essay: Jessica Adams, Gaurav Desai, Rebecca Mark, Molly Rothenberg, and Felipe Smith.

1   William Styron, *The Confessions of Nat Turner* (New York: Vintage International, 1967).

2   For a detailed analysis of the events and arguments involved in the controversy surrounding Styron's novel, see especially Albert E. Stone, *The Return of Nat Turner: History, Literature, and Cultural Politics in Sixties America* (Athens: University of Georgia Press, 1992).

3   Charles V. Hamilton, "Our Nat Turner and William Styron's Creation," in *William Styron's Nat Turner: Ten Black Writers Respond,* ed. John Henrik Clarke (Boston: Beacon Press, 1968), 74.

4   Alvin F. Poussaint, *"The Confessions of Nat Turner* and the Dilemma of William Styron," in *William Styron's Nat Turner: Ten Black Writers Respond,* ed. John Henrik Clarke (Boston: Beacon Press, 1968), 21.

5   The website of the American Psychiatric Association explains the change in the formal classification of sexual orientation:

In 1973 the American Psychiatric Association confirmed the importance of the new research by removing the term 'homosexuality' from the official manual that lists all mental and emotional disorders. In 1975 the American Psychological Association passed a resolution supporting this action. Both associations urge all mental health professionals to help dispel the stigma of mental illness that some people still associate with homosexual orientation. Since original declassification of homosexuality as a mental disorder, this decision has subsequently been reaffirmed by additional research findings and both associations.

6   Poussaint, "Dilemma of William Styron," 21–22.

7   Leo Bersani, *Homos* (Cambridge, Mass.: Harvard University Press, 1995), 149–50.

8   Ibid., 150.

9   Styron, *Confessions*, 208.

10 Many critics read Nat's abandonment of sexual contact in the name of God in variously moral terms that devalue the importance of the scene in relation to the rest of the novel. Daniel W. Ross argues that Nat's "fear of women" has created in him a sexual "confusion" that "leads him to various compensations, including homosexuality," as though Nat's pleasure in the scene were somehow false and the whole encounter were simply a temporary deviation from both the narrative and his true sexuality (Ross, "'Things I Don't Want to Find Out About': The Primal Scene in *The Confessions of Nat Turner*," *Twentieth Century Literature: A Scholarly and Critical Journal* 39.1 [1993]: 86). Vincent Harding takes a more accusatory position and argues that "it is obviously his sense of guilt over the act which drives Nat into the river for Baptism" just after his climax with Willis (Harding, "You've Taken My Nat and Gone," in *William Styron's Nat Turner: Ten Black Writers Respond*, ed. John Henrik Clarke [Boston: Beacon Press, 1968], 26–27). And David Hadaller claims that Nat's encounter with Willis is a convenient sin that shows Nat his need to repent and study religion: "After he has enjoyed mutual masturbation with Willis, [Nat] immediately baptizes the young man and then himself, promising to sin no more" (Hadaller, *Gynicide: Women in the Novels of William Styron* [Madison, Wis.: Fairleigh Dickinson University Press, 1996], 118).

11 For example, he believes that his master's wife, Miss Sarah Travis, treats him with generosity and kindness because she recognizes his basic humanity. Yet despite his personal affection for her, he decides not to save her. Indeed, his remarks on Miss Sarah are full of guilt and regret that he would have to kill her even though he thinks that killing her would be wrong (273, 369). This same guilt is even more prominent in his misgivings about Margaret Whitehead, the only person Nat kills with his own hands. As Daniel W. Ross notes, "Margaret had come closer than any other white person to accepting Nat for what he was, often seeking his friendship and spiritual guidance . . . [even though she] had failed to see Nat in his most elemental form— as a fully sexual man" (Ross, "Things," 94). By killing her, he violently severs the closest thing to a community that he ever truly had with a white person. Yet Nat also hates Margaret for "flaunting her sexuality" in front of him as though he really were the asexual being that slavery defines him as (94). Thus, in addition to needing to prove his leadership abilities to the other slaves, he decides to kill her in order to reassert his humanity and masculinity. Instead of sparing her because they both genuinely like each other, his resentment of the racialized difference between their gender identities makes him regard this gender difference as an insurmountable barrier that no revolution could equalize.

12 The only other person in the novel that Nat decides to save is Judge Jeremiah Cobb. When Cobb meets Nat before Nat starts the insurrection, he offhandedly tells Nat how much he despises the entire institution of slavery because of the dehumanizing effects it has both on the land and on every person living within its influence, whether slave or free. At the same time, he refuses to express any sympathy or pity for slaves

because, as his role as the judge in Nat's trial proves, he doesn't believe they deserve any special compensation to rectify or excuse their slave status. While his resentment of the material and social effects of the plantation's hierarchies shows that he does not regard slaves as inhuman inferiors who deserve their misery, his refusal to care shows that he is not willing to reassert their differences by treating them as a special class of people who do *not* deserve their misery. Thus, Nat decides to spare Cobb for basically the same reasons that he decides to spare Brantley, even though Cobb is a widower instead of a sodomite. Nat bases his decision to spare him on the profoundly anti-hierarchical sentiment that leads Cobb to disregard all others through a mask of uncaring and that consequently sets him apart as a kind of outlaw within his own hierarchical community.

E. L. McCallum | **Contamination's**

Germinations

In Freud's theory of sexuality, one earmark of perversion is its preference for a part over a whole. Fetishism, for instance, is commonly construed as fragmenting the object of desire (not to mention that a fetishist
is also quite particular about the fetish object he or she is partial to),
while voyeurism concentrates sexual pleasure strictly within the visual
in lieu of any other senses. Perversion in Freud is defined as a deviation of the sexual aim, either to linger in the middle or to extend sexual
pleasure to some region of the body other than the normal erogenous
zone. Perversion thus shies short of union, wholeness, in favor of finding
satisfaction in fragments or parts. In his more general discussion of the
perversions, Freud notes that they imply that "the sexual instinct may
be no simple thing, but put together from components which have come
apart again in the perversions."[1] On the one hand, Freud simply is stating that the perversions offer an illustration of components of sexual instinct, a sort of analysis (in the sense that analysis means breaking down
into parts). On the other hand, we might provocatively construe Freud
to be saying that perversion is where sexual instincts (*Sexualtrieb*) separate into forces that take on a life of their own, becoming something
distinct, detached from other instincts. If the sexual instinct components
come apart in the perversions, it behooves us to consider how perversion might effect other detachments. In this way, we might see perversion as impinging on not just sexuality per se, but also sexuality's close
relations—narrative, narcissism, knowledge. Perversion thus threatens

the coherence of the individual subject, not to mention the illusory fullness of subjects' social mediations through story and self; analyzing perversion in this way reveals important aspects of the nonindividualistic
dimension of the social.

This coming apart provokes me to offer what might best be called a
perverse reading of the drive and to think further about the particle, for
particles are elements or components of a larger phenomenon that can
only be discerned as things come apart. To make these two apparently
disparate things cohere, however, I will read them through the figure of
contamination, a perversion particularly predisposed to both the drive
—as an organization of forces outside the ego—and the particle, since,
whether radioactive, chemical, or even linguistic, contamination boils
down to an introduction of unwanted foreign particles into a system
or conglomeration. This introduction of outside elements threatens to
break down—or pervert—the system, as in the case of ecological contamination, or at minimum destroy the presumption of wholeness that
the previously untainted conglomeration—for example, a contaminated
language or cultural practice—had held.

If we perceive particles as having some kind of (implicitly organized)
motion to them, rather than being purely static entities, we might call
that movement propelling. For instance, if one has particles of, say, hair
spray or paint, that one seeks to remove from a can and apply to a surface, one requires the use of a propellant. The German word for propel is
treiben, preterite form *Trieb*. So another aspect of looking at perversion
in a social schema from a particular angle focuses our attention on the
role of *Trieb*, commonly translated in anglophone psychoanalytic con-
texts as "drive," although not infrequently as "instinct." The problem
with either "drive" or "instinct" is the associations of subjectivity and
will, perhaps less so with instinct than drive, since the former's association with animals' or organisms' motivating force subverts the affinity
to consciousness that "drive" might evoke. It is as if "drive" or *Trieb*
somehow provides the glue that holds the particles together, the force
that directs them.

The drive, however, is not the same as perversion, because perversion
is on the side of desire. Rather, what I mean by perversion is this effect of
or emphasis on fragmentation, partiality, coming apart, dispersion. I'm
curious as to how that structure could still be allied with or organized by

some drive, not simply as an expression of that drive, but as a channel to which the unity or coherence that perversion disperses might have been displaced, where the particles can be maintained in some form of organization, be it more chaotic than linear. Psychoanalytically, the drive is associated with the organism's relations outside itself, but as psychoanalysis has been taken up in literary studies, the drive has come to be connected with narrative, which might seem a vantage point by which the impersonality of the drive is more clearly viewed. In fact, narrative's juxtaposition with the drive ends up obscuring the fact that there is no individual in either narrative or the drive. And yet, narrative is inherently social; the telling of stories is unavoidably embedded in our social organization, our relations to one another. Thus my interest in this essay is in how narrative's sociality could possibly work on a nonindividualist paradigm, and I suggest that for narrative to do so requires perversion's partiality, dispersion. The drive provides a theory or inevitable detour through which we can work out the question of how there can be perverse narrative. Contamination, deeply perverse itself, as the nonhumanist, nonindividualist paradigm of driven dispersion, presents the epigrammatic figure for my concern. To begin, then, let us consider narratives of contamination and their work on or with the drive(s).

In the postmodern canon, Don DeLillo's 1984 novel *White Noise* offers the most likely literary example of the culture of contamination; the featured impurity is the Airborne Toxic Event, which takes up the middle section of the novel.[2] But there's another text that uncannily has almost exactly the same features as *White Noise:* an airborne toxic event, presented by the protagonists in a first-person narration that emphasizes the quotidian, at times ventures upon meditation, or is interrupted by the media, with the specter of Nazism in the background and the Germans in the fore, and a narrative drive toward closure at the end of the day—be it sunset or nightfall. This text is Christa Wolf's *Accident: A Day's News* (1987).[3] Perhaps it was just what was in the air in the mid-eighties, but I think something more drives the convergence of these two novels' realization of contamination. What novel realization about the drive germinates in the convergence of these two contaminations?

There's little question, at first glance, that Jack Gladney, protagonist/narrator in Don DeLillo's *White Noise,* exhibits a strong death drive; it is easy to see his obsession with death, with who—he or his wife Babette—is going to die first, with the Dylar experimental drug that supposedly assuages the fear of death, or even with his choice of object of study, Hitler. This thanatos drive is, as Freud tells us in *Beyond the Pleasure Principle,* a drive toward stasis, or as Peter Brooks reinscribes it in "Freud's Masterplots," a drive toward the completion of the narrative. This drive is connected to repetition, which Brooks, in his reading of Freud, posits harnesses energy in the service of mastery: "Repetition works as a process of *binding* toward the creation of an energetic constant-state situation which will permit the emergence of mastery and the possibility of postponement."[4] In other words, repetition offers the promise of control, management, and thus implies a sort of agency.

And while the very last word of the novel is "dead"—and thus renders the novel a most fitting example of Brooks's claim that the death drive in narrative aims toward the conclusion—I do not offer *White Noise* here to posit it as a textbook manifestation of drive theory, but instead for the illusions of individuality and the complications of drive theory that the novel sketches. Its comparison to *Accident,* moreover, illustrates the limitations of both control and the model of individual subjectivity. But first, let us consider the underlying theoretical model, as elucidated in Freud.

In both *Beyond the Pleasure Principle* and *The Ego and the Id,* Freud defines two types of instincts: the death drive and the life drive. The life drive or sexual instinct "by bringing about a more far-reaching combination of the particles into which living substance is dispersed, aims at complicating life and at the same time, of course, preserving it,"[5] while the death instinct is, as I mentioned already, a drive towards stasis, "that is, it is a kind of organic elasticity or, to put it another way, an expression of the inertia inherent in organic life."[6] Joan Copjec has already remarked on this curious articulation of the death drive by Freud, noting how contradictory it is to reconcile "organic elasticity" and "inertia" as synonyms (a point Freud himself addresses in the next sentence, if only implicitly, by commenting on how "strange" it is to think of instincts as conservative rather than "impelling towards change"). Leaving aside the remarkable appearance of "particles" in Freud's definition of the life drive, what I find striking about Freud's formulation of thanatos, here, is its presentation as repetition; the "that is" and "or, to put it another way" signal even out of context that the passage reiterates—twice—an earlier definition. Brooks makes it clear that the issue of repetition is very much bound up in the symbolic register: "Repetition is a symbolic enactment referring back to unconscious determinants, progressive in that it belongs to the forward thrust of desire, and is known by way of desire's workings in the signifying chain, but regressive in its points of reference."[7] Brooks plays a bit fast and loose with "desire" and "drive," but his focus on the role of "textual energetics" throughout *Reading for the Plot* is instructive, and the point here is that Freud's account of repetition leads him to the proposition of the death instinct as an urge to restore a prior state of existence.

Taking things to the symbolic level, and given Freud's insistence on the stasis of the death drive, it might seem odd to link thanatos to narrative, which is fundamentally about transformation, succession, progress rather than stasis or equilibrium. Indeed, Brooks himself has to balance the role of the death drive in narrative—working toward the end, binding the text's freely mobile energy to the conclusion and its quiescence—with the plot's necessary deferral of the end. The story goes something like this: "Narratable existence is stimulated into a condition of narratability, to enter a state of deviance and detour . . . before returning to the quiescence of nonnarratable existence."[8] But this account renders narrative as the drive to the nonnarratable, without accounting for how transformation might occur, or differences in the nonnarratable itself. Poetic forms like the villanelle or the pantoum that hinge on repetition are, in fact, construed to be anti-narrative, and would thus seem more likely sites of expression of the death drive in discourse. Part of the issue, however, is the very division of the drive into two forms; Lacan will later posit in his reading of Freud that there is only one drive, but the limits of Brooks's reading suggest that there might be something more at stake in drive theory than the life drive's combinatory powers and the death drive's quiescence. Like the contradictions of the drive, narrative involves the tension between telos and deferral, between closure and divagation.

Although I am not the first to link the drives to narrative, I want to consider how these narratives render contamination as itself a symptom of a different, possibly even perverse, drive, veering off course from either coalescence or stasis. To do so requires that we parcel out the drive even further, provisionally positing yet another form of instinct. This is not a drive that is reckoned in Brooks's narrative theory, although if confronted by such a possibility he might allow that it figures in Freud's *Beyond the Pleasure Principle*, given Brooks' claim that "it is indeed so difficult to say what Freud is talking about in this essay—and especially what he is not talking about."⁹ Indeed, the death instinct and the life instinct are not the only drives Freud elucidates: he also briefly distinguishes epistemophilia, the drive to know. As a way toward sketching out what this other dimension of drive might be, and to emphasize the linguistic dimension of the drive in general, I'd like to begin by positing, perhaps too glibly, that both *White Noise* and *Accident* are undergirded not by a *Todestrieb*, or death drive, but by *Deutschestrieb*, or as I would perversely prefer to translate it, Teutonophilia—the drive to be German, or to be with Germans, to, in short, engage in German.

In *Accident*, the Teutonophilia germinates in the cloud, in the radioactive particles from the Ukraine driven to Germany on prevailing winds, but at another level we see Teutonophilia in the text's repetitious concern with recent German history, the reverberations from World War II—the wartime actions of neighbors, the friends who had been exiled by Hitler, the immediately postwar typhoid epidemic, the emergence of nuclear power that is now, in 1986, plaguing them. This German drive—dare I call it *fahrvegnugen?*—circulates in the text but is not an individual impulse. The parallel should underscore the notion that drive is not something individual or willful, but a force that arises and might even work through permeation rather than propulsion.

In *White Noise*, by contrast, the Teutonophilia aligns with the protagonist, Jack Gladney, given that Jack's obsessions function around things German. It is linked to the text's manifest concern with the death drive. Jack Gladney's repetition compulsion, seen for instance in his obsession with watching his children sleep, is clearly a textbook case of staving off the threat of death, or at least change; watching them sleep punctuates his trajectory from crisis to crisis, providing a stable moment to return to, but it also manifests his own longing to return to stasis, sleep, quiescence. The threatened change, however, is not death, not the effects of the Airborne Toxic Event, nor even the constant stream of new products in the commercial market with which change is equated in the terms of the text. The threat of change is the threat of the narrative climax, the moment that portends the end of the narrative.

The plot's order makes it clear that the Airborne Toxic Event is not the climax of *White Noise*, since this event occurs, almost self-contained, in the second of three sections of the novel, but ending exactly halfway to the end of the text. With the third section picking up on threads from the first, the narrative seems as though it will culminate with the conference in Hitler studies. Hosting this conference is ostensibly what has triggered Jack's compensatory obsessions. He both wants the attention his role as host of this Germanically focused conference promises to afford him and fears that his utter ignorance of German will reveal him as a hoax. At one level, the mastery he seeks is not some immortal capability but simply the sense that he is who he is reputed to be, that he can live up to the image he feels he projects with his academic robe and dark glasses, the intellectual man of mystery. His anxiety is narcissistic, focused on the hope that, as Copjec describes narcissism, his "own being exceeds the imperfection of its image."[10] This narcissism is linked with Jack's Teutonophilia, indicating that this narcissism is deeper, drive-oriented. But this link does not mean that the drive to be with Germans is about Jack individually; rather, the narcissism angle is already aligned with Jack's dispersion, which the narrative drive of Teutonophilia effects over the course of the text. Precisely because the novel does not end here, at the Hitler studies conference, it's not about Jack consolidating his identity and mastery—and thus not about the death drive—but rather about how Jack is dispersing into particles, driven to see himself, his family, his social situation, as "particle-ized."

Thus, rather than end the novel, Jack's comic failure to master the ceremony or the language in his conference address propels him toward another Teutonic situation. Only when he learns that his rival, Willie Mink, is in nearby Iron City's Germantown—indeed, only when he learns that Iron City even *has* a Germantown[11]—does Jack finally pursue the dispenser of Dylar with whom his wife Babette has slept. Even though he has known of Babette's infidelity and indeed cajoled from her the adulterer's name, and even though this man is the source for Babette's acquisition of a drug that dispels the fear of death, what catalyzes him out of his ambivalence into action is not the information, but the Teutonophilic drive.

Gladney's drive to find Mink hurtles him willy-nilly to act against his desire for stasis, quiescence, repetition; it is a drive that is quite literally a drive since he steals the neighbors' car to arrive smack in the midst of the old Germantown in Iron City, carrying the German-made gun, a "25-caliber Zumwalt automatic" (253) his father-in-law gave him. Obsessively and remarkably, as he closes in on Willie Mink, Jack both narrates his plan and announces it as his plan, as if in a desperate hope that his plan might become performative, enacted through its enunciation: "My plan was this" (312) or "This was my plan." Only in the first iteration is the plan in the present tense: "Here is my plan" (304). All the subsequent announcements of the plan are in the past tense, while all the expositions of the plan are in the present. The splitting of the tense might signal the splitting of the drive, between the repetition compulsion, which seeks a previous state, and eros, which rejuvenates. But I prefer to see this tense shift as the marker that shows the transformation of the life drive into the death drive, and that it is precisely this transformation that makes it impossible for Gladney to carry off the murder. Killing Mink would drive toward too great a change, would in fact conjoin the two characters to create something new. At the same time, the explicit fragmenting of the narrative into levels of showing and telling, the conscious highlighting of the process of narration through the permutations of "this was my plan," signals how the narrative is beyond Jack's control. It is one (albeit critical) sign that Jack's individuality is driving toward particle-ity.

So in the face of threatened change, the narrative retreats into repetition and resolves to end. Only here, because the narrative is not undergirded by the death drive but by what I have been calling Teutonophilia, the repetition serves to disperse rather than consolidate. The pursuit ends at a hospital, where Jack and Willie are both treated for their gunshot wounds by German nuns. Jack seeks to gain favor with the nuns by speaking German. Their repartee of simple German words escalates into a vertiginous volley of existentialist exchange in English, and Jack's interrogation culminates in a reversal of the power dynamic, putting him back on the bottom, subjected to a torrent of German: "She was spraying me with German. A storm of words. She grew more animated as the speech went on. A gleeful vehemence entered her voice. . . . I began to detect a cadence, a measured beat. She was reciting something, I decided. Litanies, hymns, catechisms. . . . Taunting me with scornful prayer. The odd thing is I found it beautiful" (320). This torrent provides a perverse resolution for the novel and for Jack, reaffirming his place on the edge of the mastery of German, not entirely outside language, but definitely more subjected to than in control of it. It is perverse, because it fragments, sprays, storms. To speak, to be subject to the force of discourse, but not fully within narrative—because narrative requires an end, a point from which its action can be retroactively recalled—is to seek to seal the gap between narration, the moment of the telling, and the action or state narrated. Narrative's own iterability—the fact that narrative must always, structurally, be repeatable—guarantees against this gap being sealed. Narrative is thus always already fragmented—the drive that structures narrative, however, might be working against or toward that fragmentation. The spray of German affirms not just Jack's drive to engage German, but what Teutonophilia figures in the novel: the perverse drive to dispersion of the individual subject, and of the narrative itself. Rather than a drive to be German, it is a drive to be a germ.

Using *White Noise*'s Teutonophilia as a paradigm of the drive should not mislead us, therefore; as *Accident*'s Teutonophilic cloud reminds us, the drive is not contained in some particular individual, even if it serves ostensibly to individualize or particularize. Jack Gladney's struggle toward mastery seems like it would illustrate the individualization of the drive, yet the alignment between character and agency is too easy. Rather, Jack's ambivalent understanding of German—restricting himself in his conference address to words and forms that are primarily the same in either language, for instance—provides a paradigm for us to understand the Teutonophilic drive as a vector running on the edge between subjects and language, not the directive impulse of a discrete individual organism. That we don't know or particularly cue into the Teutonophilia in either text underscores the textual rather than the subjective location of the drive; its rhythms pulse in the cadences of the text, not so much in its melody. As Freud himself notes of the death instinct, it manifests itself indirectly, in contrast to the obviousness of the life instinct. We don't even see any German in the DeLillo novel: except for one line of "Gut, besser, best," it is all narrated rather than shown in dialogue.

If we return to *Accident* with this expanded view Teutonophilia affords of the perversity of the drive, not specifically as a German thing, but as the instinctual tensions between subjects and language that threaten to disperse as much as they serve to cohere, we see that Jack's adulterated German speech is reprised as *Accident*'s narrator, a writer, also encounters instability in language. Despite the distractions of her brother undergoing neurosurgery and the cloud of radioactivity moving across her town, she tries to work: "I sat down on my swivel chair, looking through the pages, reading individual sentences, and found that they left me cold. They, or I myself, or both of us had changed and I was reminded of certain documents where the true, the secret writing appears only after chemical treatment, whereby the original, deliberately irrelevant text is revealed to be a pretext. I saw the writing on my pages fade and possibly disappear under the effect of radiation."[12] The subject's instability — "they, or I myself, or both of us" — is as ambivalent and slippery as Jack's command of German and situation. The conjunction of *Accident*'s and *White Noise*'s linguistic crises suggests that it's not simply a matter of Gladney's failure to master German speech, nor of *Accident*'s narrator failing to master German writing, but rather that if we are viewing contamination through the drive, language is at issue — serving either as the prophylaxis so we can contend with contamination, or as much a function of the contamination itself.

The hope that "the true, the secret writing" might appear only after the page is contaminated by chemicals reveals a rather perverse desire that something true will be revealed in this airborne toxic event. This hope is one that Jack likewise desperately seeks, and arguably thinks he finds either in discreetly watching his son Heinrich master the situation in the evacuation hall by authoritatively fielding the questions and concerns of a growing crowd of evacuees, or in his subsequent rounds of doctor visits, thinking that the means of his own death — the ultimate truth for each of us — was revealed when his exposure to the cloud was registered on the medical evaluation instruments at the evacuation center. Jack is sure he's going to come down with some kind of long-term contamination, but his belief is also never confirmed. In both instances, the perverse hope homes in on the moment of transformation, when the agent acts to rearrange the organization of cells, crowds, text, and thus meaning. This drive toward transformation, then, is what is really at stake in the novels' Teutonophilia. It is a transformation that must transpire outside the realm of conscious or human agency, which is why we must perceive it to be mapped at the level of the drive.

What's so interesting about *Accident* and *White Noise* is that their articulation of contamination and drives juxtaposes the possibility of the agency of objects or particles with the predicament of the action of language and narrative. These views both explicate and complicate our understandings of ourselves as desiring subjects. Subjects, in this paradigm, are simply one site in which confrontation takes place, but a particularly important and dense site, since we are the nexus of language and object relations. In or as this nexus, however, subjects function as both incomplete and excessive; subjects are radically discerned from determined meaning—that is, disconnected from being fixed by fate—and because of that finite being, unlimited in their desire. But subjects are also subject to narrative, inescapably relating to one another in the social through narrative. Thus it is necessary to examine not simply the incoherence of individuals but the dynamics of groups and systems. As Copjec succinctly puts it, "One thing comes to be substituted for another in an endless chain only because the subject is cut off from the essential thing that would complete it."[13] Jack Gladney's Teutonophilia plays out this sequence of substitutions via the death drive, but at the same time reworks—and thereby transforms—the death drive's narrative repetitions from being recurrent impulses toward stasis into a dispersal of pieces of language: sentence fragments, advertising slogans, lists of brand names, announcements of narration.

It might help to examine this moment of transformation through a different lens, one we also find at the intersection of narrative and the drive: cause. Contamination itself is certainly a phenomenon that invokes causality, if only in its colloquial conception; when a contamination occurs, the first things we want to know are its cause and effects. For instance, the Chernobyl contamination hinged on failures of the system to maintain its integrity in the face of electrical power fluctuations. Like narrative, like the drive itself, contamination seems, thus, bound up in regressive, retroactive orientation and a forward, progressive impulse. But contamination is often mysterious, indefinite, and something of a failure—as Lacan notes, "There is cause only in something that doesn't work."[14] Within this tension, contamination forces us to recognize the nonindividualist paradigm of the drive, and the possibility of nonindividualist agency. What links contamination to narrative and language, then, is its perverse connection to causality, understood through a non-

198 E. L. McCallum

individualist paradigm of the drive and its links to repetition and the symbolic.

Lacan describes cause as having "something anti-conceptual, something indefinite,"[15] a point that Joan Copjec picks up in relation to the death drive. Although her reading hinges more on Lacan's than, as my focus has been, exclusively on Freud's views of the drive, her emphasis on the fragment, fraction, part—signaled in her very title, "Cutting Up"—renders her considerations of the drive and the role of failure relevant here. For Copjec's reading of cause unites Lacan's with mid-century philosophical views of causality that link it to failure rather than succession, conjunction, or sequence. On this reading, cause comes to be seen as perverse—a deviation from normal circumstances. If a fire breaks out, as it did in the Chernobyl reactor, its immediate cause is not the oxygen that is nonetheless necessary for the fire to exist. Cause also links to narrative through this juncture of deviance and the death drive, for as Brooks notes, "Deviance is the very condition for life to be narratable";[16] any adherence to normal circumstances, any lack of failure, is not narrative.

Copjec claims that Lacan's reading goes beyond H. L. A. Hart's and A. Honoré's, in *Causality and the Law,* to place cause at the level of the materiality of language, not at the level of a subject's conscious intentionality. Indeed, Copjec concludes that "the cause which must necessarily exist is never present in the field of consciousness that it effects,"[17] which is precisely why her account goes by way of the drive, as the forces that organize outside the conscious field. For her, the drive—and specifically the death drive—governs the relation between the psychic and the social. The link is linguistic: in Lacan's view the death drive prevails over the signifying chain, or as he calls it, *automaton,* because semiotic meaning happens regardless of human intention. Copjec points out that this is the same term Aristotle uses to describe coincidence, what occurs "as a result of a collision of separate events."[18] Since *automaton* concerns how language produces effects independently of intention, *automaton* presents a paradigm of nonhuman agency, and this chain is both social and incomplete. The death drive, which Copjec conflates with the reality principle, intervenes to delay: The reality principle "maintains desire beyond the threats of extinction presented by satisfaction. The death drive does not negate the pleasure principle, it extends it."[19]

The death drive maintains this extension in part through its reliance on repetition, but concomitantly through its correlation with the symbolic register. While Copjec's and Lacan's views hinge on language, their delineations parallel Brooks's mapping of the role of the drive in narrative to defer, delay the end. Like perversion, and perverse as it is, this view of cause radically thwarts the conception or sustenance of an individual subject.

Cause, then, is some failure within the compulsion of repetition; narrative, in contrast, is a combination of this failure to repeat—cause—and the organization of the excess or side effects of signification of the *automaton.* Narrative may be punctuated by repetition but can never be purely repetition, for repetition becomes nonnarratable. Narrative, therefore, is as fundamentally engaged in the life drive as in the death drive. But more, narrative must involve transformation, and the role of perverse fragmentation in relation to transformation may become clearer if we examine this life drive at work in the contamination texts.

The instinctual effect of contamination in *Accident* is, as we saw in the passages cited earlier, a disorientation in language. The fragments produced by perversion are even more obvious in *Accident* than in *White Noise.* Instead of smoothly linked forms—sentences, phrases, narrative—the narrator encounters words, vocabulary lists, particles. "The scientific word is 'contaminated.' I'm learning new words while you sleep, brother," she intimates early on; "nuclids—another word I have just begun to learn."[20] But as the day progresses the ineffable becomes more her concern: "Everything I have been able to think and feel has gone beyond the boundaries of prose."[21] Yet if the words fragment, become discrete and static, the words also coalesce and germinate new meanings. Hearing the reports of people leaving from Chernobyl that noon, the narrator remarks: " 'Evacuation,' brother, is one of those words which we won't be able to separate from our own experience for the rest of our lives."[22] The life drive's combinatory powers work through language, meaning sedimented upon meaning, even as the death drive's stasis seeking pushes on through narrative, stripping the accumulated meanings back to one, returning to the current moment, the story at hand. In this instance, the life drive's binding might be seen to work against narrative as a singularly directional impulse, instead pushing toward the nonnarratival or multiply narrative. "Evacuation" must be restricted to the news reports of the airborne toxic event; reverberations from the mid-century war or even the typhoid epidemic divert the narrative from its appointed end.

This double drive structure plays out in the text's trajectory of events. Against the advancing cloud, *Accident* plots the narrator's brother undergoing brain surgery for a tumor. The skilled precision of the surgeons contrasts with the diffuse drive of the tumor cells and their parallel in the particles coming from Chernobyl and the narrator's meditations on the self. Freud tells us that "the ego is the precipitate of abandoned object-cathexes and . . . it contains the history of those cathexes."[23] *Accident*'s narrator shares Freud's science-influenced view of the precipitated ego, as she muses on the "connectors between the neurons called 'synapses' below the cellular level of the brain—the connections which bring us life";[24] together these descriptions present a pixelated view of what had seemed whole, coherent. Notably, this pixelation is depicted on the paperback's cover, which has a veil of dots—are they radioactive particles or newsprint pixels?—over a bucolic scene. Pixels are things we are not supposed to see as individuated; we look through or past them as they constitute the image we are supposed to see—like radioactivity, which is also invisible. The conjunction of pixelation and precipitate here recalls the particle; without going so far as to collapse these into the same thing, in all three there is this sense of individuated components that in themselves might be insignificant, but their organization unites into a completely different, efficacious force. The important thing, then, is the mode of organization, and this is precisely why the drive, why narrative, and why perversion are important; they all serve as modes of organization. Where the emphasis is on fragments, pixelation, it becomes more difficult to perceive the force of the drive. That is why structural diffusion, this pixelation, makes *Accident* seem less, shall we say, driven than *White Noise*.

But the narrative does have an aim toward which it drives; not only is the narrator's mind focused on her brother's surgery as she involves herself in quotidian activities of gardening, meal preparation, errands, and bicycling, but the narrative wraps itself around the convention of a day in the life. This temporal organization is stronger in *Accident* than in *White Noise*, which, though its final chapter details a sunset, nonetheless simultaneously unknots the closure even as it ties things up. *Accident* has proleptic moments, such as when we are told the brother will be fine but lose his sense of smell, but for the most part we are kept in the present, be it morning, afternoon, evening, or night. Most importantly, however, for our sketch of the drives, is that structurally the text pushes toward closure, resolution, an end to the day, knowledge of the success of the surgery, completion of activities. Although any day-in-the-life-of text has a predetermined ending—nighttime, but occasionally dawn—what are we to make of this death-drive structure of conclusion, given that *Accident*'s concern with radioactive contamination is by definition not a one-day gig? This death-drive structure, therefore, turns out to be perverse: as we arrive at the end, the narrative fragments, particle-izes, condenses meanings, rather than resolves into quiescence.

The tension between the limit of the day-in-the-life genre and the subject of radioactive contamination goes beyond simply a tension between form and content. As I noted earlier, Brooks insists that narrative's death drive aims toward conclusion. In *Accident* the destination is already reached at the outset as the novel begins in the future perfect. "On a day about which I cannot write in the present tense, the cherry trees will have been in blossom. I will have avoided thinking 'exploded,' the cherry trees have exploded, although only one year earlier I could not only think but also say it readily, if not entirely with conviction."[25] The future perfect is a perverse tense, positing origin from the vantage of what is ahead. If the signifier always gains its signification retroactively, the future perfect perfectly reverses that temporality of meaning. It seeks to unify the moment of narration with the moment narrated, to close the gap between telling and tale. Like contamination itself, the future perfect relies on contiguity, but where contamination's contiguity is spatial, the future perfect's is temporal. Contiguous temporality is admittedly a bizarre notion, since spatiality is the dimension through which contiguity conventionally operates; contiguous temporality seems to divvy up time's flow into particles. Temporality, moreover, is more often viewed as a smooth trajectory, in which certain moments might be singled out of the flow, but nonetheless the sense of the dynamics of time relies on a non-pixelated, non-fragmented understanding. Analepsis and prolepsis in narrative can serve to fragment time and disrupt the flow. Like the sedimentations of meaning around certain fragments of language—words or phrases activated by the radio, as we saw above—that signal the workings of the life drive's combinatory powers, a contiguous temporality of the future perfect indicates the life drive at work in time as well as space of the narrative. Overcoming the gap between the time of narrating and the time narrated perverts the life drive.

The future perfect tense in this passage denies the perfection of the future—compromised as it is by contamination—and binds us to the particularity of a moment, an impossible present, just as the death drive's repetition compulsion seeks to bind to the instance in the past. In that sense we might understand this drive as one toward a coalescence in time rather than space. Freud indicates that one contrast between the instincts is that thanatos seeks to discharge a tension—*seeking* quiescence, reducing—whereas eros strives to heighten a tension in order to "live it off,"[26] but the future perfect muddies this distinction. The future perfect here serves to raise the bar, to heighten tension (Why can't she write about it in the present tense? Isn't she writing now, according to our conventions of narrative?), and to promise that moment of discharge, that one day things will return to their prior state of existence, to stasis (Certainly she will have written, since we hold the book). But can we not seek to bind to a future event, work to bind or return to a state that will be? Is that the drive of narrative? Why can't this narrator simply tell us about this day in the past, then, if she cannot write about it in the present?

It is precisely because of this verb-tense tension that *Accident* thus seems to work against the scheme of the drives that so easily fits *White Noise*. Wolf's narrative, which has already projected its conclusion from the outset, might seem to be the anti-example of the drive toward resolution. Nor does Wolf's narrative so neatly exemplify the drive toward things and affiliations German, because it is already in Germany—unless, of course, we see its Teutonophilia as a form of narcissism. But *Accident* raises the question of how viewing the drive as a coalescence in time changes our presuppositions of what the life drive means, particularly when we return to Freud's idea of the ego as precipitate of abandoned ego-cathexes. Is that not a coalescence in time?

Let us recall that in *Beyond the Pleasure Principle*, Freud takes the example of unicellular organisms to elucidate his theory of the life drive, or eros, as the life preserving and rejuvenating effect of temporary coalescence.[27] Remember, too, that our first mention of the life drive, from *Ego and the Id*, also formulated it in terms of particles. Instead of seeking quiescence or the return to a previous state, the life drive seeks reinvigoration, connection, and change. But rather curiously Freud speaks of germ cells exhibiting narcissistic behavior in their conjugation: "The germ-cells themselves would behave in a completely narcissistic fashion."[28] Why put this behavior in terms of narcissism?

If germs cells can be narcissistic, rather than seek to consider the prosopopoeic implications of this, let us think rather of the complications for individualism this raises, and the consequences for understanding narcissism—and drive, particle, agency—from a nonindividualistic vantage. The formulation of narcissistic germ cells emphasizes the direction or libidinal aim of the energetic investment; narcissistic libido is not directed at other objects, but is turned toward the self. Freud claims to derive the "narcissistic libido of the ego from the stores of libido by means of which the cells of the soma are attached to one another."[29] So it is striking that narcissism, which would seem to isolate a cell from others because its libidinal focus would be on itself, is bound up with a drive that foments connection, conjugation. Such terms are as remarkably contradictory as Freud's torqued use of the non-synonyms "organic elasticity" and "inertia" in his formulation of the death drive. Wouldn't narcissism be more what one would expect from the death drive, a static focus on the self, a seeking to return to a prior state, to restore the lost wholeness of an earlier conception of self—not a reaching out to combine with or connect to others, seeking change?

If *White Noise* presents a textbook case of the death drive, *Accident* illustrates this interconnected view of the life drive, depicting it through the siblings. The connection between the narrator and her brother goes beyond language. The link she projects early on, when she imagines him slipping away and chastises him for "going against the agreement," or her sudden burst into the "Ode to Joy" at 1:45 P.M., which she later corroborates with him: "I decided to ask you later, brother, just when you actually awoke from the anaesthetic that day which will have become the past. 1:45? you will say."[30] These moments of connection beyond language rely on time for their corroboration, but though they are harnessed within the confines of this rational paradigm, they push us beyond the temporal principle. The uncanny coincidences, moreover, evoke a sense of mysterious and impossible connections, as if the siblings are indeed linked through sharing the same germ-plasm. They reinscribe precisely that convergence of the *automaton* that Copjec values in Lacan and Aristotle. What is important here, however, is that in contrast to the death drive, the life drive is that principle that exceeds language; we might posit that it is the "beyond" of the Teutonophilic principle. Coincidence only operates within a field of dispersion.

Yet, just as *White Noise*'s apparent delineation of the death drive is not so direct after all, *Accident* is not a straightforward text. And what would seem to be most deadly on the thematic level—a cloud of radioactivity moving across the countryside, contaminating as it goes—turns out, on further analysis, to be more closely connected to the text's delineation of the life drive: the cloud's drive to merge with the greens, the milk, the fats stored in the body of the German in 1986. The narrative's complications drive us to understand how contamination instigates a reversal of our notions of thanatos and eros. Although we are more likely to associate contamination with death, not love or life, this day's news suggests that the binding force of particle seeking particle, the discharge of a toxic cloud, might be more deeply embedded in our eros than language or narrative will countenance. It might leave us with another, more familiar but perverted Freudian question: What does contamination want?

Contamination inevitably bodes change, and the response to contamination arguably incites the death drive, the attempt to resolve the disruption and return to a previous equilibrium; paradoxically, then, contamination would be opposed to the death drive. Moreover, since contamination's change is independent of human intentionality—contamination may be an accident, or an inadvertent side effect of better living through chemistry—it offers a compelling figure of a nonindividualized agency. The particles of contamination are driven by that force of contamination to transform, not to end or to rejuvenate. Shifting from individuals to particles presents a model for examining perversion that does not rely on the subject for its basis, but on the systems and forces in which subjects are constructed and embedded, the very systems that either guarantee or disrupt the subject's coherence. Undergirding this drive of transformation, which works upon both the death drive and the life drive, is a paradigm of life as pixelated, the various particles seeking to bind—but in what combinations? what manner? what ways?—and our sense of self, agency, and mastery only pieced together like a view of a Seurat painting from afar.

Accident demarcates the traces of the life drive's combinatory intrigues and favors a dissolution of the boundaries between self and other that airborne toxic events similarly give the lie to on a national scale. The text is punctuated by reports on the radio—itself no less a diffusive medium than the radioactive cloud, functioning just as much to bond, conjugate, transform. If the radio is an obvious parallel to the radioactive cloud— both sharing the first five letters, both particles of sound or matter operating in a combination of diffusion and focused coalescence—the text also features a less obvious parallel in the telephone calls that pepper the text. The telephone particle-izes: it restricts the sound traveling between two specific parties, caller and receiver, to a narrow bandwidth of information; it interrupts the flow of the narrative or of life; it invades without seeming invasive. Both the radio and the telephone, as the mirror of the contamination drive of the invisible cloud, offer us the difference of discourse, but more importantly narration. Through the telephone calls, the narrator can bring us the ongoing story of the brother's surgery; through the radio the narrator brings us the representation of the contamination. Insofar as both communications technologies serve as language vectors, they function to contaminate, to disperse meaning across the boundaries of individuals spatially separated from one another.

Joan Copjec has claimed that *"it is the real that unites the psychical to the social,* that this relation is ruled by the death drive."[31] If she's right, what does this mean for perversion? And how might this affect our reading of contamination, which, if I may conflate the psychoanalytical with the colloquial, could not be more real. Copjec's argument emphasizes the linchpin role of the death drive—but what does it mean to rule the relation between the psychical and the social? Here's where my crackpot notion of Teutonophilia comes in. I was obviously glib when I posited above that the radioactive cloud, the airborne toxic event, was Teutonophilic; certainly the affinity for things German is a convenient paradigm for an instinct to bond that models a nonhuman agency or subjectivity. And the claim that we understand Teutonophilia not as a drive to be German but to be a germ passed perhaps too quickly as well; it illustrates the fragmentation, particle-ization of dispersion at the expense of calling attention to the transformative effects of germs. But what Teutonophilia in these texts indicates is the drive to disperse change through language, and this is in some ways inherent in the drive to narrate.

Narration is inherently social; it seeks to bond narrator and audience, but at the same time it necessarily must transform that relation, disturb if not disrupt. If Brooks wants to claim the death drive for narrative, he can do so only for the aims and end of narrative. But both of these narratives, *Accident* and *White Noise,* have a perverse relation to their ends, precisely because they deal with contamination, which persists chronically, without ending or resolution, without continuation or renewal. They thus illustrate a different aspect of the drive—the compulsion to disperse, to ride the edge between language and narrative, knowledge and meaning, is not at all comparable to stasis or growth. Contamination offers the site for change, the transformation that Todorov found essential to narrative, but change in itself does not produce narrative; narrating produces narrative. The reading of Teutonophilia in each text brings us to the edge between language and subject, and of all the things that cannot be said, all the moments in each text that break down into particles of language—a word, a list of brand names, an advertising slogan—these all are produced within what can be said, the story that is the telling of what cannot be expressed. It is not the indirect representation of the ineffable, but the narration of the impossibility of representing that is told, a narrative that is truly perverse. The mode of perverse narration—and not every narrative is perverse—presents an opportunity to stage the threat to cohesive individual subjectivity within a context that does not threaten human life. Perverse narration makes perversion safe for the social; or to be less sloganistic, if the real does unite the psychical and the social, the death drive does not rule alone.

To illustrate this claim, let us pause to consider the ambivalent, perverse relation of the novels to their ends. *Accident,* I have already discussed, perversely begins with its projected end, with a moment beyond the narrative's moment of enunciation, so that when the day ends, the convention brings us to nightfall and the end, we have only the impossibility of continuing to narrate, to speak. The narrative trajectory moves from being embedded in the process of narrating, aware of itself as narration, to the edge of the infinite and unknown, and the problem of representing in any medium. The narrator recounts being awoken in the middle of the night by a voice and a crying; this voice called from far away and is counterbalanced by her realization that "the crying came from me, as I noticed after quite some time."[32] By contrast to this rim-

ming the edge of the verbal and the expressive, distancing and imme-
diacy, the narrator says that "very close to me, in my dream, a giant,
nauseatingly putrescent moon had swiftly sunk down below the hori-
zon. A photograph of my dead mother had been fastened to the dark
night sky."[33] Here the distance of the voice is supplanted by a radical
dedistancing of the moon, and being awake is swapped with dream. The
spatial disorientation—between closeness and distance, real and imaginary space—evinced by such exchanges in this passage enacts the very
dispersion of the perverse drive. Moreover, the replacement of the moon
by the mother's representation rehearses the association of the moon
with death, and marks a shift from the relative and prophylactic safety
of language to the more contiguous, seductive, magical mode of visual
representation. There is no resolution, only a resolve to continue. The
final line, set apart in its own paragraph, reads, "How difficult it would
be, brother, to take leave of this earth."[34]

For its part, White Noise ends with a turn toward particles, and waves.
The last chapter opens with a wild drive, one parallel to Jack Gladney's
Teutonophilic journey to Iron City, but performed by his son Wilder on
his tricycle. Wilder takes off on his own and miraculously crosses a busy
highway, only to tumble into a muddy inlet of the highwayside creek,
rescued by a "passing motorist, as such people are called."[35] The chapter concludes with Jack's musing on the newly rearranged supermarket
shelves, a disruption that re-particle-izes the clientele. "They walk in a
fragmented trance, stop and go, clusters of well-dressed figures frozen in
the aisles, trying to figure out the pattern, discern the underlying logic,
trying to remember where they'd seen the Cream of Wheat."[36] The elements of the formerly smoothly working shopping trajectory have broken down into their components, re-formed as the cluster, the fragment;
people themselves are no longer humanist agents capable of mastering
and navigating their surroundings, but elements in the system, subordinated to some other organization, some other drive. "But in the end,"
Gladney tells us, drawing to the literal end of the story, "it doesn't matter what they see or think they see. The terminals are equipped with
holographic scanners, which decode the binary secret of every item, in-
fallibly. This is the language of waves and radiation."[37]

There is something to the fact that the narrative of White Noise drives
toward particle-ization, only to then be subsumed into wave. This hap-

pens in *Accident,* as well, only through its anxious vacillation around the theme of contamination—a cloud of particles serves as the occasion by which the narrator can ponder the wave connections in which she is embedded, familially, historically, linguistically, technologically, globally, networks that exist beyond her own immediate existence, beyond language, beyond the separation imposed by distance and death. The binary that is decoded on the products at the end of *White Noise* has the dual nature of particles and waves: On the one hand, it is simply the bar code on the product, but on the other hand, it is that which particle-izes the shoppers and the items seemingly indiscriminately.

A perverse narrative would be, then, not simply the narrative that dallies in the middle, but one that posits an end only to transform it—like a particle to a wave—into something else, into a Möbius strip of a story, narrating the edge of what can be told. We need perversion as a narrative, beyond what narratives of perversion already exist—in Freud, for instance, and now more widely in queer studies. Perversion as a narrative figures a space where the narrator is telling a story that is a problem being figured out, not where he or she already knows the end and wants to tell you how we arrived there. These perverse narratives do not drive toward a static, prior state of existence, untroubled knowledge, or an identificatory union between narratee or reader and narrator or protagonist. Rather, they drive epistemophilically toward the in-between, the edge where the language sometimes obtrudes as particles, fragmenting and dissolving narrative, and other times as waves, seamlessly carrying forward on the narrative drive. The perversity of these novels is precisely that *White Noise* could be a textbook case of the death drive as narrative, or *Accident* an exemplar of the life drive. At the same time, each provides a textbook case of a perverse narrative, driven by the structures outside of consciousness, the particles/waves that scan the codes of writing, bar codes, tumors, life, and death.

Notes

1   Sigmund Freud, *Three Essays on the Theory of Sexuality,* trans. and ed. James Strachey (New York: Basic, 1962), 28.
2   Don DeLillo, *White Noise* (New York: Penguin, 1986).
3   Christa Wolf, *Accident: A Day's News,* trans. Heike Schwarzbauer (New York: Noonday, 1989).

4   Peter Brooks, *Reading for the Plot: Design and Innovation in Narrative* (New York: Vintage, 1984), 101.

5   Sigmund Freud, *The Ego and the Id*, trans. Joan Riviere, ed. James Strachey (New York: Norton, 1962), 30.

6   Sigmund Freud, *Beyond the Pleasure Principle*, trans. and ed. James Strachey (New York: W. W. Norton, 1961), 43.

7   Brooks, *Reading for the Plot*, 124.

8   Ibid., 108.

9   Ibid., 97.

10 Joan Copjec, *Read My Desire: Lacan against the Historicists* (Cambridge, Mass.: MIT Press, 1994), 37.

11 DeLillo, *White Noise*, 301.

12 Wolf, *Accident*, 23.

13 Copjec, "Cutting Up," *Read My Desire*, 61.

14 Jacques Lacan, *The Four Fundamental Concepts of Psycho-Analysis*, trans. Alan Sheridan, ed. Jacques-Alain Miller (New York: Norton, 1981), 22.

15 Ibid.

16 Brooks, *Reading for the Plot*, 139.

17 Copjec, *Read My Desire*.

18 Ibid., 48.

19 Ibid., 54.

20 Wolf, *Accident*, 5, 8.

21 Ibid., 58.

22 Ibid., 57.

23 Freud, *The Ego and the Id*, 19.

24 Wolf, *Accident*, 40.

25 Ibid., 3.

26 Freud, *Beyond the Pleasure Principle*, 67.

27 Ibid., 60.

28 Ibid.

29 Ibid.

30 Wolf, *Accident*, 56.

31 Copjec, *Read My Desire*, 39.

32 Wolf, *Accident*, 109.

33 Ibid.

34 Ibid.

35 DeLillo, *White Noise*, 324.

36 Ibid., 325.

37 Ibid., 326.

Works Cited

American Psychiatric Association. *Diagnostic and Statistical Manual of Mental Disorders* [DSM-III-R]. Washington: American Psychiatric Association, 1987.

American Psychological Association. "Answers to Your Questions about Sexual Orientation and Homosexuality." *http://www.apa.org/pubinfo/orient.html*.

André, Serge. *L'Imposture perverse*. Paris: Seuil, 1993.

Bach, Sheldon. *The Language of Perversion and the Language of Love*. Northvale, N.J.: Aronson, 1994.

Bataille, Georges. *The Accursed Share: An Essay on General Economy*. New York: Zone Books, 1988.

———. *The Trial of Gilles de Rais*. Translated by Richard Robinson. Los Angeles, Calif.: Amok, 1991.

———. *Le procès de Gilles de Rais*. Paris: Jean-Jacques Pauvert, 1965.

Bataille, Michel. *Gilles de Rais*. Paris: Mercure de France, 1972.

Baudrillard, Jean. *The Mirror of Production*. St. Louis, Mo.: Telos Press, 1975.

Benedetti, Jean. *Gilles de Rais*. New York: Stein and Day, 1972.

Bersani, Leo. *Homos*. Cambridge, Mass.: Harvard University Press, 1995.

Bibler, Michael P. "Cotton's Queer Relations: Homosexuality, Race, and Social Equality in the Literature of the Southern Plantation, 1936–1968." Unpublished dissertation, 2002.

Bossard, Eugène, abbé. *Gilles de Rais, maréchal de France dit Barbe-Bleue*. Paris: Champion, 1886.

Bozovic, Miran. "Diderot and l'âme-machine." *Filozofski vestnik* (Ljubljana) 3 (2001).

Brennan, Claire. *The Poetry of Sylvia Plath*. Cambridge, Mass.: Icon Books, 2000.

Bronfen, Elisabeth. *The Knotted Subject*. New York: Columbia University Press, 2000.

Brooks, Peter. *Reading for the Plot: Design and Innovation in Narrative*. New York: Vintage, 1984.

Buck-Morss, Susan. *Dreamworld and Catastrophe: The Passing of Mass Utopia in East and West*. Cambridge, Mass.: MIT Press, 2000.

Burroughs, William S. *Cities of the Red Night*. New York: Holt, 1981.

——. *Re/Search: William S. Burroughs, Brion Gysin, Throbbing Gristle*. San Francisco, Calif.: Re/Search Publications, 1982.

——. *The Western Lands*. New York: Penguin, 1987.

Butler, Judith. *Gender Trouble: Feminism and the Subversion of Identity*. New York: Routledge, 1990.

Calasso, Roberto. *The Ruin of Kasch*. Cambridge, Mass.: Belknap Press, Harvard University Press, 1994.

Casanova, Giacomo. *History of My Life*. 3 vols. Translated by Willard R. Trask. Baltimore, Md.: Johns Hopkins University Press, 1997.

Chomsky, Noam. *Pirates and Emperors: International Terrorism in the Real World*. New York: Claremont Research & Publications, 1986.

Copjec, Joan. *Read My Desire: Lacan against the Historicists*. Cambridge, Mass.: MIT Press, 1994.

——, ed. *Radical Evil*. London: Verso, 1996.

de Lauretis, Teresa. *The Practice of Love: Lesbian Sexuality and Perverse Desire*. Bloomington, Ind.: Indiana University Press, 1994.

Deleuze, Gilles. *Masochism and Coldness*. New York: Zone Books, 1993.

Deleuze, Gilles, and Felix Guattari. *A Thousand Plateaus*. Minneapolis, Minn.: University of Minnesota Press, 1987.

DeLillo, Don. *White Noise*. New York: Penguin, 1986.

Diderot, Denis. *Les Bijoux indiscrets*. In *Oeuvres complètes*, vol. 3. Paris: Hermann, 1978.

Diken, Bulent, and Carsten Bagge Laustsen. "Enjoy Your Fight!—*Fight Club* as a Symptom of the Network Society." Unpublished manuscript.

Dolan, Frederick. "The Poetics of Postmodern Subversion: The Politics of Writing in William S Burroughs's *The Western Lands*." *Contemporary Literature* 32 (1991): 534–51.

Dollimore, Jonathan. *Sexual Dissidence: Augustine to Wilde, Freud to Foucault*. Oxford: Oxford University Press, 1991.

Dor, Joël. *Structure et perversion*. Paris: Denoël, 1987.

Drugstore Cowboy. Dir. Gus Van Sant. Avenue Pictures, 1989.

Feldstein, Richard, Bruce Fink, and Maire Jaanus, eds. *Reading Seminars I and II: Lacan's Return to Freud*. Albany: SUNY Press, 1996.

——. *Reading Seminar XI: Lacan's Four Fundamental Concepts of Psychoanalysis*. Albany: SUNY Press, 1995.

Fink, Bruce. *A Clinical Introduction to Lacanian Psychoanalysis: Theory and Technique*. Cambridge, Mass.: Harvard University Press, 1997.

——. *The Lacanian Subject: Between Language and Jouissance*. Princeton, N.J.: Princeton University Press, 1995.

Foster, Dennis. *Sublime Enjoyment*. Cambridge, Mass.: Cambridge University Press, 1997.

Foucault, Michel. *The History of Sexuality, Volume I*. Translated by Robert Hurley. New York: Vintage, 1980.

Freud, Sigmund. *Beyond the Pleasure Principle*. Edited and translated by James Strachey. New York: W. W. Norton, 1961.

——. *Drei Abhandlungen zur Sexualtheorie*. Frankfurt A.M.: Fischer, 1965.

——. *The Ego and the Id*. Edited by James Strachey. Translated by Joan Riviere. New York: Norton, 1962.

——. "Fetishism." In *The Standard Edition of the Complete Psychological Works of Sigmund Freud*, XXI. Translated and edited by James Strachey. 24 vols. London: Hogarth Press, 1953–74.

——. *Group Psychology and the Analysis of the Ego*. The Standard Edition, XVIII.

——. *The Standard Edition of the Complete Psychological Works of Sigmund Freud*. 24 vols. Edited and translated by James Strachey et al. London: The Hogarth Press and The Institute of Psycho-Analysis, 1961.

——. *Studies on Hysteria*. The Standard Edition, II.

——. *Three Essays on the Theory of Sexuality*. Translated and edited by James Strachey. New York: Basic, 1962.

Fuchs, Cynthia. Review of *Exotica* and Interview with Atom Egoyan. *http://www.inform.umd.edu/EdRes/Topic/WomensStudies/FilmReviews/exotica-fuchs*.

Given, James B. *Inquisition and Medieval Society: Power, Discipline, and Resistance in Languedoc*. Ithaca, N.Y.: Cornell University Press, 1997.

Goldberg, Jonathan. *Sodometries: Renaissance Texts, Modern Sexualities*. Stanford, Calif.: Stanford University Press, 1992.

Hadaller, David. *Gynicide: Women in the Novels of William Styron*. Madison, Wis.: Fairleigh Dickinson University Press, 1996.

Hamilton, Charles V. "Our Nat Turner and William Styron's Creation." In *William Styron's Nat Turner: Ten Black Writers Respond*. Edited by John Henrik Clarke. Boston, Mass.: Beacon Press, 1968.

Harding, Vincent. "You've Taken My Nat and Gone." In *William Styron's Nat Turner: Ten Black Writers Respond*. Edited by John Henrik Clarke. Boston, Mass.: Beacon Press, 1968.

Hart, H. L. A., and A. Honoré. *Causation and the Law*. Oxford: Clarendon, 1959.

Heers, Jacques. *Gilles de Rais. Vérités et légendes*. Paris: Perrin, 1994.

Hegel, G. W. F. *Phenomenology of Spirit*. Translated A. V. Miller. New York: Oxford University Press, 1977.

Hernandez, Ludovico. *Le procès inquisitoriale de Gilles de Rais*. Paris: Curieux, 1921.

Herubel, Michel. *Gilles de Rais et le déclin du Moyen-Age*. Paris: Librairie académique Perrin, 1962.

——. *Gilles de Rais ou la fin d'un monde*. Paris: J. Picollec, 1993.

Hollier, Denis. *Against Architecture: The Writings of Georges Bataille*. Cambridge, Mass.: MIT Press, 1989.

——. *La prise de la concorde*. Paris: Gallimard, 1974.

Hyatte, Reginald. *Laughter for the Devil: The Trials of Gilles de Rais, Companion-in-Arms of Joan of Arc (1440)*. London: Associated University Presses, 1984.

Kristeva, Julia. "Women's Time." In *The Kristeva Reader*. New York: Columbia University Press, 1986, 187–213.

Kuberski, Philip. *The Persistence of Memory.* Berkeley: University of California Press, 1992.

Lacan, Jacques. *Écrits.* Paris: Seuil, 1996.

——. *The Four Fundamental Concepts of Psycho-Analysis.* Edited by Jacques-Alain Miller. Translated by Alan Sheridan. New York: Norton, 1978.

——. "Intervention sur le transfert." *Écrits.* Paris: Seuil, 1966.

——. "Kant with Sade." Translated by James B. Swenson Jr. *October* 51 (1989): 55–104.

——. "L'Étourdit." *Scilicet* 4 (1973): 23.

——. Seminar IV, *La relation d'objet, 1956–1957.* Edited by Jacques-Alain Miller. Paris: Seuil, 1994.

——. Seminar VI, *Le Désir et son interprètation, 1958–1959.* Privately published by and for the members of L'Association freudienne internationale. Paris: I.S.I., 1994.

——. Seminar VII, *The Ethics of Psychoanalysis.* Translated by Dennis Porter. Edited by Jacques-Alain Miller. New York: Norton, 1992.

——. Seminar IX, *L'identification, 1961–1962.* Unpublished.

——. Seminar X, *L'Angoisse, 1962–1963.* Unpublished.

——. Seminar XX, *Encore, On feminine sexuality: the limits of love and knowledge, 1972–1973.* Edited by Jacques-Alain Miller. Translated by Bruce Fink. New York: W.W. Norton & Company, 1998.

Laplanche, Jean, and Jean-Baptiste Pontalis. *The Language of Psychoanalysis.* Translated by D. Nicholson-Smith. New York: Norton, 1973; London: Karnac Books and The Institute of Psycho-Analysis, 1988.

Lea, Henry Charles. *A History of The Inquisition of the Middle Ages.* 3 vols. New York: Harper, 1888.

Lewis, D. B. Wyndham. *The Soul of Marshal Gilles de Rais.* London: Eyre and Spottis-woode, 1952.

MacLean, Paul D. "Brain Evolution Relating to Family, Play, and the Separation Call." *Archives of General Psychiatry* 42 (1985): 405–17.

Mannoni, Octave. *Clés pour l'Imaginaire, ou l'Autre Scène.* Paris: Points, Editions du Seuil, 1969.

——. "Le Théâtre du point de vue de l'Imaginaire." *La Psychanalyse* 5 (1960): 164.

Marcuse, Herbert. *One Dimensional Man: Studies in the Ideology of Advanced Industrial Society.* London: Routledge, 1964.

McCallum, E. L. *Object Lessons: How to Do Things with Fetishism.* Albany: SUNY Press, 1998.

Merleau-Ponty, Maurice. *Humanism and Terror: The Communist Problem.* Oxford: Polity Press, 2000.

Miles, Barry. *William Burroughs: el hombre invisible.* New York: Hyperion, 1992.

Miller, Jacques-Alain. "On Perversion." In *Reading Seminars I and II: Lacan's Return to Freud.* Edited by Richard Feldstein, Bruce Fink, and Maire Jaanus. Albany: SUNY Press, 1996.

Morgan, Marabel. *The Total Woman.* New York: Pocket-Simon and Schuster, 1973.

Nancy, Jean-Luc. *The Inoperative Community.* Edited by Peter Connor. Translated by Peter Connor, Lisa Garbus, Michael Holland, and Simona Sawhney. Minneapolis, Minn.: University of Minnesota Press, 1991.

Pascal, Blaise. *Les lettres provinciales*. Edited by Louis Cognet. Paris: Garnier, 1965.

———. *Pensées de Blaise Pascal*. Paris: J. Vrin, 1942.

Porton, Richard. "Family Romances." *http://members.cruzio.com/~akreyche/frintro.html*. Originally published in *Cineaste* 23 (1997): 2.

Poussaint, Alvin F. "*The Confessions of Nat Turner* and the Dilemma of William Styron." In *William Styron's Nat Turner: Ten Black Writers Respond*. Edited by John Henrik Clarke. Boston, Mass.: Beacon Press, 1968.

Reinach, Salomon. "Gilles de Rais." *Cultes, mythes et religions* 4.8 (1912): 267–99.

Reliquet, Philippe. *Le Moyen-Age. Gilles de Rais: maréchal, monstre et martyr*. Paris: Editions Pierre Belfond, 1982: 244–45.

Rorty, Richard. "Ethics without Principles." In *Philosophy and Social Hope*. New York: Penguin, 1999.

———. "Philosophy as a Kind of Writing: An Essay on Derrida." *Consequences of Pragmatism: (Essays: 1972–1980)*. Minneapolis, Minn.: University of Minnesota Press, 1982.

Rosello, Mireille. "Jésus, Gilles et Jeanne: 'Qui veut noyer son chien est bien content qu'il ait la rage.'" *Stanford French Review* 13.1 (spring 1989): 81–95.

Ross, Daniel W. "'Things I Don't Want to Find Out About': The Primal Scene in *The Confessions of Nat Turner*." *Twentieth Century Literature: A Scholarly and Critical Journal* 39.1 (1993): 79–98.

Rothenberg, Molly Anne. *Re-Thinking Blake's Textuality*. Columbia: University of Missouri Press, 1993.

Rotman, Brian. *Signifying Nothing: The Semiotics of Zero*. Stanford, Calif.: Stanford University Press, 1987.

Roy, Jules. *La Bataille de Dien Bien Phu*. Paris: René Julliard, 1963.

Russell, Bertrand. *The Autobiography of Bertrand Russell*. London: Routledge, 2000.

Santner, Eric. "Miracles Happen: Benjamin, Rosenzweig, and the Limits of the Enlightenment." Unpublished paper, 2001.

Schwartz, Nina. *Dead Fathers: The Logic of Transference in Modern Narrative*. Ann Arbor: University of Michigan Press, 1994.

Seitz, Don Carlos. *Under the Black Flag*. New York: The Dial Press, 1925.

Seltzer, Mark. *Serial Killers: Death and Life in America's Wound Culture*. New York: Routledge, 1998.

Sloterdijk, Peter. *Critique of Cynical Reason*. Translated by Michael Eldred. Minneapolis: University of Minnesota Press, 1987.

Stevens, Wallace. *The Collected Poems of Wallace Stevens*. New York: Knopf, 1954.

Stone, Albert E. *The Return of Nat Turner: History, Literature, and Cultural Politics in Sixties America*. Athens: University of Georgia Press, 1992.

Styron, William. *The Confessions of Nat Turner*. New York: Vintage International, 1967.

Talayesva, Don C. *Sun Chief: The Autobiography of a Hopi Indian*. Edited by Leo W. Simmons. New Haven, Conn.: Yale University Press, 1942.

Todorov, Tzvetan. *The Poetics of Prose*. Translated by Richard Howard. Ithaca, N.Y.: Cornell University Press, 1977.

Tournier, Michel. *Gilles et Jeanne*. Paris: Gallimard, 1983.

Voltaire, François- Marie Arouet de. *Essai sur les moeurs et l'esprit des nations et sur les principaux faits de l'histoire depuis Charlemagne jusqu'à Louis XIII.* Paris: Garnier, 1963.

Wilson, Thomas. *Bluebeard: A Contribution to History and Folk-lore.* New York: The Knickerbocker Press, 1899.

Wolf, Christa. *Accident: A Day's News.* Translated by Heike Schwarzbauer. New York: Noonday, 1989.

Wolf, Leonard. *Bluebeard: The Life and Crimes of Gilles de Rais.* New York: Clarkson N. Potter, 1980.

Žižek, Slavoj. *The Metastases of Enjoyment: Six Essays on Woman and Causality.* London: Verso, 1994.

——. *The Plague of Fantasies.* London: Verso, 1997.

——. *The Sublime Object of Ideology.* London: Verso, 1989.

Contributors

Michael P. Bibler teaches at Tulane University. This essay comprises part of his unpublished larger work "Cotton's Queer Relations: Homosexuality, Race, and Social Equality in the Literature of the Southern Plantation, 1936–1968."

Bruce Fink is Professor of Psychology at Duquesne University and a practicing psychoanalyst. He is the author of *The Lacanian Subject: Between Language and Jouissance,* the translator of several of Lacan's seminars, and the coeditor of two collections of papers on Lacan.

Dennis Foster is the chairman of the English department at Southern Methodist University, where he holds the D. D. Frensley chair in English. Among other things, he has published *Sublime Enjoyment,* a critical study of the constitutive role of perversion in literary representations of American communal life (Cambridge: Cambridge University Press, 1997).

Octave Mannoni was an eminent psychoanalyst and theorist.

E. L. McCallum teaches in the Department of English at Michigan State University. She is the author of *Object Lessons: How to Do Things with Fetishism* (SUNY Press, 1998) and has published articles in journals such as *Camera Obscura, The New Centennial Review, Genders,* and *Poetics Today.*

James Penney is currently a Lecturer in the Department of French at the University of Nottingham in England. His work has appeared in *Paragraph, Journal for the Psychoanalysis of Culture and Society,* and *Umbra.* His current project, *The Structures of Love,* deals with the politics of the transference and the psychosocial dynamics of radical social change.

Molly Anne Rothenberg is Associate Professor of English at Tulane University and a practicing psychoanalyst. She is the author of *Re-Thinking Blake's Textuality* (Columbia, Mo.: University of Missouri Press, 1993), and her published psychoanalytic work includes articles in journals such as *Critical Inquiry, Camera Obscura,* and *Gender and Psychoanalysis.* She is completing a book on psychoanalysis and ethics.

Nina Schwartz is Associate Professor of English at Southern Methodist University. Her book, *Dead Fathers: The Logic of Transference in Modern Narrative*, was published in 1994 (Ann Arbor: University of Michigan Press). This essay is part of a larger project that considers contemporary literature and films representing the relations of violence and desire in situations of social and personal extremity.

Slavoj Žižek is Senior Researcher at the Institute for Social Studies, Ljubljana, Slovenia. His numerous other books include *The Sublime Object of Ideology, The Plague of Fantasies,* and *The Metastases of Enjoyment.* He is the editor of the series SIC, Duke University Press.

Index

Library of Congress Cataloging-in-Publication Data
Perversion and the social relation / Molly Anne Rothenberg,
Dennis Foster, and Slavoj Žižek, editors.
p. cm. — (SIC ; 4)
Includes bibliographical references and index.
ISBN 0-8223-3085-7 (cloth : alk. paper)
ISBN 0-8223-3097-0 (pbk. : alk. paper)
1. Sexual deviation in literature.   2. Sexual deviation.
3. Psychoanalysis and literature.   4. American fiction—20th century—History and
criticism—Theory, etc.   I. Rothenbert, Molly Anne.   II. Foster, Dennis A.   III. Žižek,
Slavoj.   IV. SIC (Durham, N.C.) ; 4.
PN56.S53 P47 2003   809'.933538—dc21   2002153875